# ANXIETY FREE

# ANXIETY FREE

A 12-WEEK
SELF-HELP GUIDE
FOR MANAGING
ANXIETY

## Dr. Dave Ferruolo

Dr. Dave Books

Dr. Dave Books
New Hampshire
*drdavebooks.com*

ANXIETY FREE: A 12-Week Self-Help Guide for Managing Anxiety

ISBN: 9781963834222 (Paperback)

Printed in the USA
9 8 7 6 5 4 3 2 1 0

First Printing, 2024

# Contents

v

**PART III**

# Final Words

# Introduction to Anxiety

# ANXIETY FREE

Welcome to *ANXIETY FREE*, your 12-week self-help guide for managing anxiety. Embarking on this journey, you've made a pivotal choice—to understand and manage anxiety. *ANXIETY FREE* is designed to be a supportive self-help companion over the next 12 weeks, offering a blend of knowledge, practical strategies, and exercises to empower you. We aim to equip you with the skills to navigate anxiety more effectively.

Understanding anxiety is needed to manage it effectively. Anxiety is not just a condition or a fleeting state of mind. It's a natural and universal response to stress. It functions as an alarm system designed to alert you to potential threats and prepare your body to face them. This response is anthropologically rooted in our survival instincts, serving as a protective mechanism throughout human history.

However, when anxiety becomes more than an occasional response —when it turns into an overwhelming or persistent force—it can significantly impact your daily life. It can cloud your thoughts, influence your decisions, and affect your physical health. This is where the challenge lies: finding a balance that allows you to recognize and respond to genuine threats without letting anxiety dominate your life.

Our objective in *ANXIETY FREE* is to help you achieve that balance.

By getting to know anxiety—its triggers, its manifestations, and its effects—you can begin to address it constructively. You will never elevate the stress response entirely; instead, you will learn to manage it in a way that it no longer elevates to anxiety and prevents you from living your life to its fullest.

We will explore the various facets of anxiety, from its physical symptoms to its psychological impacts. Understanding these aspects will assist you in recognizing the signs of heightened stress in yourself and taking appropriate action to curtail full-out anxiety.

This guide is structured to provide you with the knowledge and tools to navigate anxiety more effectively. Through a combination of evidence-based strategies and practical exercises, you'll learn how to lessen anxiety's grip on your life. The goal is to foster a healthier, more balanced approach to dealing with stress and fear, enabling you to face challenges with resilience and clarity.

Structured over 12 weeks, the guide introduces you to a series of themes, activities, and reflections to tackle the various aspects of anxiety. Here's how to engage with it effectively:

1. **Set Aside Time**: Commit specific times daily to work through the activities and reflections to ensure consistency.
2. **Journaling**: Keep a journal for your thoughts, emotions, and observations. This will be a valuable tool for tracking your journey.
3. **Openness**: Embrace each section with willingness. Some parts may be challenging, but they're all steps toward progress.
4. **Support**: While this guide is structured for independent use, consider reaching out for additional support from professionals or your support network when needed.

As we venture into the self-help guide, it's essential to establish realistic expectations about managing anxiety. This journey will help you develop and refine coping mechanisms to navigate anxiety more effectively. However, completely eradicating it from your life is unrealistic.

It's essential to recognize that navigating anxiety is a nonlinear path, filled with its highs and lows.

There will be moments of significant progress where you feel a strong sense of control and understanding over your anxiety. Conversely, there will also be times of setbacks, where challenges might seem to overshadow your achievements. These fluctuations are a natural and expected part of the process. They do not signify failure but are learning opportunities that contribute to your overall growth and understanding of managing anxiety.

This guide is structured as a 12-week program, but viewing it as a 12-segment trek is more accurate. Each segment represents a critical area of learning and development, and the time you spend on each can vary greatly. For some, a segment might unfold over a few days; for others, it might stretch into months. It's possible to experience substantial improvements and even remission of anxiety symptoms within 90 days; however, for some, progress may be slower, extending over multiple months or more.

With this variability in progress, patience, resilience, and a commitment to self-compassion are paramount. Celebrate every step, no matter how small, and view setbacks as integral parts of the learning process. These experiences provide invaluable insights into your patterns of anxiety, enabling you to recognize and overcome challenges more effectively over time.

Approach this guide with an open mind and a heart ready for the triumphs and trials. Remember, the goal is not to achieve a state of no anxiety but to cultivate a life where you are equipped with the tools and knowledge to manage it successfully. Your journey through these 12 segments is unique to you, and embracing it fully, with all its ups and downs, is key to fostering a deeper, more empowering understanding of how to live harmoniously with anxiety.

As you stand at the threshold of this transformative journey, mentally and physically preparing yourself becomes paramount to harnessing the full benefits of this program. Let's explore how you can set the stage for a productive and enlightening journey through anxiety management.

## Mental Readiness

- *Embrace Challenge*: Embarking on this journey requires stepping outside your comfort zone. Anticipate challenges and understand that each one offers an opportunity for growth. Cultivating a mindset that views obstacles as pathways to learning will empower you through the highs and lows of this process.
- *Cultivate Openness*: New experiences, especially those that push us into unfamiliar territory, can be daunting yet immensely rewarding. Approach each segment of this guide with an open heart and mind, ready to absorb new knowledge and engage with new practices. This openness is your key to unlocking profound personal insights and breakthroughs.
- *Commitment to the Process*: Progress in managing anxiety is achieved through consistent effort and dedication. Commit to fully engaging with each exercise and reflection, even when challenging. Your commitment will fuel your journey and lead to meaningful change.
- *Self-Compassion*: Be kind and patient with yourself throughout this process. Recognize that growth occurs at your own pace, and setbacks are part of the journey, not indicators of failure. Practicing self-compassion will nurture your mental resilience and support your progress.

## Physical Environment

- *Create a Comfortable Space*: Identify a space where you can engage with the program's activities undisturbed. This could be a quiet corner of your home, a dedicated room, or any safe and comfortable area. A conducive physical environment can significantly enhance your focus and engagement with the material.

- *Organize Necessary Materials:* Ensure you have all the necessary materials before beginning. A journal or notebook is essential for recording thoughts, reflections, and progress. Consider also having pens, highlighters, or other tools to aid learning and reflection.
- *Minimize Distractions:* In our digitally-driven world, distractions are ever-present. Make a conscious effort to minimize these during your dedicated program time. This might mean turning off your phone, using apps to block distracting websites, or informing others of your engagement times to ensure privacy.
- *Comfort Measures:* Consider incorporating elements that enhance comfort and focus, such as comfortable seating, adequate lighting, or even background music that helps you relax. Personalize your space to suit your needs, making it a haven for your journey through this guide.

Preparing yourself both mentally and physically sets a strong foundation for your journey through managing anxiety. It equips you with the right mindset and environment to fully engage with and benefit from the program's teachings. Remember, this preparation is an act of self-care, a commitment to your well-being and growth. As you step forward, carry the readiness to explore, learn, and transform.

This guide is the culmination of years of effective clinical practice by the author, reflecting a deep understanding of anxiety and its myriad effects on individuals' lives. The information and strategies contained herein are more than theoretical concepts. They are evidence-based and distilled from practices and processes proven successful in helping people lead more balanced, less anxiety-driven lives.

Drawing from a rich pool of knowledge, this guide integrates insights from those who have navigated the complexities of anxiety and from the author and his professional peers who have dedicated their careers to understanding and alleviating stress. The coping skills, strategies, and processes outlined over the next 12 weeks are tried and true, having been utilized in thousands of clinical appointments. The author carefully selected these tools and meticulously organized them to provide a comprehensive tool for managing anxiety effectively.

As we embark on this journey together, take solace in knowing that every step you take is grounded in a deep understanding of anxiety management. Each segment of this guide is designed to bring you closer to a life where anxiety is a manageable part of your experience, not overwhelming. The strategies you will learn and the insights you will gain have helped countless people before you to achieve greater control and understanding of their anxiety.

Let this guide help you navigate the sometimes turbulent waters of managing anxiety. With every chapter, every exercise, and every reflection, you are moving toward growth, comprehension, and empowerment.

Let's begin this journey by embracing the potential of a more balanced, anxiety-free life.

## 2

# *The Science of Anxiety*

In this chapter, we will explore the biological underpinnings of anxiety. This exploration is crucial for anyone aiming to grasp and manage anxiety more effectively. By diving into the physiological and neurological aspects of anxiety, we equip ourselves with the insights necessary to navigate this complex condition.

We will uncover how anxiety transcends mere emotional turmoil, impacting both the mind and body in multifaceted ways. You'll gain an understanding of the critical brain structures, such as the amygdala, prefrontal cortex, and hippocampus, and their roles in the anxiety response. The chapter will elucidate the fight-or-flight response, a primitive mechanism designed to protect us from perceived threats, and its effects on our contemporary lives.

Recognizing the physical manifestations of anxiety is equally vital. Anxiety prompts a series of bodily reactions—like an accelerated heartbeat and increased alertness—geared toward safeguarding us in dangerous scenarios. Nonetheless, when these responses are persistently triggered without any actual danger, they may lead to adverse health outcomes over time.

Furthermore, we delve into the significance of neurotransmitters, the brain's chemical messengers, and how their imbalances can affect our anxiety levels. This knowledge not only aids in understanding the condition but also highlights the importance of diverse treatment strategies, including medications, therapy, and lifestyle adjustments.

The primary goal of this chapter is to lay a foundational understanding that anxiety is deeply rooted in our biology. This understanding demystifies the condition, paving the way for empathy and effective management strategies. By recognizing the physiological and neurological dimensions of anxiety, we approach our path toward managing it with informed optimism and resilience.

As we navigate the science behind anxiety, we unlock an essential tool against it, illuminating a more balanced and serene pathway.

## Understanding Anxiety: More Than Just a Feeling

Anxiety is an innate mechanism and has evolved over millennia. It aims to safeguard us from perceived threats. This complex response system equips our bodies to confront challenges directly or escape potential dangers. Manifesting through feelings of apprehension, worry, or unease, anxiety is complemented by physical symptoms such as elevated heart rates, sweating, and increased alertness. Fundamentally, it operates as our body's alarm system, urging us to be vigilant and act prudently when faced with threats.

Yet, the essence of anxiety stretches beyond a mere fleeting sensation or temporary state of concern. It encompasses a broad spectrum of emotional, physical, and cognitive reactions, varying significantly in intensity, duration, and influence on our lives. In everyday contexts, anxiety can arise from concerns about a forthcoming job interview, the nerves before a public speech, or the discomfort about a medical visit. These instances of anxiety are common and serve a practical purpose by motivating us to prepare thoroughly or excel in our performances.

## Everyday Stress vs. Anxiety Disorders

Distinguishing between everyday stress and anxiety disorders is important for understanding and management. Everyday stress responds to specific stressors or threats and is generally proportionate to the situation, often resolving once the stressor has passed or is addressed. For instance, experiencing stress before a significant exam is normal and usually diminishes following the exam.

Conversely, anxiety disorders are marked by more intense, enduring feelings that may arise without an apparent stressor. This form of anxiety can severely disrupt daily life, relationships, and overall well-being. Characterized by persistent, excessive worry disproportionate to the level of actual threat, those with anxiety disorders might find their worry uncontrollable, leading to symptoms like fatigue, muscle tension, and sleep issues.

Various anxiety disorders exist, including generalized anxiety disorder (GAD), panic disorder, social anxiety disorder, and specific phobias, each with distinctive symptoms and triggers. Unlike everyday stress, which is a facet of daily life, anxiety disorders necessitate professional intervention and management strategies to support individuals in achieving a balanced, fulfilling life.

Understanding the distinction between everyday stress and anxiety disorders is key to knowing when to seek help and the approach to treatment. Acknowledging that anxiety is more than a transient feeling, that it involves an intricate interplay of emotions, physical sensations, and thoughts, opens the door to deeper insights into our mental health and wellness.

### The Brain's Role in Anxiety

Anxiety's manifestation is not merely abstract; it is rooted in the complex structure and chemistry of the brain. A closer examination of the brain reveals specific structures integral to the anxiety response: the amygdala, prefrontal cortex, and hippocampus. Each plays a distinct role yet interacts closely, influencing how anxiety is experienced.

- *The Amygdala*: Known as the brain's "alarm system," the amygdala is central to processing emotions like fear and anxiety. It triggers a response cascade, preparing the body to react to perceived threats. In those with anxiety disorders, the amygdala may respond excessively to minor or nonexistent threats.

- *The Prefrontal Cortex*: Involved in higher-order functions such as decision-making and impulse control, the prefrontal cortex helps modulate anxiety by evaluating threat levels and regulating the amygdala. Optimal functioning allows for perspective and reduced alarm, but anxiety can hinder this regulatory ability.

- *The Hippocampus*: Essential for memory, the hippocampus encodes threatening situations into memories, influencing responses to similar future scenarios. Anxiety can enhance fear memories' persistence and, with chronic stress, impact the hippocampus, affecting memory and learning.

Anxiety's effect on brain function is profound, altering areas responsible for decision-making, memory, and emotional regulation. For instance, an overactive amygdala can perpetuate fear, impeding the prefrontal cortex's rational decision-making capabilities. Additionally, anxiety's influence on the hippocampus may bias memory formation, reinforcing anxious thoughts.

Understanding the brain's involvement in anxiety transcends academic interest, bearing practical implications for managing the condition. By recognizing these underlying mechanisms, individuals can better comprehend their anxiety experiences, pursuing strategies that regulate brain function. Techniques fostering relaxation and mindfulness can calm the amygdala, whereas cognitive-behavioral methods can bolster the prefrontal cortex's governance over anxious thoughts. This awareness equips individuals to actively engage in their mental health, using insights into brain function to address anxiety effectively.

### The Physiology of Anxiety: Fight-or-Flight Response

Central to comprehending anxiety is the fight-or-flight response, an intrinsic physiological reaction to perceived danger, threat, or harm.

This mechanism, first elucidated by Walter Cannon in the early 20th century, is a function of the sympathetic nervous system, gearing an individual to either confront or evade a threat. It is an ancient survival strategy stemming from a primal urge for self-preservation.

Upon perceiving a threat, the amygdala signals the adrenal glands, triggering the release of stress hormones like adrenaline (epinephrine) and cortisol. Adrenaline quickens your heartbeat, raises blood pressure, and enhances energy, preparing your body for action. Cortisol, the chief stress hormone, elevates blood sugar levels, improves the brain's glucose utilization, and suppresses non-critical or harmful functions in a fight-or-flight scenario.

The release of these hormones can lead to various physical symptoms commonly linked to anxiety:

- *Elevated heart rate and palpitations*: Priming muscles for action by increasing blood circulation.
- *Accelerated breathing* (*hyperventilation):* Boosting oxygen supply to the blood for quick muscle response.
- *Sweating:* Cooling the body due to an increased metabolic rate.
- *Trembling or shaking:* Resulting from muscle tension and heightened nervous system activity.
- *Dizziness or lightheadedness:* Occurring as blood is channeled to major muscle groups, potentially reducing cerebral blood flow.
- *Digestive discomfort:* Blood flow is diverted from the digestive tract, leading to nausea or upset.

While these symptoms may be unsettling, they are functional in a genuine fight-or-flight context, equipping the body to face the threat directly or escape.

Adrenaline and cortisol are primary factors in the fight-or-flight response and, consequently, anxiety. The immediate impact of adrenaline prepares the body for instant action against threats, while cortisol sustains alertness and readiness over a more prolonged period.

In today's environment, where physical dangers are less frequent, this response can be activated by non-life-threatening situations such as public speaking or job interviews. Continuous or repeated activation of this response, leading to regular or extended stress hormone spikes, can result in persistent anxiety. This ongoing exposure to cortisol and other stress hormones can disturb nearly all bodily functions, elevating the risk of various health issues, including heart conditions, sleep problems, digestive disorders, depression, and cognitive impairments.

Grasping the fight-or-flight response and stress hormones' role in anxiety is vital. It not only clarifies the nature of anxiety but also guides us toward managing its physical effects. Practices like deep breathing, relaxation techniques, and mindfulness can diminish the body's stress reaction, alleviating the intense physical sensations associated with anxiety.

### Beyond Fight-or-Flight: The Freeze and Fawn Responses

The common understanding of the body's primary reaction to stress —the fight-or-flight response—is just the beginning. Human stress responses also encompass "freeze" and "fawn" reactions, both instinctual for survival and significantly influencing how individuals handle anxiety in diverse scenarios.

*Understanding the Freeze Response*: The freeze response is triggered when an individual perceives a threat but determines that neither resistance (fight) nor escape (flight) is feasible. In such instances, the body may "freeze" as a protective measure. This can appear as physical immobility, where one cannot move or speak, or as a mental detachment or dissociation, feeling separated from the immediate reality. This state is believed to minimize pain during an attack and render the individual less detectable to predators.

In contemporary life, the freeze response might manifest in intensely stressful moments where one feels swamped or powerless. For instance, during a panic attack, a person may become immobilized or, when confronting a traumatic event, might dissociate, psychologically distancing themselves from the threat.

*The Fawn Response Explained*: The fawn response is identified as a compulsion to avert conflict or danger by placating or appeasing the perceived threat. This reaction involves an immediate inclination to fulfill the needs, desires, or demands of others to sidestep conflict or criticism, rooted in the belief that safety is attainable by becoming indispensable or endeared to the source of threat.

In situations that provoke anxiety, those who naturally resort to the fawn response may excessively strive to please others, shun confrontation at any cost, or neglect their own needs and emotions. This behavior might be observable in relationships where one partner habitually capitulates to the other's demands to maintain harmony or in professional settings where someone assumes extra responsibilities to evade criticism or conflict.

Both the freeze and fawn responses can profoundly affect individuals dealing with anxiety. The freeze response may lead to a sense of helplessness or immobility, hindering the effective management of anxiety-provoking situations. Over time, this can intensify anxiety, as the person might feel incapable of altering their situation or response.

Conversely, the fawn response may cultivate behavioral patterns that amplify anxiety. Consistently prioritizing the needs of others above one's own can result in exhaustion, resentment, and a diminished sense of self, all contributing to the cycle of anxiety.

By broadening our understanding to include these additional stress responses, we deepen our insight into human behavior under stress and danger. Recognizing when one is exhibiting a freeze or fawn response is a critical first step toward adopting healthier management strategies. Acknowledging these reactions and their effects enables individuals to explore more adaptive coping methods, such as establishing boundaries, practicing assertive communication, and employing grounding techniques, thus navigating through anxiety with greater efficacy.

**Chronic Anxiety and Its Impact on the Body**

Chronic anxiety transcends mental distress, exerting a significant toll on the physical body as well. When anxiety persists over time, the body's continuous readiness to respond to stress can induce a range of health complications across various bodily systems. Acknowledging the far-reaching implications of chronic anxiety is vital not just for mental wellness but for maintaining comprehensive physical health.

Persistent stress from chronic anxiety keeps the body in an enduring state of vigilance, which can tax the body in numerous ways:

- *Cardiovascular Health:* Chronic anxiety can elevate heart rate and blood pressure, imposing extra burden on the heart and circulatory system. This heightened cardiovascular strain can escalate the risk of developing heart-related conditions, such as coronary artery disease, arrhythmias, and myocardial infarction. Also, prolonged stress hormone secretion may cause vascular inflammation and arterial modifications, augmenting the risk of heart disease.
- *Digestive System:* The digestive tract is particularly vulnerable to the effects of anxiety, with symptoms ranging from mild (nausea, stomach cramps) to severe conditions like irritable bowel syndrome (IBS), characterized by ongoing pain, diarrhea, and constipation. Chronic anxiety can also intensify symptoms of gastroesophageal reflux disease (GERD) and contribute to the formation of ulcers.
- *Musculoskeletal System:* Anxiety-induced muscle tension can evolve into chronic pain conditions. Individuals might endure persistent headaches, migraines, or widespread muscular pain, often linked to fibromyalgia.
- *Immune Function:* Chronic anxiety can compromise immune response, heightening susceptibility to infections and illnesses. Elevated cortisol levels over extended periods can inhibit immune effectiveness, diminish lymphocyte counts, and slow wound healing.

- *Neurological Effects:* Long-term anxiety can alter brain structure and functionality, especially within regions governing mood regulation, like the amygdala and prefrontal cortex. Such changes may increase the likelihood of mood disorders, including depression. Extended stress hormone exposure can also impair memory and cognitive functions, affecting concentration, decision-making, and memory recall.

The link between sustained anxiety and physical health is reciprocal; chronic anxiety can precipitate various health issues, and existing physical conditions can intensify anxiety, fostering a self-sustaining cycle of worsening health and anxiety.

For example, an individual with chronic anxiety may develop IBS, further heightening their anxiety due to discomfort and health worries. Similarly, chronic pain can restrict activities and life quality, fueling frustration, depression, and anxiety.

Recognizing chronic anxiety's impact on physical health emphasizes the need for holistic management approaches that consider both mental and physical facets of the condition. Strategies like regular exercise, stress reduction techniques, a balanced diet, and professional counseling can alleviate anxiety's physical effects and enhance overall health. It's crucial for those experiencing chronic anxiety to seek comprehensive support to safeguard their mental and physical well-being.

### The Role of Neurotransmitters in Anxiety

Neurotransmitters, the brain's chemical messengers, modulate mood, behavior, and mental well-being. In the realm of anxiety, the equilibrium and functionality of particular neurotransmitters—specifically serotonin, gamma-aminobutyric acid (GABA), and dopamine—are of significant importance. Variations or imbalances in these neurotransmitters can affect the manifestation of anxiety, either by initiating or intensifying it.

*Serotonin:* Dubbed the "feel-good" neurotransmitter, serotonin plays a vital role in mood regulation, appetite, and sleep, which are intricately connected to anxiety. A serotonin deficiency is linked to heightened anxiety and depression. Several treatments for anxiety and depression, including selective serotonin reuptake inhibitors (SSRIs), aim to boost serotonin levels, thereby aiding in alleviating anxiety symptoms. The impact of serotonin on anxiety is multifaceted, affecting mood regulation and the modulation of anxiety responses within the brain's neural pathways.

*GABA:* As the brain's primary inhibitory neurotransmitter, GABA's function is to mitigate neural activity. Its capacity to induce calm is crucial for managing fear and anxiety during neuronal hyperactivity. Lower levels of GABA are associated with increased anxiety, restlessness, and challenges in achieving relaxation. Anxiety treatments that enhance GABA activity, like benzodiazepines, are effective for acute anxiety relief, amplifying GABA's calming influence on the nervous system and promoting a state of relaxation.

*Dopamine:* Dopamine, linked with the brain's reward mechanism, oversees pleasure, motivation, and concentration. Although its direct connection to anxiety is less pronounced than serotonin and GABA, imbalances in dopamine can influence general mood and well-being, thereby affecting anxiety. For example, diminished dopamine levels can result in apathy, decreased motivation, and heightened stress, aggravating anxiety symptoms. Dopamine also contributes to stress responses and how individuals manage stress-inducing situations.

The delicate balance of neurotransmitters is essential for mental health, with imbalances potentially leading to significant anxiety implications. For instance, reduced serotonin may precipitate mood disorders and amplify anxiety, while insufficient GABA might prevent effective relaxation and mental calmness. Moreover, dopamine discrepancies can alter stress perception and response, possibly elevating anxiety.

Additionally, the interaction among these neurotransmitters implies that an imbalance in one could influence the others, engendering complex mood and behavioral shifts. For example, low serotonin could indirectly affect dopamine production, further altering mood and anxiety.

Recognizing neurotransmitters' role in anxiety underscores the necessity for comprehensive treatment strategies. These may include medication targeting specific neurotransmitter systems, lifestyle modifications to affect neurotransmitter levels, and psychotherapy to tackle cognitive and emotional facets of anxiety. Through addressing neurotransmitter imbalances, individuals may experience relief from anxiety, enhancing their mental health and life quality.

### Understanding Anxiety Disorders

Anxiety disorders represent the most widespread category of mental health issues globally, impacting countless lives. Unlike routine stress experienced by many, anxiety disorders are marked by their intensity, persistence, and the significant interference they cause in daily activities. These disorders encompass a broad range of conditions, each with unique triggers, symptoms, and physiological impacts. This section delves into several prevalent anxiety disorders: Generalized Anxiety Disorder (GAD), Panic Disorder, Phobias, and Social Anxiety Disorder.

GAD involves chronic, exaggerated worry about everyday life that seems disproportionate to the actual likelihood of the anticipated problems. Those with GAD struggle to control this worry and often anticipate adverse outcomes, even in benign situations. The condition can manifest physically as restlessness, muscle tension, and disturbances in sleep patterns. GAD is associated with a persistent sense of dread and heightened neural activity in areas related to emotion processing, such as the amygdala and the prefrontal cortex, reflecting the brain's ongoing anticipation of negative events.

Panic Disorder is defined by the occurrence of spontaneous panic attacks—intense bouts of fear or discomfort that escalate rapidly, accompanied by physical symptoms like heart palpitations, sweating, and dizziness. In panic disorder, the brain's threat detection mechanism is overly sensitive, triggering an exaggerated fight-or-flight response even without a real threat. This heightened alertness to bodily sensations can perpetuate and escalate the panic cycle.

Phobias are characterized by an irrational fear of specific objects, situations, or activities that are generally not dangerous. The avoidance behavior associated with phobias can significantly disrupt daily functioning. The fear response to phobias is localized in the brain, with the amygdala playing a crucial role in triggering immediate anxiety or fear reactions, often out of proportion to the actual danger presented by the feared subject.

Social Anxiety Disorder involves an intense fear of being negatively evaluated or rejected in social or performance situations. This fear can be so overwhelming that it impedes normal daily activities and leads to avoidance of social interactions. Brain imaging reveals that individuals with this disorder exhibit increased activity in regions responsible for processing social and emotional stimuli, such as the amygdala and prefrontal cortex, highlighting the profound anxiety experienced in social contexts.

While all anxiety disorders are united by excessive fear or worry, the physiological and neurological responses vary across different conditions. For example, panic disorder triggers an immediate and intense physical reaction, akin to facing an imminent threat, whereas GAD is marked by a more continuous state of tension and preparedness. The response in phobias is acutely specific to particular stimuli, and social anxiety disorder is closely linked to the processing of social and emotional signals.

Recognizing these variances is essential for the effective treatment and management of anxiety disorders. Customizing interventions to address the distinct characteristics of each anxiety disorder can enhance treatment efficacy, improving life quality for those affected by these conditions.

### The Plasticity of the Brain

One of the most encouraging insights from neuroscience in the context of mental health and anxiety management is the concept of neuroplasticity. This principle reveals the brain's remarkable ability to reorganize and adapt by forming new neural connections throughout a person's life, influenced by experiences, behaviors, thoughts, and emotions. For those facing anxiety, neuroplasticity offers hope, illustrating that the brain is not fixed but capable of transformation. This means that anxiety-driven thought patterns can potentially be reshaped into healthier, more balanced ones.

Contrary to the outdated belief that the adult brain remains unchanged, current research confirms the brain's dynamic nature. It continually adjusts and forms new connections between neurons, reacting to novel information and experiences. This adaptability indicates that the brain's response to anxiety, including overactivity in areas like the amygdala and changes in the prefrontal cortex and hippocampus, isn't irreversible. Through specific therapies and practices, it's possible to foster the development of new neural pathways, reducing anxiety's grip on the mind.

Various therapeutic strategies, including Cognitive Behavioral Therapy (CBT), mindfulness, and certain medications, employ neuroplasticity principles to address anxiety. For example, CBT encourages the identification and restructuring of anxious thoughts and behaviors, effectively rewiring the brain to lessen its reaction to stressors. Similarly, mindfulness and meditation strengthen brain regions linked to attention and emotion regulation, calming an overactive amygdala and promoting engagement of the rational prefrontal cortex.

Furthermore, embracing new experiences and learning can enhance neuroplasticity, serving as a powerful tool against anxiety. Activities like physical exercise not only foster new neural connections but can also increase the size of brain regions, playing a crucial role in alleviating anxiety symptoms and underscoring the link between physical and mental health.

Grasping the nuances of anxiety and the brain's transformative capabilities can empower those living with anxiety. It reframes anxiety as a transitionary state and a condition that can be altered through understanding and targeted action. This perspective encourages individuals to take an active stance in managing their mental health exploring treatments that promote neuroplastic changes.

Armed with knowledge about neuroplasticity, individuals are better positioned to choose treatments that do more than alleviate anxiety symptoms temporarily—they contribute to the brain's long-term adaptability and resilience. This shift from merely enduring anxiety to actively cultivating a brain environment that fosters calm and well-being is profoundly liberating.

Neuroplasticity's revelation provides a beacon of hope for those affected by anxiety, signifying that with intentional practice and therapeutic intervention, modifying the brain's predisposition to anxiety is within reach. It highlights our brains' dynamic essence and inherent ability to evolve, laying a solid foundation for achieving a balanced, anxiety-free existence.

### The Path Forward

In wrapping up our exploration of anxiety's science, it becomes evident that grasping how anxiety operates within the brain and body transcends mere scholarly interest—it's a critical step toward empowerment and healing. Throughout this chapter, we've delved into anxiety's complexities, from the fundamental fight-or-flight response to the intricate impact of neurotransmitters such as serotonin, GABA, and dopamine. We've examined the varied manifestations of anxiety disorders, shedding light on the unique challenges each presents in the brain, thereby recognizing the broad spectrum of anxiety experiences. Crucially, we've encountered hope through neuroplasticity, the brain's astonishing capacity for adaptation and change, offering genuine prospects for managing and transcending anxiety.

### Key Insights Recap:

- *Fight-or-Flight Response:* An essential survival mechanism that, when persistently triggered, forms the basis of anxiety.
- *Neurotransmitter Dynamics:* The significant influence of serotonin, GABA, and dopamine imbalances on our emotional and anxiety states.
- *Anxiety Disorders Spectrum:* Understanding the distinct features and brain activities in conditions such as GAD, panic disorder, phobias, and social anxiety disorder is vital.
- *Neuroplasticity:* The brain's ability to evolve, providing a solid foundation for therapeutic measures to transform our neural architecture to alleviate anxiety.

Grasping anxiety's scientific underpinnings clarifies that the feelings and thoughts that often seem insurmountable are, in fact, identifiable physiological and neurological processes, manageable with appropriate knowledge and interventions.

This fundamental comprehension is essential not just for those experiencing anxiety but also for changing societal views on mental health. It underscores that anxiety isn't a matter of choice or mere willpower deficiency but results from a complex blend of genetic, environmental, and psychological factors. Such understanding fosters empathy towards oneself and others and underscores the significance of research-backed treatments.

Equipped with this insight, individuals are better prepared to address their anxiety proactively. Whether through therapy, medications, lifestyle modifications, or a combination thereof, understanding anxiety's underlying science can lead to more informed and effective management choices.

Progressing forward means expanding our knowledge of anxiety science and advocating for and engaging with evidence-based treatments. It entails creating a personal and societal environment conducive to mental health awareness, comprehension, and intervention.

As we proceed, let's utilize the knowledge and insights from this chapter as empowerment tools. The journey through anxiety is profoundly personal and varies from one person to the next, yet it's a journey no one should navigate in isolation. With adequate understanding and support, managing anxiety becomes an achievable goal. Let this chapter act as a beacon towards a future where anxiety no longer holds sway over our lives but rather where we possess the insight and strategies to manage it with confidence and resilience.

# 3

# *Living with Anxiety*

Living with anxiety can often feel like being trapped in a relentless storm, where the memory of calm seems a distant dream. This condition, characterized by persistent worry, unease, and fear, affects many people, each in profoundly personal ways. It influences daily life, relationships, and personal growth extensively. Understanding not only the general nature of anxiety but also your specific triggers is crucial for managing it effectively and reducing its impact on your life.

Anxiety, as discussed in Chapter 2, is a natural response to perceived threats or stressors. This response activates the body's fight-or-flight mechanism, an evolutionary adaptation that prepares us to react swiftly to environmental dangers. However, when this alarm system becomes overactive, it leads to persistent and excessive worry, fear, and physical symptoms, even in the absence of actual threats. Understanding the difference between normal situational stress and a clinical anxiety disorder is crucial.

Normal stress is an emotional reaction to challenging situations that demand a response, such as facing an upcoming deadline, preparing for an exam, or engaging in public speaking. This type of stress often serves as a motivator, providing a burst of energy and focus that dissipates once the stressful situation is resolved. In contrast, an anxiety disorder is characterized by a dysfunctional stress response that is disproportionate to the circumstances. Individuals with an anxiety disorder experience overwhelming and persistent anxiety that can significantly impair their daily functioning and quality of life, even when no objective danger is present.

The triggers for anxiety disorders are diverse and reflect a complex interplay of biological, psychological, and environmental factors. Work-related pressures such as excessive workloads, tight deadlines, or conflicts with colleagues can heighten stress levels and contribute to anxiety. Similarly, strains in relationships—whether in romantic partnerships, family dynamics, or social circles—can also be potent triggers, mainly when communication breaks down or trust is compromised.

Major life transitions, such as starting a new job, relocating to a different city, or becoming a parent, often bring about significant uncertainties and challenges that can fuel anxiety disorders. Moreover, significant life events, both positive, like marriage or a promotion, and negative, such as the loss of a loved one or financial setbacks, can disrupt established routines and require substantial adaptation, thus increasing vulnerability to anxiety.

For individuals with pre-existing mental health conditions, such as depression, obsessive-compulsive disorder, or post-traumatic stress disorder, anxiety disorders can be a common comorbid condition, further exacerbating symptoms and complicating treatment approaches. Additionally, cognitive distortions and perceptual biases, such as the misattribution of benign situations or stimuli as threats and distorted perceptions that overestimate the likelihood or severity of risks, can also contribute to the experience of disproportionate anxiety responses.

Our 12-Week Self-Help Guide explores these cognitive errors in detail and provides strategies to address them effectively. Identifying one's unique patterns and triggers of anxiety is crucial for effective management. By recognizing the specific situations, thoughts, or environments that provoke disproportionate anxiety responses, individuals can better anticipate potential difficulties and implement coping strategies to minimize disruptions to their daily functioning and overall well-being.

Managing and overcoming anxiety is a deeply personal journey that requires an approach tailored to your unique experiences and triggers. To support you in this transformative process, *ANXIETY FREE* offers a comprehensive 12-week self-help guide with practical strategies and profound insights for overcoming anxiety.

### Initial Weeks: Building a Foundation.

The program begins by establishing a solid mindfulness and relaxation techniques foundation in the first week. These initial steps are designed to help you regain control over your anxiety response and cultivate a sense of calm amidst life's turbulence. In the second week, the focus shifts to managing acute anxiety symptoms and panic attacks, providing you with specific techniques to handle these intense situations.

### Mid-Program: Deepening Understanding and Skills.

Weeks three and four introduce the principles of Cognitive Behavioral Therapy (CBT), a well-established method for identifying and challenging the negative thought patterns that perpetuate anxiety. You'll engage in exercises to restructure your thinking, setting the stage for improved mental health. Week five explores deeper psychological concepts, encouraging you to reflect on your personal meaning schema, worldviews, and the role of cognitive distortions and defense mechanisms. This introspective period is crucial for understanding how your beliefs and coping mechanisms shape your anxiety.

### Exploring Therapeutic Modalities.

The program continues to expand in week six by exploring Internal Family Systems (IFS), offering a framework to understand and harmonize the conflicting parts of your psyche. In week seven, Acceptance and Commitment Therapy (ACT) is introduced, emphasizing the importance of accepting difficult thoughts and emotions while committing to actions aligned with your values.

**Practical Applications and Emotional Intelligence.**

Week eight is dedicated to practical problem-solving strategies, providing tools to address issues contributing to your anxiety. Week nine emphasizes emotional intelligence development, helping you better understand and regulate your emotional responses.

**Holistic Well-being and Personal Meaning.**

The guide recognizes the holistic nature of well-being, dedicating week ten to self-care practices and nurturing supportive social connections. Week eleven focuses on the profound impact of finding personal meaning and purpose, guiding you to align your life with your deepest values.

**Preparing for the Future.**

The final week prepares you for life beyond the program, offering strategies for identifying triggers, managing setbacks, and sustaining your progress toward an anxiety-free life. This last week is pivotal, equipping you with the tools to maintain your gains and embrace future challenges with resilience.

Throughout this 12-week journey, practical exercises, reflections, and guidance support you in integrating these transformative strategies into your daily life. The goal extends beyond symptom management; it aims to cultivate a resilient mindset that empowers you to navigate life's complexities with confidence, clarity, and enduring inner peace.

Embarking on this 12-week self-help journey to overcome anxiety is not just about following a structure; it's about committing to a profound personal transformation. This path requires unwavering courage and dedication as it delves deep into self-exploration and growth. You may face aspects of your psyche that you have long avoided or denied, challenging deeply held beliefs, confronting painful emotions, and learning to embrace vulnerability.

However, you are not without guidance. The strategies this book introduces are based on well-established methods such as Cognitive-

Behavioral Therapy (CBT) and mindfulness techniques, which have been shown to effectively help countless individuals regain control of their lives from the clutches of anxiety. The key to harnessing their full potential lies in your active participation and willingness to engage deeply with the process.

Transformation through this program is most effective when you fully commit to the exercises, reflections, and practices recommended. Real progress stems not from merely absorbing information but your steadfast commitment to apply these strategies, even when consistently challenging.

It's also important to recognize when additional support is needed. While the guide provides a comprehensive framework, navigating deep-rooted anxiety might require the support of a qualified mental health professional. A therapist can offer personalized insights, accountability, and a neutral perspective, greatly enhancing your ability to achieve and maintain anxiety-free. Should you or anyone else experience severe anxiety that leads to thoughts of self-harm, it's crucial to contact emergency services immediately.

Ultimately, the journey you are about to undertake is one of deep personal discovery and growth. It invites you to confront your fears, challenge your limiting beliefs, and step into a new, more authentic way of living. The journey can be demanding, but the rewards—a life lived with authenticity and free from the constraints of anxiety—are truly invaluable. As you approach this path, keep an open mind, muster your courage, and commit wholeheartedly to your well-being. You are on your way to becoming a stronger, more resilient version of yourself.

### Moving Forward

Living with anxiety is just one chapter of your life story—it doesn't define you. By understanding your triggers and equipping yourself with effective strategies, you can transform your relationship with anxiety. This journey towards an anxiety-free life involves continuous learning and adaptation. Set achievable goals, incorporate the discussed strategies into your daily routine, and celebrate every victory. You can achieve personal growth and fulfillment with patience, dedication, and a commitment to your well-being.

As you embark on this path, it's important to remember that progress in overcoming anxiety is rarely straightforward. You might face setbacks and unexpected challenges, but each step you take, no matter how small, is a move toward building a stronger, more resilient version of yourself. These steps might include practicing the relaxation techniques introduced in the first week, challenging negative thought patterns through cognitive behavioral therapy exercises, or simply recognizing when it's time to seek support from others.

Remember, the journey toward an anxiety-free life is continuous, and learning to manage anxiety is a skill that you will improve over time. Start by setting small, achievable goals and gradually incorporate the strategies discussed into your daily routine. Celebrate every victory, learn from each challenge, and remain patient and committed to your path.

By redefining your relationship with anxiety not as a barrier but as a part of your life that you can manage and control, you will open up new possibilities for personal growth and fulfillment. Let this be the moment you step forward with courage, equipped with the knowledge and tools you need to cultivate a peaceful, empowered, and anxiety-free existence.

# 4

# Tracking Progress

Tracking Progress in managing anxiety is about discovering new layers of self-awareness and adopting effective healing strategies. This journey, less about empirical methods and more about an intuitive process, invites you to deeply self-reflect to understand your feelings and perceptions about your progress. Realizing that achieving a life free from anxiety is a goal that may not fully materialize until you've reached it, this approach helps you delve beyond tangible symptoms to explore your thoughts and emotions.

This intuitive approach transcends the tangible symptoms and targets, delving into your thoughts and emotions about your path. It acknowledges that progress milestones are often internal and subjective rather than externally measurable or visible. This method enables you to map your journey in a way that resonates with your personal experiences and emotional landscape, even if the clear outline of an anxiety-free life is still forming.

We introduce the metaphor of a bridge to visualize your journey. Picture a bridge stretching over a serene river, symbolizing your transition from the grip of anxiety to the hopeful path of tranquility. Unlike a conventional bridge marked by clear signs and measures, your crossing is guided by your inner sense of growth and movement.

You're encouraged to reflect on your current position on this bridge weekly. It's a chance to pause, observe, and feel where you are in your emotional journey. Consider:

- How do I *feel* about my progress this week?
- Do I sense movement forward, backward, or stasis, and why?
- Where on the bridge do I find myself now?

There are no incorrect responses. Tune into your intuition and emotional truths to authentically chart your journey.

Maintain a journal or use the bridge illustration on these pages for weekly reflections, marking your location on it. This can be a simple dot, symbol, or color reflecting your current state. Over time, this visual will evolve into a map of your emotional journey, adorned with the unique markers of your progress.

**Navigating Uncertainty with Hope**

Facing doubt or uncertainty about your progress is a natural part of healing. Sometimes, it may feel like you are regressing, but remember, healing is not linear. Each shift, whether forward or backward, is integral to your journey. These moments are not setbacks but essential parts of your path, offering insights and deepening your understanding of the healing process. Each week's reflection on your position on the metaphorical bridge is a learning opportunity, regardless of where you find yourself.

As you continue this intuitive process, you'll gradually construct a detailed map of your journey. While the destination may not yet be in sight, your sense of advancement will guide you. The bridge metaphor reminds you that, step by step, you are moving towards a life where anxiety's hold diminishes, making way for new experiences, emotions, and well-being currently beyond imagination. Trust in this journey, for each step on the bridge, directed by your intuition and emotions, brings you closer to discovering what an anxiety-free life means.

Professionals can also employ clinical measures to help track your progress. Professionals are always recommended to provide guidance and support. Additionally, the use of weekly scales is helpful. Each week, you will be asked to place your anxiety on a scale of 0 to 10, with zero being no anxiety at all and 10 being the most intense anxiety you've ever experienced. This scale, alongside the metaphor of the bridge, will serve as a gauge for progress, helping determine whether to slow down, revisit previous strategies, or seek professional help if no improvement is observed.

Before beginning to manage anxiety, it's crucial to establish a base-line of your current state. This initial assessment is your starting point, enabling you to measure your progress throughout the 12-week *ANXIETY FREE* guide. Below, you'll find instructions on how to chart yourself on the metaphorical bridge and the anxiety scale. Remember, these tools are designed to reflect your personal experience and growth accurately.

### Placing Yourself on the Bridge

At the bottom of this chapter, there's an illustration of a bridge. This bridge represents your journey from the current state of living with anxiety to reaching a place of peace and control over your anxiety.

1. **Reflect**: Spend a moment reflecting on your current emotional state and the challenges you're facing with anxiety. Consider the impact of your anxiety on daily activities, relationships, work, and your sense of well-being.
2. **Identify Your Position**: Look at the bridge illustration and imagine where you would place yourself. Are you at the very start, somewhere in the middle, or nearing the other side? There's no right or wrong place to be; this is about acknowledg-ing where you are.
3. **Mark Your Spot**: Using a pen or marker, place a dot on the bridge where you feel you currently stand. You can also use

stickers or draw a small symbol that resonates with you. This mark represents your starting point on this journey.

## Determining Your Position on the Anxiety Scale

Below the bridge illustration, you'll find an anxiety scale ranging from 0 to 10, where 0 indicates no anxiety at all, and 10 represents the most severe anxiety you've ever experienced.

1. **Assess Your Anxiety**: Take a moment to assess your general level of anxiety over the past week. Consider the intensity, frequency, and impact of your anxiety on your life.
2. **Choose Your Number**: Based on your reflection, choose a number on the scale that best represents your current state of anxiety.
3. **Record Your Number**: Write down your chosen number in your journal or on paper. This number is your baseline anxiety level before starting the self-help guide.

**Embracing the Non-linear Journey**

Understanding that your journey through anxiety is highly personal and non-linear is crucial. The 'weeks' outlined in this guide may represent different durations in real-time—days, months, or more—depending on your pace. The essence of this journey lies not in relentless forward movement, but in the depth of understanding, healing, and growth you achieve at each step. As you navigate this path, remember that the circuitous route is a process of continuous learning and adaptation, uniquely shaped by your experiences and insights.

As you embark on this journey, remember the non-linear and circuitous path through anxiety, a process of continuous learning and adaptation. Your pace, your experiences, and the insights you gain are uniquely yours. Let these initial steps of charting your current position serve as a grounding reminder of your starting point, from which you'll navigate through the twists and turns toward a life where anxiety is no longer in control.

# 12 Week Self-Help Guide

# 5

# Mindfulness Relaxation

Welcome to the first week of your anxiety-freedom guide. The focus of this first week is mindfulness and relaxation techniques. We will delve into the biological and psychological underpinnings of anxiety, exploring how our bodies and minds react to stress and perceived threats. Understanding these responses forms the basis for why and how mindfulness and relaxation techniques can be so effective.

**Understanding Eustress**

Before we go into the negative aspects of anxiety, let's look at how stress can be positive. Eustress, or positive stress, plays an important role in our lives by enhancing performance, motivation, and overall well-being.

Eustress is derived from the Greek prefix 'eu-' meaning 'good' and refers to the positive cognitive response one feels when confronting a fulfilling challenge. Unlike distress, which is associated with anxiety and potential harm, eustress is characterized by feelings of excitement, fulfillment, or satisfaction derived from overcoming a meaningful challenge.

Eustress can be experienced in various scenarios. For instance, starting a new job or receiving a promotion can induce eustress, as these events are challenging yet provide significant opportunities for personal and professional growth. Similarly, students often experience eustress during exams or when engaging in challenging projects that stretch their abilities and create a sense of accomplishment.

Athletes often experience eustress during competitions, where the adrenaline rush and the challenge of the event can lead to peak performance. Additionally, personal milestones such as weddings, moving to a new home, or preparing for a family gathering can produce eustress, offering both joy and a sense of achievement.

Eustress is beneficial as it provides the energy and mental alertness needed to perform tasks effectively. The stress response involved in eustress helps to focus attention and mobilize energy, improving efficiency and output. It also motivates individuals to face challenges head-on and strive for success, reinforcing the drive for achievement and fulfillment.

Regular exposure to eustress can help build psychological resilience. Individuals develop confidence and adaptability by continually overcoming challenges, which are crucial for handling future stresses. Achieving goals and overcoming obstacles provides a sense of accomplishment, a factor in personal satisfaction, and a positive self-image.

While eustress is generally positive, managing it effectively ensures it doesn't become distress. Balancing challenging tasks with adequate rest and recovery and setting realistic goals are essential. Maintaining a supportive social network can help manage eustress. Recognizing personal limits and avoiding excessive pressures can help maintain eustress as a positive force.

Understanding that not all stress is detrimental allows us to approach challenges with a more balanced perspective, recognizing the potential for positive outcomes. By learning to harness eustress, we can improve our daily functioning and enhance our quality of life, turning challenges into opportunities for growth.

Later in Week 1, we will discuss cognitive distortions, which may unintentionally reattribute good stress to something negative, creating anxiety. But this week, we will focus on mindfulness and how it can help us with anxiety responses. To understand how mindfulness helps, let's refresh ourselves with the fight-flight-freeze response.

## The Fight-Flight-Freeze Response

We discussed in detail the fight-flight-freeze response in Chapter 2. To review, anxiety is a physiological reaction that occurs in the presence of something terrifying, either mentally or physically. The response is triggered by the HPA axis, an essential part of the neuro-endocrine system that controls reactions to stress and regulates many body processes, including digestion, the immune system, mood and emotions, sexuality, and energy storage and expenditure.

The HPA axis engages in our defense by releasing stress hormones like cortisol, which primes your body to fight the danger, flee from it, or freeze in anticipation of further action. This was incredibly useful in our evolutionary past, when physical threats were a regular part of daily life. However, in our modern lifestyle, the same response can be triggered by situations that are not directly life-threatening—like public speaking, deadlines at work, or social interactions. Unfortunately, perceived threats are as real as actual danger in our brains.

When the fight-flight-freeze response misfires, is activated too frequently, or has a prolonged response, it can lead to chronic stress or anxiety disorders. The constant release of cortisol and other stress hormones can wreak havoc on the body, leading to a host of physical and psychological health issues, including heart disease, diabetes, depression, and a weakened immune system. Understanding how this response works is the first step in learning to manage it effectively through mindfulness and relaxation techniques.

## The Impact of Modern Life

In modern life, where physical threats are less frequent, the fight-flight-freeze response can often feel like an overreaction to daily stressors. Although life can be stressful, it rarely requires the intense physical action for which our bodies are preparing. This is an example of misattribution of the situation, leading to a perception of impending harm. And, of course, one should be anxious in the face of a real threat. To repeat, cognitively, there is no difference between perceived and actual threats. It responds similarly and activates the fight-flight-freeze response.

While vital for our ancestors in life-threatening situations, the fight-flight-freeze response often misfires in today's world, where physical threats are less common. This adaptive mechanism, which served to protect from predators and other dangers, now activates in situations where no physical danger exists.

In contemporary settings, what triggers our stress response is often not an immediate threat to our physical safety but psychological stress. For instance, receiving a barrage of emails, facing deadlines, or navigating social interactions can initiate this reaction. The body responds as though these are threats to survival, releasing a flood of stress hormones like adrenaline and cortisol.

This biological reaction includes increased heart rate, rapid breathing, and heightened muscle preparedness—changes advantageous in an actual fight or flight scenario but unnecessary and harmful when the "threat" consists of non-threatening everyday challenges. These responses are exaggerated because the physiological changes are far greater than needed for dealing with modern stressors.

When the fight-flight-freeze response is repeatedly triggered without actual physical threats, it can lead to a state of chronic stress. This constant state of alert can strain the body, particularly the cardiovascular and immune systems. Over time, this strain can manifest as chronic anxiety, high blood pressure, digestive issues, and a weakened immune response. Furthermore, overexposure to cortisol and other stress hormones can disrupt almost all your body's processes, increasing the risk of numerous health problems.

Our health and well-being depend on learning how to appropriately calibrate our responses to stress. Understanding that these physiological reactions are often disproportionate to modern-day stressors is the first step in managing them effectively. By recognizing these patterns, individuals can begin to implement mindfulness and relaxation techniques that help mitigate these responses, aligning the body's reactions more closely with the actual level of danger or demand presented by modern life.

### Recognizing the Signs of Stress Responses

We need to know how our bodies show signs of stress and the significance of noticing these signs early. Identifying these signs helps us manage stress more quickly and effectively.

**Physiological Responses:** Physiological responses to stress, specifically rapid heartbeat and shallow breathing, serve as the body's primary defense mechanisms when faced with a perceived threat. Here's a more detailed look at these responses:

When stressed, the body releases stress hormones like adrenaline and cortisol. These hormones stimulate the heart muscle, causing it to beat faster. This accelerated heartbeat is known as tachycardia. The purpose of this response historically was to increase blood circulation quickly, ensuring that oxygen and vital nutrients reached critical areas such as muscles and the brain, thereby preparing the body for quick, strenuous actions required in fight or flight situations.

In contemporary environments, however, this physical reaction often occurs when no immediate physical action is necessary, such as during intense discussions at work or in traffic jams. While this response might have been adaptive for survival in the face of physical threats like predators or enemies, its utility is less in modern-day stressors that typically do not require a physical fight or flight.

Alongside a rapid heartbeat, shallow, rapid breathing or hyperventilation often occurs during stress. This type of breathing increases the body's oxygen intake and prepares it for action. Initially, this would have been beneficial by providing the muscles with the oxygen needed for fighting or fleeing. However, unlike deep breathing, which is calming, shallow breathing can decrease the level of carbon dioxide in the blood, which may lead to symptoms such as dizziness or a tingling sensation in the limbs, further exacerbating feelings of distress rather than alleviating them.

In modern scenarios, these physiological responses can seem like overreactions because they activate without real physical danger. For example, a rapid heartbeat and shallow breathing during a stressful meeting or while driving do not serve a protective or beneficial role. Instead, they can contribute to increased feelings of anxiety and stress, making it harder to focus, make decisions, or handle interpersonal interactions effectively.

Understanding these physiological responses helps to recognize them when they occur and manage them effectively. Techniques such as deep breathing exercises, mindfulness meditation, or physical activities like walking or stretching can help regulate the heart rate and deepen breathing, thus mitigating the body's stress response and helping maintain composure and focus even during potentially stressful situations.

**Muscle Tension and Sweating:** Muscle tension, or muscular hyperactivity, occurs as part of the body's automatic preparation for the fight-or-flight response. When faced with a perceived threat, the body's muscles tense up, readying themselves for physical action, such as running or fighting. This response is mediated by the nervous system, which sends signals to the muscles to increase readiness. Historically, this preparedness was essential for survival, enabling quick and powerful movements necessary in a hostile environment.

However, such physical reactions are less often required in today's context. For instance, muscle tension during a stressful work presentation or in a traffic jam does not aid in resolving these situations and can instead lead to discomfort. Chronic muscle tension can result in physical ailments such as headaches, migraines, and chronic pain disorders, particularly in the back and neck.

Sweating is another primitive response designed primarily for thermoregulation—helping the body maintain its optimal temperature during intense physical activity or in response to environmental heat.

When stressed, the body also sweats as part of the sympathetic nervous system's activation. The release of stress hormones stimulates sweat glands, particularly those around the armpits, palms, and soles, leading to increased perspiration.

While sweating has its roots in physical exertion and temperature control, it's more often a manifestation of emotional or psychological stress in contemporary settings. For example, sweating during a challenging negotiation or a public speaking engagement is typically a reaction to psychological stress rather than physical exertion. Although it's a natural and healthy bodily function, excessive sweating under non-physical stress can be uncomfortable and sometimes embarrassing, potentially exacerbating the stress experience.

Mindfulness techniques that focus on calming the mind and reducing emotional arousal can be beneficial for managing stress-induced sweating. These practices help decrease the overall activation of the sympathetic nervous system, thereby reducing sweat production linked to stress.

Incorporating these strategies into daily life helps manage these specific physiological responses. It contributes to a broader resilience against stress, enhancing overall health and well-being in modern life. By acknowledging these responses as natural yet often outdated reactions to contemporary stressors, we can better equip ourselves to handle them through mindful intervention and proactive stress management.

**Emotional and Psychological Responses:** Stress impacts us physically, emotionally, and psychologically. The experience of stress can manifest through various emotional responses such as feelings of anxiety, restlessness, or being overwhelmed. These reactions are often the body's immediate response to perceived threats, which, in today's world, are more likely to be psychological than physical threats.

When we're stressed, we may feel an undercurrent of anxiety that keeps us on edge, making us anticipate negative outcomes even when there's no real danger. This anxiety is often accompanied by restlessness an inability to relax or stay still, which can disrupt everyday routines and decrease productivity. Another common emotional response is feeling overwhelmed, where the challenges and demands of daily life seem too much to handle, leading to a sense of helplessness or loss of control.

Psychologically, stress can lead us into a cycle of excessive worry about the future, constantly contemplating worst-case scenarios. This mental state makes concentrating difficult, as our minds are cluttered with concerns, and our thoughts are pulled in many directions simultaneously. Over time, this continuous strain can lead to mental fatigue, where we feel emotionally and cognitively drained, unable to engage effectively with our daily tasks or make decisions efficiently.

Understanding how stress manifests emotionally and psychologically can significantly improve how we manage it. Techniques involving cognitive-behavioral approaches help by restructuring our thinking patterns, teaching us to challenge negative thoughts and focus more on realistic outcomes rather than worst-case scenarios. This shift in thinking can alleviate anxiety and reduce the feeling of being overwhelmed. However, as mentioned, we must be calm to use these higher cognitive functions.

Practicing mindfulness brings our focus back to the present, allowing us to disengage from distressing thoughts. They help cultivate a state of mind where we can address tasks individually, improving concentration and reducing the clutter in our thoughts.

Ensuring we get enough rest is necessary for recovering from mental fatigue. A well-rested mind is more resilient and better equipped to handle stress. In some cases, the intensity of emotional and psychological responses to stress might require professional intervention. Therapists and counselors can offer support tailored to individual circumstances, providing strategies to manage stress more effectively.

By addressing the emotional and psychological facets of stress, we not only mitigate the immediate symptoms but also strengthen our long-term ability to cope with future stressors, enhancing overall mental health and stability.

By recognizing these signs early, we can mitigate the stress response before it escalates. Mindfulness and relaxation techniques can effectively calm these physiological reactions, helping the body regain balance.

### Strategies to Regulate Our Stress Response

Week 1 explores various mindfulness and relaxation techniques that help regulate this response. Deep breathing, progressive muscle relaxation, and guided imagery can help calm the body's stress response and bring our systems back to equilibrium. These practices encourage a state of calm and balance, making it easier to manage stress in high-pressure situations.

By managing the fight-flight-freeze response effectively, we reduce the frequency and intensity of our stress reactions and lay a foundation for improved overall well-being. This proactive approach to stress management ensures that we are better equipped to handle the challenges of modern life without compromising our health.

Through the knowledge and techniques shared this week, we will enhance our ability to maintain calmness and balance amidst the fast-paced and often stressful modern environment. This understanding and these skills are crucial for reducing anxiety and improving our capacity to thrive in various aspects of life.

### History, Science, & Role in Managing Anxiety

Mindfulness is a practice deeply rooted in history and backed by modern science as a fundamental strategy for managing anxiety. It involves maintaining a moment-by-moment awareness of our thoughts, feelings, bodily sensations, and surrounding environment with openness and non-judgment.

Meditative practices and concepts of mindfulness have ancient roots tracing back thousands of years across multiple cultures and traditions. Some of the earliest evidence comes from ancient Hindu traditions in India, dating back to around 1500 BCE or earlier.

The Vedic texts and traditions of Hinduism describe meditation and mindfulness as pathways to enlightenment and liberation. Yoga, focusing on unifying the mind, body, and spiritual consciousness through disciplined practice, incorporates meditative techniques central to Hindu philosophy.

Around the 6th century BCE, meditative practices and mindfulness took root in Buddhism, which emerged from the Hindu spiritual culture in ancient India. The Buddha practiced and taught meditation and mindfulness as core components of the Eightfold Path to end suffering. Buddhist meditation techniques spread throughout Asia.

By the 3rd century BCE, meditative practices had been embraced by Indian philosophical traditions like Jainism, which promoted asceticism, non-violence, and liberation of the soul through disciplined meditation.

In ancient China, around the 6th century BCE, meditative practices developed in philosophical traditions like Daoism and Confucianism focused on self-cultivation, balance, and harmony. Daoist practices like zuowang incorporated mindfulness principles.

Ancient Greek schools like Pyrrhonism, Academics, and Stoicism around the 4th century BCE explored philosophical tenets related to mindfulness and meditative self-reflection to achieve well-being.

Meditative and mindfulness practices spread through the Middle East with Sufism in Islam around the 8th century CE. Sufi traditions incorporated practices like dhikr and muraqabah for spiritual growth.

Meditative and mindfulness modalities entered Western awareness in modern times through 19th/20th century influences like Hindu/Buddhist teachers and the Transcendentalist/New Age movements. Scientific research into their therapeutic benefits further boosted global adoption.

So, in essence, while taking diverse cultural forms, these contemplative practices have ancient cross-cultural spiritual roots tracing back over 3500 years across Hindu, Buddhist, Jain, Daoist, Hellenic, and Sufi traditions before achieving mainstream modern acceptance.

Scientific research into mindfulness has thrived over the past few decades. Neuroscientific studies reveal that mindfulness meditation can lead to changes in the brain areas related to perception, body awareness, pain tolerance, emotion regulation, introspection, complex thinking, and sense of self. Techniques such as MRI scans show that mindfulness enhances cortical thickness in the hippocampus, which governs learning and memory, and in some regions of the brain that play roles in emotion regulation and self-referential processing.

Additionally, studies have indicated that mindfulness reduces activity in the amygdala, the brain area responsible for fear processing, which is heavily involved in anxiety and stress responses. By dampening this activity, mindfulness helps moderate the fight, flight or freeze responses that are often inappropriate reactions to modern-day stressors.

Mindfulness is considered a first-line defense in managing anxiety primarily because it helps break the cycle of the brain's limbic system response. During high anxiety, the brain often gets stuck in a loop of fight, flight, or freeze reactions driven by the limbic system, which hinders the use of higher cognitive strategies, such as those employed in Cognitive Behavioral Therapy (CBT). If a limbic response consumes a person, they may find it challenging to engage in CBT's reflective and restructuring techniques, which require thinking through thoughts and emotions logically and rationally.

Mindfulness helps by calming the limbic system and reducing the immediacy of the stress response. This calming effect allows individuals to move out of the automatic limbic response and engage the prefrontal cortex, the brain area associated with higher-order brain functions such as awareness, concentration, and decision-making. By stabilizing the mind's response to stress and anxiety, mindfulness creates the mental space necessary to employ more complex cognitive techniques for long-term anxiety management.

Integrating mindfulness into daily life can significantly improve an individual's ability to manage stress and anxiety. We can incorporate simple practices such as mindful breathing, observation, and mindful listening throughout the day to maintain heightened, relaxed awareness. These practices reduce immediate stress and anxiety and cultivate a lasting mindfulness habit that can improve overall emotional and psychological resilience.

With its rich history, substantial scientific backing, and practical benefits, mindfulness is a powerful tool for managing anxiety and enhancing overall well-being. By starting with mindfulness, individuals can prepare their minds for deeper therapeutic work, addressing anxiety holistically and effectively.

### Mindfulness and Staying Present to Overcome Anxiety

One of the most potent ways mindfulness can help address anxiety is by anchoring us firmly in the present moment. When anxious, our minds tend to get carried away by worries about the future or rumination over past events. This mental time travel depletes our energy and compounds our anxiety.

Through mindfulness practices like breath awareness, body scans, and mindful observation, we cultivate the skill of recognizing when our minds have wandered away from the here and now. With gentleness and patience, we can then guide our attention back to present-moment awareness.

Why is being fully present so beneficial when we feel anxious? In part because anxiety is primarily fed by imagination and thoughts that are disconnected from current reality. Our anxious minds get caught up spinning worst-case scenario stories that have not occurred yet.

Mindfulness permits us to hit the pause button on this mental proliferation. We can notice the worries and fears arising but resist getting entangled in their dramatizations. Instead, we anchor ourselves in the tangible reality of the present - the sensations in our body, the sights and sounds around us in this very moment.

From this present-centered awareness, we can reflect: "At this moment, am I actually in danger? Am I truly unsafe right now?" For many of us, the truthful answer in that immediate instance is "no."

Anxiety is lying to us about an imagined threat, disconnected from current circumstances.

Mindfulness allows us to befriend reality. We use our grounding in the present moment to reassure ourselves - "Right now, in this present moment, I am okay, and I am safe." We don't have to change anything or push the anxiety away. We simply need to observe it with a calm, centered presence.

This mindful, present awareness also helps regulate and calm our physical anxiety responses like muscle tension, rapid heartbeat, or stomach upset. We can notice these distress signals compassionately, breathing into them and reminding ourselves that they are simply anxious visitors that will pass in time if we don't get overly invested in them.

Through meditative, reflective practices, we train ourselves to disentangle from the anxious storylines and instead abide in the truth of the present moment - where very little is threatening or unsafe. We strengthen our ability to pause, observe our anxious tendencies with acceptance, and return to the peaceful recognition that in this exact moment, we have everything we need to be okay.

Mindfulness is not about forcing ourselves to stop feeling anxiety, but rather, relating to it differently - with a grounded presence and kind understanding that reminds us of the transient nature of all mental states and emotional storms. From this spacious, present-moment awareness, we can ride the waves of anxiety with greater grace, never entirely drowning in its turbulence but surfacing again and again into the refuge of the here and now.

# Week 1 Self-Help Guide

## Mindfulness & Relaxation

Mindfulness and relaxation are powerful tools in managing anxiety. This seven-day self-help homework guide introduces these techniques as the foundation of an anxiety management strategy. Each day focuses on a different aspect of mindfulness and relaxation, providing practical exercises and insights.

# Week 1 Day 1

## Trigger Awareness

**Objective:** The objective of today's exercise is to enhance your understanding of what triggers your anxiety, identifying the precursors that lead to anxious moments. This insight is foundational for managing and ultimately reducing the frequency and intensity of anxiety episodes.

**Information:** Becoming aware of the early signs of anxiety is crucial. By recognizing these signals, you can intervene earlier in the anxiety process, which can help prevent or lessen the severity of an anxiety episode. Today, you will develop a "trigger" journal to record and reflect on these signals.

**Instructions:**

1. **Start a Trigger Journal:** Create a dedicated journal to note instances when you feel highly anxious.
2. **Record and Reflect:** Whenever you notice your anxiety levels rising, write down the details:
   ◦ **What were you doing, thinking, and feeling right before you noticed the anxiety?**
   ◦ **Trace Backwards:** After recording the immediate precursors, remember what you were doing or thinking before those immediate thoughts and actions. Keep tracing until you can't remember any further or until you reach a point where you felt calm.
3. **Mindfulness Practice:** Before you begin to feel anxious, practice mindfulness. This can involve deep breathing, focusing on

your senses, or meditating. The goal is to remain present and grounded, preventing escalation.

**Reflection:** At the end of the day, review your journal entries. Look for patterns or common themes in what triggers your anxiety. Reflect on:

- **The earliest signs of discomfort you noted.**
- **How effective the mindfulness techniques were in mitigating your anxiety.**

**Integration:** As you continue this exercise throughout the week, integrate the mindfulness techniques more consistently into moments you identify as potential triggers. The goal is to make these practices a reflexive part of your response to rising anxiety.

This structured approach to understanding and managing your anxiety triggers will help you regain control over your emotional responses and reduce the impact of anxiety on your daily life. Keep the journal handy and update it as soon as you notice triggers or increased anxiety, as this will enhance the accuracy and usefulness of your reflections.

# Week 1 Day 2

## Breath and Body Awareness

**Objective:** Today's exercise aims to familiarize yourself with deep breathing and full-body relaxation techniques. These techniques are valuable tools for managing anxiety, especially when you first notice the signs of triggers as identified in Day 1. By integrating breath and body awareness, you can effectively reduce the physiological and psychological effects of anxiety.

**Information:** Deep breathing and relaxation techniques help to calm the nervous system, reduce stress, and promote a state of calm. By consciously altering your breath and relaxing your body, you can counteract the body's anxiety response, often characterized by shallow breathing and muscle tension. Today's exercise also incorporates a reassuring mantra to reinforce a sense of safety and stability.

**Instructions:**

1. **Find a Quiet Space:** Find a comfortable and quiet place to sit or lie down without interruptions.
2. **Deep Breathing:**
   - **Inhale Slowly:** Breathe deeply through your nose, allowing your stomach to expand fully.
   - **Hold Your Breath:** Hold your breath for a count of four.
   - **Exhale Slowly:** Exhale completely through your mouth, feeling your stomach contract and release all tension.
   - **Repeat:** Continue this pattern for several minutes, focusing solely on your breathing.
3. **Progressive Muscle Relaxation:**

- **Tense and Release:** Tightly tense each muscle group for a few seconds, then slowly release, noticing the difference in sensation. Start from your forehead and work your way to your toes.
- **Focus on Relaxation:** With each exhale, imagine releasing stress and tension from your body, visualizing it flowing out of you and falling off you.

4. **Mantra Repetition:**
   - **Recite a Mantra:** As you breathe deeply and relax, silently repeat to yourself: "I am safe, I am okay."
   - **Believe in Your Safety:** Emphasize each word in your mind, reinforcing your emotional and physical safety.

**Reflection:** After completing the exercise, spend a few minutes in silence, allowing yourself to absorb the calmness. Reflect on how your body feels compared to before the exercise. Think about the effectiveness of the mantra in shifting your thoughts away from anxiety.

**Integration:** Practice this technique daily, especially during moments when you first notice anxiety triggers, as recorded in your Trigger Journal. Over time, aim to use these techniques automatically when you start to feel anxious, integrating them into your daily routine to maintain a state of calm and clarity.

By regularly practicing these techniques, you will enhance your ability to stay present, think clearly, and mitigate the effects of anxiety on your mind and body. This will empower you to handle stressful situations more effectively, using your breath and body awareness as tools for tranquility.

# Week 1 Day 3

## Body Scan Meditation

**Objective:** Today's focus is on mastering the body scan meditation technique. This practice enhances your ability to be present and attuned to physical sensations throughout your body, helping you identify and release areas of tension that may contribute to anxiety.

**Information:** Body scan meditation is a form of mindful meditation where you focus on different parts of your body in sequence, from head to toe. This technique is effective for developing both concentration and body awareness. It allows you to notice and release physical tension and reduce stress and anxiety by fostering relaxed awareness.

**Instructions:**

1. **Prepare Your Environment:** Find a quiet, comfortable space where you can lie down on your back with your legs slightly apart and arms at your sides, palms facing up. You can also do this seated if lying down isn't possible.
2. **Start with Deep Breathing:** Take a few deep breaths to relax your mind and body. With each exhale, feel yourself sinking deeper into relaxation.
3. **Focus on Your Feet:** Begin the body scan at your feet. Notice any sensations in your toes, the soles of your feet, and your heels. If you detect any tension, imagine it melting away with each breath.
4. **Move Up Through Your Body:** Gradually shift your focus

through different parts of your body: your ankles, calves, knees, thighs, hips, abdomen, chest, back, hands, arms, shoulders, neck, and finally your head. Spend a few moments on each area.

5. **Notice and Release Tension:** As you focus on each body part, acknowledge any discomfort, pain, or tension. Breathe into these areas and imagine the tension releasing and flowing out of your body with each exhale.

6. **Scan the Whole Body:** After reaching the top of your head, spend a few moments scanning your whole body in one piece. Notice the feeling of wholeness and the relaxed state of your entire body.

7. **Close with Deep Breathing:** Finish your body scan with a few deep breaths, feeling refreshed and calm.

**Reflection:** Reflect on the experience of the body scan. Did you notice areas of your body where tension accumulates? How did focusing on each part of your body one at a time affect your overall sense of relaxation?

**Integration:** Incorporate this body scan meditation into your daily routine, especially when you start feeling early signs of anxiety, as identified in your Trigger Journal. Regular practice can significantly enhance your awareness and control over your body's stress responses.

This body scan meditation will equip you with the tools to consciously relax various parts of your body, fostering a powerful sense of calm that can help mitigate the physical symptoms of anxiety.

# Week 1 Day 4

## The 5-5-5 Sensory Grounding Exercise

**Objective:** Today, you will learn the 5-5-5 grounding technique, an effective strategy to manage acute anxiety by engaging your senses and regulating your breathing. This exercise can be utilized during moments of high anxiety or stress to help bring you back to the present and reduce feelings of overwhelm.

**Information:** The 5-5-5 rule is a sensory grounding technique that helps interrupt the escalation of anxiety by focusing on the present moment through your senses and controlled breathing. Grounding techniques like this are widely recognized in cognitive behavioral therapy (CBT) and other therapeutic approaches for their effectiveness in managing anxiety and stress symptoms.

**Instructions:**

1. **Begin with Controlled Breathing:**
   - **Inhale Deeply:** Breathe slowly through your nose for 5 seconds, focusing solely on filling your lungs.
   - **Hold Your Breath:** Hold your breath for 5 seconds. This pause helps regulate your oxygen intake and can have a calming effect on your nervous system.
   - **Exhale Slowly:** Breathe through your mouth for 5 seconds, releasing tension and anxiety. Imagine expelling stress and worry with your breath.
   - **Repeat** this breathing pattern for a few cycles until you feel a noticeable relaxation.
2. **Engage Your Senses:**

- **Five Things You Can See:** Look around and note five things you can see. Pick items you wouldn't usually notice, like a crack on the wall, a spot on the ceiling, or how light reflects off a surface.
- **Five Sounds You Can Hear:** Close your eyes and listen carefully. Identify five different sounds around you. It might be the hum of an appliance, birds chirping outside, or distant traffic.
- **Five Objects You Can Touch:** Reach out and touch five objects within your environment. Notice their texture, temperature, and shape. It could be the fabric of your clothes, the cool surface of a table, or the grass under your feet.

**Reflection:** After completing the exercise, take a moment to reflect on your experience. How did your level of anxiety change before and after the exercise? Did focusing on your senses help distract you from anxious thoughts? How did your body physically respond to the breathing technique?

**Integration:** Make the 5-5-5 rule a go-to strategy whenever you start noticing early signs of anxiety, as tracked in your Trigger Journal. Integrating this exercise into your daily routine, especially during stressful situations, can help you maintain a sense of calm and control.

# Week 1 Day 5

## Progressive Muscle Relaxation

**Objective:** Today focuses on learning Progressive Muscle Relaxation (PMR), a technique to help you relax your muscles through a two-step process of tensing and relaxing specific muscle groups. This practice is beneficial for reducing stress and anxiety by physically releasing tension held in the body.

**Information:** Progressive Muscle Relaxation (PMR) was a technique developed by Dr. Edmund Jacobson in the early 20th century. It is based on the premise that mental calmness is a natural result of physical relaxation. PMR has been widely used to help alleviate symptoms of anxiety and stress, improve sleep, and enhance overall well-being.

**Instructions:**

1. **Find a Comfortable Position:** Lie on your back in a comfortable, quiet place. You can lie on a mat on the floor or your bed. Make sure your clothing is comfortable, and your environment is conducive to relaxation.
2. **Start with Deep Breaths:** Take a few deep breaths to relax your mind and body. Inhale slowly through your nose, hold for a few seconds and exhale through your mouth.
3. **Tense and Relax Muscle Groups:** Follow these steps for each muscle group:
   ○ **Feet:** Begin by tensing the muscles in your toes and feet. Hold the tension for about 5 seconds, then release and notice the sensation of relaxation. Pause for 10 seconds.

- **Lower Legs:** Tense your calf muscles by pulling your toes toward you. Hold, then relax.
- **Thighs and Glutes:** Tense your thighs and buttocks. Hold, then relax.
- **Stomach:** Tightly contract your stomach muscles. Hold, then relax.
- **Chest and Shoulders:** Breathe deeply to tense the chest and raise your shoulders toward your ears to tense the shoulder muscles. Hold, then relax while exhaling.
- **Arms:** Extend your arms out and clench your fists. Hold, then relax.
- **Neck and Face:** Tense your facial muscles by squeezing your eyes shut and puckering your lips, then release. Also, try to bring your chin to your chest to tense the neck muscles, then relax.
- **Forehead:** Raise your eyebrows as high as possible, hold, and relax.

4. **End with Deep Breathing:** Once you have gone through all the muscle groups, focus on your breath for a few minutes. Feel your body completely relaxed and your mind at peace.

**Reflection:** After completing the PMR session, reflect on how your body feels compared to before you started. Are there areas that still hold tension? How effective was the exercise in helping you reduce anxiety?

**Integration:** Integrate PMR into your daily routine, especially during times when you feel stressed or when you recognize early signs of anxiety. Regular practice can significantly reduce physical symptoms of stress and improve your mental clarity and emotional resilience.

# Week 1 Day 6

## *Schedule Your Worry Time*

**Objective:** Today, you will learn and implement the practice of scheduling a specific time to worry, known as "worry time." This evidence-based strategy helps manage anxiety by confining worry to a defined period, which can prevent it from overwhelming your day.

**Instructions:**

1. **Choose a Time and Place:**
   - Select a consistent 15-30 minute period each day, ideally in the morning or afternoon, to dedicate to worrying. Avoid scheduling this time right before bed to prevent sleep disturbances. Choose a place where you can be uninterrupted and that isn't associated with relaxation or sleep.

2. **Setting Up Your Worry Time:**
   - During your worry time, allow yourself to fully engage with your worries without judgment. Write down all the concerns that come to mind, no matter how big or small.
   - Use a timer to keep track of time. Once the timer goes off, conclude your worry session and move to a different activity or setting.

3. **Managing Worry Outside of Scheduled Time:**
   - If worries arise outside of the designated time, make a note of them and decide to postpone dealing with them until your next worry time. This helps train your brain to

handle worries only during the allotted times, enhancing your control over anxiety.

4. **Reflect on the Process:**
    - At the end of the week, review the worries you noted. Look for patterns or recurring themes. This reflection can help you understand your anxieties better and adjust your coping strategies accordingly.

5. **Repeat and Adjust:**
    - Continue with this practice, adjusting the duration and timing as needed based on your experience. Over time, you may find that your anxiety becomes more manageable as you train yourself to confine worries to their designated time.

**Reflection:** After practicing this technique, reflect on how segregating worry to specific times of the day affects your overall anxiety. Are you able to focus more on present tasks? Do you feel less overwhelmed by spontaneous worries throughout the day?

This technique is supported by research showing that worry can be controlled and that postponing worry to a specific time can significantly reduce its impact on your life. By practicing scheduled worry time, you give yourself permission to postpone anxiety, which can help decrease its intensity and frequency, leading to a more focused and less anxious daily experience.

# Week 1 Day 7

## *Embracing Mindfulness as a Way of Life*

**Objective:** Today's session is designed to shift your perspective on mindfulness from a practice to a way of being. The goal is to embed mindfulness into your daily life so profoundly that it becomes an integral part of who you are, enhancing your ability to manage anxiety and stress effectively.

**Information:** Mindfulness is not just a set of exercises; it's a state of active, open attention to the present moment. When you become mindful, you realize that you are not your thoughts; you become an observer of your thoughts from moment to moment without judging them. By practicing mindfulness regularly, you can change the way you think about stressful situations, ultimately leading to a reduction in anxiety.

**Instructions:**

1. **Understanding Mindfulness:**
    - Recognize that mindfulness involves being aware of your thoughts, feelings, bodily sensations, and surrounding environment in a non-judgmental and accepting way.
    - Understand that mindfulness is not just for moments of peace but is especially useful during stressful times.
2. **Practical Integration of Mindfulness:**
    - **While Driving:** Focus on the feel of the steering wheel, the sound of the engine, and the sight of the road. When

you notice your mind wandering to other concerns, gently bring your attention to the driving experience.

- **During Work:** Whether sitting at a desk or moving about, periodically pause to genuinely absorb your environment. Note the texture of your office furniture, the sounds of your workplace, and your bodily sensations – the pressure of your feet on the floor or your back against the chair.
- **While walking:** Pay attention to each step, the rhythm of your pace, and how each foot feels as it touches the ground. Observe as you breathe in and out, and notice the sensations of moving air on your face and body.
- **During Presentations:** Focus on the sound of your voice, the pace of your speech, and the feedback from the audience. Use breaths to center yourself in the moment if you feel anxious.
- **In Personal Interactions:** Be fully present during conversations, focusing on the other person's words, expressions, and tone of voice without planning your next thing to say.

3. **Daily Mindfulness Moments:**
   - Set reminders to pause a few times a day to check in with yourself. Use these moments to practice deep breathing and acknowledge and accept your feelings without judgment.

**Reflection:** Reflect on how integrating mindfulness into your daily activities has affected your stress and anxiety levels. Have you noticed a difference in how you respond to stress? How does maintaining a non-judgmental awareness influence your emotional reactions?

**Integration:** Encourage the continual practice of mindfulness throughout your day. The more you practice, the more natural it will become. Mindfulness is a powerful tool that can be seamlessly integrated into any part of your life, providing a robust mechanism to handle stress and anxiety effectively.

By the end of the week, mindfulness should start to feel less like a practice and more like a characteristic of your everyday life. This shift is crucial for long-term anxiety management and living a more engaged, present, and fulfilled life.

# Week 1 Tracking Progress

As you conclude this week's exercises, take a moment to reflect on your progress. Refer to the bridge illustration and consider where you currently stand on your journey toward managing anxiety. Place a mark on the bridge representing your position and rate your anxiety level on the provided 0-10 scale. Remember, progress is personal, and each step matters.

**Instructions:**

1. Take a moment to reflect on your progress and experiences.
2. Refer to the bridge illustration below.
3. Consider where you currently stand on your journey.
4. Place a mark on the bridge representing your current position.
5. Next, rate where your average anxiety level has been over this week.
6. Record your anxiety rating on the provided 0-10 scale, with 0 being no anxiety and 10 being the most intense anxiety you've experienced.
7. Reflect and journal.

**Reflection:** After marking your bridge position and anxiety rating, reflect on your progress. Examine skills learned, challenges faced, and changes in thoughts and behaviors. Journal your insights and observations. Identify successes, challenges, and areas requiring more attention. Determine if you need to slow down, revisit previous weeks or skills, or seek professional help to maintain progress. Assess your

overall progress and consider if professional support is needed or how it's contributing to your journey.

| 0 | 1 | 2 | 3 | 4 | 5 | 6 | 7 | 8 | 9 | 10 |

No
Anxiety

Moderate
Anxiety

High
Anxiety

# 6

# Beyond Mindfulness

In the previous chapters, we explored how mindfulness can be an incredibly powerful tool for managing anxiety and stress. By cultivating present-moment awareness and allowing thoughts and emotions to arise without judgment, mindfulness helps break the cycle of anxiety. It provides us with a way to detach from the constant stream of worries and "what-if" thinking that so often fuels anxiety.

However, there are times when anxiety becomes so intense and overwhelming that mindfulness alone is not enough to keep it in check. When our brain and body become flooded with the fight-or-flight response, rational thinking can cease, and we can lose our ability to ground ourselves in the present reality. This is what happens during a panic attack or a period of acute, incapacitating anxiety.

A panic attack is an abrupt surge of intense fear or discomfort that peaks within minutes. Physical symptoms such as racing heartbeat, shortness of breath, trembling, and dizziness are common. Psychologically, one may experience terrifying thoughts of dying, losing control or going crazy. Acute anxiety is similar but may last for an extended period - hours or even days. Both panic attacks and acute anxiety can significantly impair our ability to function normally in everyday life.

While mindfulness practices can sometimes help prevent or minimize panic attacks and acute anxiety when in the throes of such an extreme reaction, we need additional strategies. This chapter will provide practical tools to manage panic and acute anxiety when they arise, guiding you through specific coping techniques.

It's important to note that if panic attacks or acute anxiety persist or significantly interfere with your life, professional support from a therapist or counselor is recommended. While the strategies in this chapter can be beneficial, some anxiety conditions may require more intensive treatment. Don't hesitate to seek professional help if your symptoms are severe or unmanageable.

By learning to identify and respond effectively to panic attacks and acute anxiety, you can prevent these intense experiences from derailing you completely. Used in conjunction with mindfulness, the skills you'll learn will provide a comprehensive approach to overcoming anxiety and regaining a sense of calm and control, no matter how overwhelming things may feel in the moment.

## Understanding Panic Attacks

Panic attacks represent an extreme physiological and psychological response, even more intense than the general fight-or-flight anxiety reaction. They often appear out of nowhere without any apparent trigger, making them incredibly frightening and difficult to control.

Physiological Aspects: During a panic attack, the body goes into a full fight-or-flight mode without any actual danger. The sympathetic nervous system becomes dramatically overactivated, leading to a wave of physical symptoms. These can include racing or pounding heartbeat, chest pains, shortness of breath or feeling smothered, trembling or shaking, sweating, nausea, dizziness, and numbness or tingling sensations. Sometimes, these somatic symptoms can be so intense they are mistaken for a heart attack or another serious medical emergency.

Psychological Impacts: The cognitive and emotional experience of a panic attack is one of extreme, incapacitating terror, even though no actual danger is present. People often report intense fear of losing control, going crazy, or dying. There is a sense of dissociation or disconnect from reality. The world can seem unreal, dreamlike, and unfamiliar - a phenomenon known as derealization. Thoughts may race uncontrollably as the sufferer catastrophizes and spirals down into worst-case scenarios. Overall, panic attacks create an overwhelming feeling of being trapped and powerless over one's emotional and physical responses.

Causes and Risk Factors: While panic attacks can seem to strike at random, there are predispositions that increase one's risk. Having first-degree relatives with panic disorder indicates a potential genetic/biological predisposition. Excessive stress, major life changes or transitions, and environmental factors like extreme heat can trigger panic attacks. Stimulants like caffeine or certain medications are other common precipitants. Finally, panic attacks can develop into a self-perpetuating cycle - the fear of having another attack itself becomes a sufficient trigger.

Types of Panic Attacks: Panic attacks can be categorized into expected vs unexpected and cued vs uncued. Expected panic attacks are those that the sufferer anticipates or even inadvertently causes through hyper-vigilance about body sensations. Unexpected ones seem to occur spontaneously without any trigger. Cued panic attacks have a specific, identifiable trigger, such as a phobic situation, whereas uncued ones appear to happen for no discernible reason.

The different types of panic attacks are not necessarily distinct—they exist on a spectrum, and many panic sufferers experience a combination. However, it can be helpful to identify any consistent patterns or triggers that typically precipitate one's panic attacks as part of creating an effective coping plan.

## Acute Anxiety: Beyond Everyday Stress

While panic attacks are intense, acute anxiety is similarly overwhelming but often lasts for more extended periods. Unlike the sudden onset of panic, acute anxiety builds gradually over hours or days in response to a very stressful situation or trauma.

Definition and Characteristics Acute anxiety, also called anxiety panic, is marked by severe and incapacitating symptoms that are longer lasting than a panic attack episode. The intensity far exceeds everyday stresses or worries. Acute anxiety significantly impairs the ability to function normally in daily life activities. It is persistent rather than a short burst of panic symptoms.

Sources of Acute Anxiety Common triggers include traumatic experiences like accidents, assaults, or natural disasters. Phobias and excessive worries about particular situations can precipitate acute anxiety when those perceived threats become imminent. Major life stressors and sources of severe stress like divorce, job loss, death of a loved one, or chronic illnesses are also potential instigators.

Somatic Symptoms The physical manifestations of acute anxiety are similar to panic but tend to be more prolonged. These include sustained muscle tension that may lead to headaches, back pain, or jaw clenching. Acute anxiety often causes appetite changes and gastrointestinal issues like nausea, diarrhea, or stomach cramps. Fatigue, insomnia, and generalized aches/pains are common somatic effects.

Cognitive and Emotional Experience Psychologically, acute anxiety is characterized by a barrage of negative, catastrophic thoughts that seem inescapable—intense worry, fears, and rumination compound upon each other in a vicious cycle. Emotionally, sufferers often feel constantly on edge, restless, and irritable. Concentration becomes extremely difficult with the onslaught of racing thoughts. A sense of dread and impending danger is pervasive.

While panic attacks can transition into acute anxiety, it is also possible to experience high anxiety without full-blown panic attacks. No matter the trigger, any sustained and intense anxiety reaction requires intervention. Like panic, if acute anxiety persists for an extended period, it is advisable to seek professional treatment. However, the coping techniques in this chapter can provide relief for acute anxiety as well.

**Management Strategies for Panic and Acute Anxiety**

While mindfulness practices can help prevent and minimize anxiety over the long-term, when in the throes of a panic attack or acute anxiety episode, specific interventions are needed to regain control. A multi-pronged approach incorporating grounding techniques, cognitive restructuring, behavioral strategies, lifestyle adjustments, and professional support is recommended.

Grounding and Breathwork When panic or acute anxiety strikes, grounding methods can break through the overwhelming physical and emotional sensations. Belly breathing, focusing on slow, deep abdominal breaths, can rapidly calm the body's stress response. The 5-5-5 technique presented in week one is a go-to grounding exercise that redirects attention to the present reality.

Panic attacks are often maintained by catastrophic, irrational thoughts that heighten anxiety further. Cognitive restructuring helps challenge and reframe these thoughts to reflect a more rational perspective. This may involve coping statements like "This feeling is temporary" or examining evidence contrary to fears of losing control. In the coming weeks, we will cover cognitive restructuring in detail in the self-help homework guide.

Opposite-to-Emotion Action. While it's the instinct to avoid scary situations during the panic, behavioral approaches encourage facing feared stimuli through gradual exposure. This builds tolerance and realizes that anxiety naturally diminishes over time without catastrophe. Scheduling positive activities despite anxiety can also prevent excessive avoidance.

Sleep deprivation, poor nutrition, lack of exercise, and other lifestyle factors can increase vulnerability to panic and anxiety. Making adjustments like sticking to a sleep schedule, eating balanced meals, getting regular physical activity, and practicing general stress management can prevent anxiety from spiraling out of control.

If panic attacks and acute anxiety persist for extended periods and significantly impair functioning, don't hesitate to seek professional mental health treatment. Cognitive-behavioral therapy, mindfulness-based interventions, and, in some cases, anti-anxiety medication or other psychotropic drugs can be highly effective when properly pre-scribed.

A psychological and psychiatric evaluation is recommended for frequent, unmanageable panic or severe acute anxiety. These are seri-ous mental health conditions that require appropriate assessment and diagnosis to determine the optimal treatment plan. Working with a licensed therapist or counselor is advisable to understand the root causes better and develop comprehensive coping strategies.

### Preventing Relapse and Sustaining Progress

Once you have gained control over panic attacks and acute anxiety episodes through the strategies outlined, it's important to have a plan for maintaining your progress long-term. Anxiety conditions can be cyclical, so you must be vigilant against relapse.

Continued practice of mindfulness meditation, body scans, breath awareness, and other mindfulness exercises is key. These aren't tools to use only during moments of anxiety - regular practice helps reinforce pathways in the brain for being present and letting thoughts and feel-ings arise without fueling them. Mindfulness becomes a way of being, not just a coping technique.

In addition to a mindfulness routine, a healthy lifestyle supports anxiety management. Getting sufficient sleep, nutritious eating, regular exercise, limiting caffeine/alcohol, and calming self-care create a strong foundation of wellness. Be proactive about managing everyday stress through relaxation practices.

Even with diligent maintenance, setbacks can occur where anxiety temporarily regains a foothold. This is normal and okay - the key is not berating yourself but approaching it with self-compassion. Avoid panic about having a panic attack. Use your coping strategies, but don't resist the feelings. They will pass more quickly when not fighting against them.

If you find your coping strategies are no longer as effective for oc-casional relapses, reevaluate and update your coping plan. Regress this chapter's techniques or seek out new skills. Review potential triggers. Consider returning to therapy for "tune-ups" as needed. The path to overcoming anxiety is rarely linear.

The main things are not losing hope during temporary setbacks and cultivating patience and self-kindness throughout the journey. Persistence with lifestyle habits, mindfulness practices, and coping strategies will help minimize relapses and sustain your hard-earned progress over time.

In this chapter, we explored how to navigate the overwhelming experience of panic attacks and acute anxiety episodes. We defined the physiological and psychological impacts of these intense anxiety states, as well as common causes and risk factors. Crucially, we outlined a comprehensive arsenal of coping strategies to regain control during panic - including grounding techniques, cognitive restructuring, behavioral approaches, lifestyle adjustments, and knowing when to seek professional treatment.

While mindfulness practices are valuable for anxiety management, we recognized that mindfulness alone is often not sufficient when the mind and body become flooded with the fight-or-flight response characteristic of panic and acute anxiety. The techniques in this chapter provide additional tools to break through the cycle of overwhelm in those moments.

However, it's important to integrate these strategies with an ongoing mindfulness practice, not treat them as separate interventions. Mindfulness creates the foundation of present-centered awareness, allowing specific panic/anxiety coping skills to be implemented most effectively. Working in concert, mindful breathing, grounding yourself in your senses, and reframing catastrophic thoughts become much more accessible. Mindfulness and these interventions are complementary pathways to overcoming panic and acute anxiety.

Sustaining your progress is an ever-evolving process that requires adjusting your coping plan when needed. You may need to adapt strategies as anxious episodes inevitably arise from different future triggers and stressors. What's most important is developing an attitude of self-compassion - recognizing that setbacks are part of the journey but maintaining confidence that you possess the tools to manage and move through them.

With diligent practice integrating mindfulness with your panic/anxiety coping skills, you are building resilient pathways in your mind to prevent these intense experiences from derailing you completely. While the work isn't always easy, you are developing unshakable reservoirs of inner calm and clarity to navigate anxiety's turbulence effectively. Trust the process, have patience with yourself, and remain open to continuously evolving your step-by-step approach to overcoming panic and acute anxiety.

While this week's chapter provided an in-depth look at panic attacks and acute anxiety states, the good news is that you already have a robust set of tools at your disposal. The mindfulness practices, breathwork, relaxation techniques, and calming strategies you learned in week one's self-help guide can be effectively employed when anxiety becomes overwhelming. The body scan meditation, mindful observation exercises, and techniques for integrating mindfulness into your day are the skills needed to ground yourself and break free from panic's grip. So this week, we'll build upon that solid foundation with three additional panic-specific strategies. But remember, everything you've already practiced is your strongest defense when anxiety intensifies. Draw upon those ever-available mindful resources as needed.

# Week 2 Self-Help Guide

## Acute Anxiety and Panic

The next seven exercises and processes are deeply rooted in mindfulness. These meditative and relaxation techniques are designed to help address acute anxiety and panic. Often, when anxiety levels are significant, we are unable to think clearly due to the heightened stress response. These tools offer a way to help calm the body and quiet the mind so you have the ability to think through highly stressful situations and manage anxiety effectively.

# Week 2 Day 1

## Creating a Panic Attack Safety Plan

**Objective:** Today's task will empower you by creating a personal panic attack safety plan. This plan will be a go-to resource during acute episodes of anxiety or panic, providing clear steps and resources to help you manage intense moments effectively. By preparing this plan, you will equip yourself with a structured response for any acute situation, enhancing your ability to cope and regain control.

**Instructions:**

1. **Identify Warning Signs:**
   - Reflect on the early indicators that signal the onset of a panic attack or acute anxiety episode. Consider what you typically think about, what you are doing, where you are, and who you are with when these feelings surface. Document these signs clearly in your plan.
2. **List Coping Skills When Alone:**
   - Write down the coping mechanisms that have effectively managed negative emotions, especially when alone. These might include breathing exercises, grounding techniques, or engaging in a specific hobby that helps divert your thoughts. Use this book as a guide.
3. **Identify People, Places, and Situations That Provide Distraction:**
   - Consider the people who make you feel safe, valued, and happy. Also, identify places or situations that bring you

joy and comfort. Listing these can help you quickly decide where to go or whom to seek out when you feel a panic attack coming on.

4. **Compile a List of Helpful Contacts:**
   - Create a list of personal contacts—friends, family members, or colleagues—who understand your situation and are reliable in times of need. Include their contact details and possibly a brief note on how they can assist during an episode.

5. **Include Professional Support Contacts:**
   - Detail the contact information for your primary care provider, counselor, or any mental health professional you currently see. If you have a spiritual mentor or advisor, include them as well. Make sure this list is up-to-date and accessible.

6. **Safe Environment Strategies:**
   - Think about making your immediate environment safe during a panic attack. This might involve removing stressors from your vicinity, creating a calm and comforting physical space, or having certain calming items like music, stress balls, or aromatic oils readily available.

**Reflection and Integration:** After you have compiled your safety plan, spend a few moments reflecting on how having this plan makes you feel. Do you feel more prepared? Are you less anxious about potential future episodes? Consider where you will keep this plan to ensure it is easily accessible when needed. You might also want to share this plan with a trusted friend or family member who can help remind you of the steps when you're feeling overwhelmed.

**Encouragement:** Remember, the goal of this safety plan is not just to cope with panic attacks when they occur but also to give you a sense of control and preparedness, which can be incredibly empowering. Regularly updating and revising your plan as you discover what works best for you is key to making it an effective tool in your anxiety management toolkit.

# Week 2 Day 2

## *Revisiting Week 1 Skills and Recognizing Top Coping Strategies*

**Objective:** Today's session is dedicated to reviewing and reflecting on the anxiety management skills introduced in week one, with a focus on identifying which of these techniques are most effective for you during a panic attack or acute anxiety episode. We'll pinpoint the top two skills that resonate best with your needs and prepare them as your go-to strategies.

**Skills Overview:**

1. **Breath and Body Awareness:** Focuses on syncing breath with body sensations to cultivate a calming effect.
2. **Body Scan Meditation:** Involves mentally scanning your body for tension or discomfort, promoting overall relaxation.
3. **The 5-5-5 Sensory Grounding Exercise:** Utilizes your senses to anchor you in the present moment, effectively diverting attention from anxiety.
4. **Progressive Muscle Relaxation:** A systematic technique to tense and then relax muscle groups, enhancing body awareness and relaxation.
5. **Enhanced Breath and Body Awareness:** An advanced level of the first skill that integrates deeper breathing exercises with mindfulness practices.

**Instructions:**

- **Practice Each Skill:** Briefly practice each of the above techniques. As you engage with each skill, note any immediate effects on your anxiety level.
- **Evaluate Effectiveness:** After practicing each skill, evaluate how effectively it helped manage your anxiety. Consider factors such as ease of use, immediate relief provided, and overall comfort with the technique.

**Reflection:**

- **Identify Top Two Skills:** Reflect on which two skills you found most effective and why. Think about how these techniques addressed your symptoms of panic or anxiety.
- **Journaling Exercise:** Write down your thoughts about each technique in a journal. Describe what you felt before and after the exercise and why some techniques worked better.
- **Decision on Go-To Skills:** Decide which two skills will be your primary go-to techniques when you sense a panic attack or acute anxiety coming on. Consider creating easy-to-remember cues for yourself to initiate these techniques quickly.

**Integration:**

- **Prepare for Quick Access:** Plan how to make these skills quickly accessible during anxiety. It might involve setting reminders on your phone, keeping a small card with brief instructions in your wallet, or even posting notes in areas where you often experience anxiety (e.g., work desk, car).
- **Practice Regularly:** Incorporate these top skills into your daily routine to build familiarity and ease of use. Regular practice can reduce the onset intensity of panic attacks and make your responses more automatic.

By the end of today's session, you should have a clear understanding of which skills effectively mitigate your symptoms of panic and acute anxiety. With these tools ready, you can feel more prepared and confident in managing anxiety, knowing precisely what to do when symptoms appear. This proactive approach is crucial for reducing the impact of anxiety on your daily life.

# Week 2 Day 3

## Stop, Breathe, Think, Act Technique

**Objective:** Today, you will learn the "Stop, Breathe, Think, Act" technique, a structured approach to managing the onset of panic attacks and acute anxiety. This method utilizes principles from mindfulness and cognitive behavioral therapy to effectively halt escalating anxiety.

**Instructions:**

1. **Stop:**
   - At the first sign of escalating anxiety or a panic attack, immediately halt all activities. This includes stopping any action you are performing and any thoughts that are fueling your anxiety.
   - Acknowledge to yourself that this is a critical moment where your intervention through this technique can alter your experience and prevent the escalation of anxiety.

2. **Breathe:**
   - Engage in deep breathing exercises to stabilize both your mind and body. Start by taking deep, deliberate breaths: inhale slowly through your nose for five seconds, hold that breath for another five seconds, and then exhale slowly through your mouth for five seconds.
   - Repeat this breathing pattern at least five times to help foster a sense of calm and relaxation throughout your body.

3. **Think:**

- Begin a cognitive reassessment of your current state. Use calming affirmations such as "I am okay" and "I am safe."
- Recognize and acknowledge that you are experiencing a panic attack or acute anxiety. Remind yourself that you are in a safe environment, capable of managing these feelings.
- Consider the triggers that may have initiated your response. Reflect on whether the perceived threat is real or an exaggerated fear.

4. **Act:**

- Based on your reassessment, choose an appropriate and rational action to mitigate your anxiety. This could be stepping out of a stressful environment, reaching out to a supportive friend, or continuing to engage in calming practices.
- Implement your chosen action, continually reassessing and adjusting as needed while focusing on your breathing and cognitive state.
- Persist with this process until you notice a decrease in anxiety or until you feel more in control.

**Reflection:** After practicing this technique, reflect on the effectiveness of each step in helping you manage your anxiety. Consider how stopping to assess the situation helped prevent a full-blown panic attack, how breathing reduced physical symptoms, and how reassessing your thoughts provided a clearer perspective.

**Integration:** Incorporate this technique into your daily routine by practicing the breathing and cognitive reassessment steps even when not experiencing heightened anxiety. This practice will enhance your familiarity with the process, making it more effective when a real anxiety episode occurs.

# Week 2 Tracking Progress

With another week of the program complete, it's time to assess your progress. Visualize the bridge and consider how far you've come in your journey. Place a mark on the bridge signifying your current position and rate your anxiety level on the 0-10 scale. Acknowledge the work you've done and the skills you've acquired.

**Instructions**:

1. Take a moment to reflect on your progress and experiences.
2. Refer to the bridge illustration below.
3. Consider where you currently stand on your journey.
4. Place a mark on the bridge representing your current position.
5. Next, rate where your average anxiety level has been over this week.
6. Record your anxiety rating on the provided 0-10 scale, with 0 being no anxiety and 10 being the most intense anxiety you've experienced.
7. Reflect and journal.

**Reflection**: After marking your bridge position and anxiety rating, reflect on your progress. Examine skills learned, challenges faced, and changes in thoughts and behaviors. Journal your insights and observations. Identify successes, challenges, and areas requiring more attention. Determine if you need to slow down, revisit previous weeks or skills, or seek professional help to maintain progress. Assess your

overall progress and consider if professional support is needed or how it's contributing to your journey.

| 0 | 1 | 2 | 3 | 4 | 5 | 6 | 7 | 8 | 9 | 10 |

No
Anxiety
          Moderate
          Anxiety
          High
          Anxiety

**7**

# *Understanding and Managing Anxiety*

This chapter delves into the cognitive and behavioral aspects of anxiety, providing insights and tools rooted in the principles of Cognitive Behavioral Therapy (CBT).

### The Essence of Perception in Anxiety

At the heart of the anxiety experience lies the complex interplay between perception and reality. Our perceptions, molded by our distinctive worldviews, schemas, and life experiences, serve as lenses through which we interpret and navigate the world around us. In the realm of anxiety, these perceptions can become distorted, leading to an overestimation of threat and an underestimation of one's coping abilities.

To illustrate this concept, let's consider a typical everyday example: the experience of a job interview. For an individual prone to anxiety, the perception of this event can be significantly skewed. They might view the interview as a high-stakes situation where their entire worth and future are on the line. They may imagine worst-case scenarios, such as stumbling over their words, being judged harshly, or facing rejection. These thoughts can quickly spiral into a sense of overwhelming threat, triggering intense anxiety symptoms like a racing heartbeat, sweaty palms, and difficulty concentrating.

A job interview is an opportunity to showcase one's skills and experience. While important, it is not a definitive measure of one's value. Many factors contribute to the outcome of an interview, and even if it doesn't lead to a job offer, it doesn't negate an individual's worth or potential. However, the anxious mind's perception of the situation as catastrophic and underestimating one's ability to handle the outcome can create a distorted sense of reality.

Another relatable example is the perception of social interactions for someone with social anxiety. They may perceive a friendly gathering as a minefield of potential embarrassment and rejection. Making small talk or being the center of attention can feel like an insurmountable threat. They might worry about saying the wrong thing, being judged, or not fitting in. As a result, they may avoid social situations altogether or endure them with intense discomfort.

Most social interactions are not as high-stakes as they feel to someone with social anxiety. People are often more focused on their own experiences and are generally forgiving of minor social missteps. Many people experience nervousness in social situations, which doesn't define their overall social competence or likability. Yet, the anxious mind's perception of social interactions as highly threatening can lead to a distorted view of reality and a diminished sense of one's ability to navigate these situations effectively.

These examples highlight how anxiety can color our perceptions, making everyday experiences feel more daunting and threatening than they objectively are. The anxious mind tends to zoom in on potential dangers while minimizing one's coping resources, creating a skewed reality that fuels the cycle of anxiety.

Understanding this dynamic is a crucial step in managing anxiety. By recognizing that our perceptions can be distorted by anxiety, we can start to challenge these thoughts and reframe our experiences in a more balanced way. This involves questioning the evidence for our anxious perceptions, considering alternative perspectives, and reminding ourselves of our strengths and successes in navigating challenging situations.

Through this process of cognitive reappraisal, we can gradually shift our perceptions to more accurately reflect reality. We can learn to see job interviews as opportunities for growth rather than threats to our self-worth. We can approach social interactions with the understanding that most people are not as critical as we fear and that we have the skills to handle these situations.

By understanding the essence of perception in anxiety and actively working to align our perceptions with reality, we can break free from the distorted lens of anxiety and engage with the world in a more balanced, confident, and fulfilling way.

## Worldviews and Schemas: The Building Blocks of Anxiety

Worldviews are the overarching mental frameworks that contain our core beliefs, attitudes, and values. They form the lens through which we perceive and make sense of our lives and the world around us. Worldviews shape our interpretations of events, influence our emotional responses, and guide our actions in various situations. They are like a mental map that helps us navigate the complexities of life.

For example, someone with an optimistic worldview might believe that challenges are opportunities for growth and that setbacks are temporary. They may approach difficulties with resilience and a problem-solving mindset. In contrast, someone with a pessimistic worldview might see challenges as insurmountable obstacles and setbacks that confirm their negative expectations. They may feel helpless and discouraged in the face of adversity.

In the context of anxiety, worldviews can significantly impact how we perceive and respond to anxiety-provoking situations. An individual with an anxiety-prone worldview might believe that the world is a dangerous and unpredictable place, that they are fundamentally flawed or incapable, and that they have little control over their life. These beliefs can amplify anxiety by making everyday situations feel more threatening and overwhelming.

Schemas are the cognitive building blocks that make up our worldviews. They are mental structures that help us organize and interpret information based on past experiences. Schemas act as shortcuts that allow us to quickly make sense of new information by comparing it to similar experiences we've had before.

For instance, if someone had a positive experience with dogs growing up, they may have developed a schema that dogs are friendly and lovable. When encountering a new dog, their schema helps them quickly categorize the animal as likely safe and approachable. However, suppose someone had a frightening experience with a dog. In that case, they may have formed a schema that dogs are dangerous and unpredictable. This schema can make them feel anxious and on guard around dogs, even if the current dog exhibits no signs of aggression.

In anxiety, maladaptive schemas can contribute to distorted thinking patterns that fuel anxious feelings. These schemas are often based on negative experiences or learned beliefs overgeneralized and rigidly applied to new situations, even when they don't fully fit.

For example, someone with a schema that making mistakes is unacceptable and leads to rejection might become highly anxious about completing tasks perfectly. They may spend excessive time checking their work, procrastinating for fear of failure, or avoiding challenges altogether. This perfectionism schema can maintain a cycle of anxiety, as the individual's rigid expectations are rarely met, leading to further self-criticism and worry.

Another example is a schema related to control. An individual with anxiety may have a schema that they must be in control at all times to prevent bad things from happening. This schema can lead to excessive worry, micromanaging behaviors, and difficulty tolerating uncertainty. When faced with situations outside their control, they may experience heightened anxiety and engage in futile attempts to control the uncontrollable.

Recognizing and understanding our worldviews and schemas is a crucial step in managing anxiety. By becoming aware of our core beliefs and the ways they influence our perceptions and responses, we can start to question and challenge the ones that contribute to our anxiety.

This process involves examining the evidence for and against our beliefs, considering alternative perspectives, and gradually updating our schemas to be more flexible and adaptive. For instance, someone with a perfectionism schema can practice self-compassion and remind themselves that mistakes are a normal part of learning and growth. They can set more realistic expectations and focus on progress rather than perfection.

Similarly, someone with a control schema can work on accepting that some things are beyond their control and focus on what they can influence. They can practice relaxation techniques and develop coping statements to manage anxiety in the face of uncertainty.

By modifying our worldviews and schemas to be more balanced and realistic, we can reduce the frequency and intensity of anxious thoughts and feelings. We can cultivate a more resilient and adaptable mindset to face life's challenges more confidently and efficiently.

Worldviews and schemas are the foundational elements that shape our perception and experience of anxiety. By understanding and actively working with these building blocks, we can create a more supportive and empowering mental framework for managing anxiety and living a fulfilling life.

## Three Critical Dimensions of Worldviews in Anxiety:

*Self-Perception*: Self-perception refers to the beliefs and attitudes individuals hold about themselves. In anxiety, self-perception often becomes distorted, characterized by negative self-beliefs and a critical inner voice. These negative self-perceptions can fuel anxious thoughts and behaviors, creating a vicious cycle.

For example, someone with anxiety may have a self-perception that they are incompetent or inadequate. They may constantly doubt their abilities, even in areas where they have demonstrated success. This negative self-belief can lead to a fear of failure, causing them to avoid challenges or overcompensate by working excessively hard.

Another common self-perception in anxiety is the belief that one is fundamentally flawed or unlovable. This can manifest as a fear of rejection or abandonment, leading to people-pleasing behaviors or difficulty setting boundaries. The individual may constantly seek validation from others while simultaneously doubting any positive feedback they receive.

These negative self-perceptions are often not realistically and objectively grounded. They stem from past experiences, negative self-talk, and internalizing external criticism or expectations. Challenging and reframing these distorted self-perceptions is a key aspect of managing anxiety. This involves practicing self-compassion, acknowledging one's strengths and accomplishments, and developing a more balanced and realistic view of oneself.

***Perception of the World***: *Perception of the world* refers to beliefs and assumptions individuals hold about the nature of reality and how the world functions. With anxiety, the perception of the world can become skewed, characterized by a sense of unpredictability, danger, or overwhelming demands.

For instance, someone with generalized anxiety may perceive the world as a series of endless worst-case scenarios. They may constantly worry about potential disasters, from minor inconveniences to catastrophic events. This perception of the world as inherently threatening can lead to chronic feelings of apprehension and unease.

Another example is the perception of the world as unpredictable and uncontrollable. Individuals with anxiety may struggle with uncertainty, believing that they must have control over every aspect of their lives to feel secure. This can lead to rigid planning, difficulty adapting to change, and helplessness when faced with unexpected situations.

Additionally, some individuals with anxiety may perceive the world as overly demanding or judgmental. They may feel like they are constantly being evaluated and that any mistake or imperfection will have negative consequences. This perception can result in perfectionism, social anxiety, and a fear of criticism.

Shifting these distorted perceptions of the world involves learning to tolerate uncertainty, challenging catastrophic thinking, and developing a more balanced and realistic outlook. This can include practicing mindfulness to stay grounded in the present moment, exposing oneself gradually to feared situations to build confidence, and reframing negative thoughts about the world in a more neutral or positive light.

***Self in the World***: The dimension of *self in the world* refers to how individuals perceive their place and role within the larger context of society and relationships. Anxiety can significantly impact this perception, leading to feelings of disconnection, insecurity, and difficulty navigating social interactions.

For example, someone with social anxiety may perceive themselves as an outsider or misfit in social situations. They may believe that they are fundamentally different from others and that they incur judgment or rejection. This perception can lead to avoidance of social events, difficulty forming and maintaining relationships, and loneliness or isolation.

Another example is the perception of oneself as powerless or vulnerable in the face of external challenges. Individuals with anxiety may feel like they lack the resources or abilities to cope with life's demands, leading to a sense of helplessness or dependence on others. This perception can manifest as difficulty making decisions, avoidance of responsibility, or a constant need for reassurance.

Moreover, anxiety can impact an individual's sense of purpose or meaning in the world. They may question their place in the grand scheme of things, leading to existential anxiety or a feeling of being adrift. This perception can contribute to emptiness or a lack of direction in life.

Adjusting these perceptions of self in the world involves building self-efficacy, assertiveness skills, and a sense of connectedness. This can include practicing self-advocacy, setting healthy boundaries, and engaging in activities that foster a sense of mastery and accomplishment.

It also involves challenging beliefs about one's worth and purpose, exploring personal values and goals, and cultivating supportive relationships.

By understanding and addressing these three critical dimensions of worldviews - self-perception, perception of the world, and self in the world - individuals can gain insight into the underlying beliefs and assumptions contributing to their anxiety. Through cognitive reframing, behavioral experiments, and self-reflection, they can gradually reshape these perceptions to be more balanced, realistic, and empowering, paving the way for greater emotional well-being and resilience in the face of anxiety.

## The Dynamic Nature of Worldviews in Anxiety

Recognizing that worldviews are not static but dynamic and context-dependent is crucial. Individuals' perceptions of themselves and the world vary across different life domains and situations. For example, someone may feel confident and competent in their professional life but experience intense anxiety in social settings. This variability highlights the multifaceted nature of anxiety and the importance of addressing it across various contexts.

## The Role of Perception in Shaping Reality

Perception plays a crucial role in shaping our experience of reality, especially in the context of anxiety. How we perceive and interpret the world directly influences our thoughts, emotions, and behaviors. In anxiety, the path from perception to reality often involves the creation of subjective stories—personalized narratives that blend factual information with individual biases, beliefs, and past experiences.

Let's consider an example to illustrate this process. Imagine you're preparing for a job interview. The objective reality is that you have an upcoming meeting with a potential employer to discuss your qualifications and fit for the role. However, your perception of this situation may be heavily influenced by your anxiety.

You might create a subjective story filled with worst-case scenarios and self-doubt. Your internal narrative might sound something like this: "I'm not qualified enough for this position. I'll probably stumble over my words and make a fool of myself. The interviewer will see right through me and realize I'm a fraud. I'll never get this job, and my career will be ruined."

Notice how this subjective story blends some factual information (the upcoming interview) with individual biases (self-doubt, impostor syndrome), beliefs (I'm not qualified), and past experiences (fear of rejection). This personalized narrative significantly influences your emotional and cognitive responses, triggering anxious thoughts and feelings.

You may feel nervous, with your heart racing and palms sweating. You might have trouble sleeping the night before the interview, as your mind is filled with worries and negative self-talk. These anxious thoughts and physical sensations can then feed back into your perception, reinforcing that the interview is a threat and you're incapable of handling it.

In this way, your perception of the situation shapes your reality. Your subjective story becomes your lived experience, even though it may not accurately reflect the objective reality of the interview. This process can create a self-fulfilling prophecy, where your anxious thoughts and behaviors inadvertently sabotage your performance, making your fears more likely to come true.

Another example is how social anxiety can shape the perception of social interactions. Let's say you're invited to a party where you don't know many people. The objective reality is that you've been asked to a social gathering with an opportunity to meet new people and potentially make friends.

However, your social anxiety may lead you to create a subjective story that focuses on potential rejection and embarrassment. Your inner narrative might be this: "I won't fit in with these people. They'll think I'm boring or awkward. I'll say something stupid, and everyone will laugh at me. It's safer to just stay home and avoid the whole situation."

Again, this subjective story blends factual information (the party invitation) with individual biases (fear of rejection), beliefs (I'm socially awkward), and past experiences (memories of social discomfort). This narrative triggers anxious thoughts and feelings, such as worry about being judged or embarrassed.

As a result, you may decline the invitation or, if you do attend, you might engage in safety behaviors like sticking close to the people you already know, avoiding eye contact, or leaving early. These anxious behaviors reinforce your perception that social situations are threatening and you cannot handle them.

Understanding the role of perception in shaping reality is key to recognizing and challenging anxiety-provoking thoughts. By becoming aware of how our subjective stories influence our emotions and behaviors, we can start to question the accuracy and helpfulness of these narratives.

This involves learning to separate objective facts from subjective interpretations. In the job interview example, the objective facts are that you have an upcoming meeting to discuss your qualifications. Your subjective story about not being good enough or ruining your career is an interpretation, not a fact.

Once we recognize this distinction, we can start to challenge our anxiety-provoking perceptions. We can ask ourselves: "What evidence do I have for and against this thought? Is there another way to look at this situation? What would I say to a friend who had this thought?"

We can create a more balanced and realistic perception of the situation by questioning our subjective stories and considering alternative perspectives. We can remind ourselves of our strengths, past successes, and coping skills. We can reframe the situation as an opportunity for growth and learning rather than a threat.

Over time, this practice of challenging and reframing our perceptions can help us break the cycle of anxiety. By changing our subjective stories, we can change our emotional and behavioral responses, leading to a more positive and empowering experience of reality.

The role of perception in shaping reality is a crucial concept in understanding and managing anxiety. Our subjective stories, based on our biases, beliefs, and experiences, significantly influence our thoughts, emotions, and behaviors. By becoming aware of these stories and learning to challenge them, we can create a more balanced and realistic perception of the world, paving the way for greater emotional well-being and resilience in the face of anxiety.

## The Subjectivity of Experience: Examples of Anxiety Perception

To illustrate the subjectivity of experience in anxiety, consider the scenario of three individuals standing on the edge of a bridge, wearing their bungee jumping equipment, preparing to take the leap. Each person's perception and emotional response to this situation can vary greatly, highlighting how anxiety can color one's interpretation of the same objective experience.

Person A is excited and eager to jump. They have been looking forward to this moment, seeing it as an exhilarating challenge and an opportunity for personal growth. Their perception of the situation is one of adventure and thrill-seeking. They attribute the physiological sensations they're experiencing, such as a racing heart and butterflies in their stomach, to anticipation and excitement.

Person B, on the other hand, appears apprehensive but ready. They recognize the potential risks of bungee jumping but have chosen to face their fears and push themselves out of their comfort zone. Their perception of the situation is one of calculated risk-taking and self-improvement. They attribute their physiological responses, similar to Person A's, to nervousness and determination.

In contrast, Person C is experiencing high levels of anxiety. Despite the safety measures in place and the reassurance of the bungee jumping staff, they perceive the situation as highly threatening. Their mind is flooded with worst-case scenarios, imagining the bungee cord snapping or the harness failing. They attribute their racing heart, sweaty palms, and shallow breathing to impending danger and a lack of control.

Objectively, all three individuals are in the same situation, wearing the same safety gear and facing the same physical challenge. Their bodies are all experiencing similar physiological responses, such as increased heart rate, adrenaline rush, and heightened alertness. These physiological responses are a natural reaction to the perceived risk and excitement of the situation, preparing the body for action.

However, what sets these individuals apart is their subjective perception and attribution of these physiological sensations. Person A interprets their body's responses as positive and energizing, fueling their excitement for the jump. Person B sees these sensations as a sign of their body preparing to face a challenge, helping them stay focused and determined. Person C, however, perceives these same sensations as a warning sign of imminent danger, reinforcing their anxiety and fear.

This example highlights how the same objective situation and physiological responses can be interpreted and experienced differently based on individuals' perceptions and attribution. Anxiety can significantly influence this process, causing individuals to perceive neutral or even positive situations as threatening and attributing physiological responses to danger or lack of control.

Another example that illustrates the subjectivity of experience in anxiety is public speaking. Imagine three individuals preparing to give a presentation to a large audience. Person X is excited and confident, seeing the presentation as an opportunity to share their knowledge and engage with the audience. They attribute their increased heart rate and energy to enthusiasm and readiness.

Person Y feels slightly nervous but mostly prepared. They recognize that public speaking can be challenging. However, they have practiced their presentation and feel confident about delivering it effectively. They attribute their nervousness to the natural anticipation of a performance but feel in control and ready to face the challenge.

Person Z, however, is overwhelmed with anxiety. They perceive the presentation as a threat to their self-esteem and fear being judged or criticized by the audience. They attribute their racing heart, trembling hands, and dry mouth to their fear of failure and humiliation.

Again, all three individuals are facing the same objective situation of giving a presentation. Their bodies respond with similar physiological reactions, such as increased adrenaline and heightened alertness. However, their subjective perceptions and attributions of these sensations differ greatly, influencing their emotional experience and behavior.

Understanding the subjectivity of experience in anxiety is crucial for recognizing and challenging anxiety-provoking thoughts. By becoming aware of how our perceptions and attributions shape our emotional responses, we can question the accuracy and helpfulness of these interpretations.

Person C could challenge their catastrophic thoughts in the bungee jumping example by reminding themselves of the safety measures and the thousands of successful bungee jumps that occur each year. They could reframe their physiological sensations as a normal response to a thrilling situation rather than a sign of danger.

Similarly, in the public speaking scenario, Person Z could reframe their nervousness as a sign of caring about their performance rather than a sign of impending failure. They could remind themselves of their preparation and past successes, focusing on the opportunity to share their knowledge rather than the fear of judgment.

By recognizing the subjectivity of experience and learning to challenge anxiety-provoking perceptions and attributions, individuals can develop a more balanced and realistic view of the situations they face. This shift in perspective can help reduce the intensity and frequency of anxiety symptoms, allowing individuals to engage with the world in a more confident and empowered way.

The subjectivity of experience in anxiety highlights how the same objective situation and physiological responses can be perceived and interpreted differently by individuals based on their thoughts, beliefs, and emotional states. By becoming aware of this subjectivity and learning to challenge anxiety-provoking perceptions and attributions, individuals can start to break the cycle of anxiety and develop a more resilient and adaptive mindset.

## The Mechanism of Confirmation Bias in Anxiety

Confirmation bias is a cognitive tendency to seek out, interpret, and recall information in a way that confirms one's pre-existing beliefs or hypotheses. In the context of anxiety, confirmation bias can play a significant role in maintaining and exacerbating anxious thoughts and feelings. The brain functions as a confirmation machine, constantly seeking evidence to support existing beliefs and worldviews, even when these beliefs are irrational or unhelpful.

Let's consider an example to illustrate how confirmation bias operates in anxiety. Imagine a college student named Sarah who struggles with social anxiety. Sarah believes that she is socially awkward and that others will reject or judge her negatively in social situations. This belief has led her to avoid social gatherings and to feel intense anxiety when she does engage in social interactions.

One day, Sarah attends a party with her classmates. Throughout the evening, she interacts with several people, some of whom seem engaged and friendly. In contrast, others appear more reserved or distracted. However, due to her confirmation bias, Sarah's attention is drawn to any signs that seem to confirm her belief about being socially awkward.

For instance, when Sarah is talking to a classmate, and there is a brief lull in the conversation, she immediately interprets this as evidence that she is boring and that the other person is not interested in talking to her. When another classmate glances at their phone while Sarah is speaking, she takes this as a sign that she is not worth listening to and is being judged negatively.

On the other hand, when a classmate laughs at one of Sarah's jokes or expresses interest in something she has said, she tends to discount these positive interactions. She might think, "They're just being polite," or "They probably didn't mean it." As a result, Sarah's confirmation bias leads her to selectively focus on and remember the interactions that confirm her negative beliefs about herself while discounting or ignoring evidence that challenges these beliefs.

This selective attention and interpretation of social cues reinforce Sarah's anxiety and maintain her negative self-image. Constantly seeking confirmation of her anxious thoughts strengthens the neural pathways associated with these beliefs, making them more automatic and habitual.

Another example of confirmation bias in anxiety is in the context of health anxiety, also known as hypochondriasis. Let's consider the case of David, a middle-aged man who has a persistent fear of developing a serious illness despite repeated reassurances from his doctor that he is in good health.

David's confirmation bias makes him hypervigilant for bodily sensations or symptoms that could be interpreted as signs of illness. When he notices a slight ache in his chest, he immediately thinks, "This could be a heart attack." When he feels a bit tired or dizzy, he jumps to the conclusion that he must have a brain tumor.

David spends hours researching his symptoms online, seeking out information that confirms his fears. He focuses on stories of people who had similar symptoms and were later diagnosed with serious illnesses while ignoring the countless examples of people who had these symptoms and were perfectly healthy. He interprets ambiguous or neutral information, such as a doctor's suggestion to monitor a symptom, as evidence that something must be seriously wrong.

This confirmation bias fuels David's health anxiety, causing him to experience frequent panic attacks and to spend a significant amount of time and energy worrying about his health. Despite multiple medical tests and reassurances, his anxiety persists because his brain is constantly seeking and interpreting information in a way that confirms his fears.

Understanding the mechanism of confirmation bias in anxiety is essential for developing effective strategies to challenge and overcome anxious thoughts. One key strategy is actively seeking evidence that disconfirms one's anxious beliefs. For Sarah, this might involve actively focusing on and remembering her positive social interactions rather than dwelling on perceived rejections or judgments. She might keep a journal of successful social experiences or ask trusted friends for feedback on her social skills.

For David, challenging his confirmation bias might involve limiting his online research and exposure to anxiety-provoking information. He might work with a therapist to develop a more balanced and realistic perspective on his health, learning to interpret bodily sensations in a less catastrophic way and to trust the medical evidence that indicates he is healthy.

Another important strategy is to practice cognitive reappraisal, which involves reframing anxiety-provoking situations or thoughts in a more neutral or positive light. For example, when Sarah notices a lull in conversation, instead of assuming this means she is boring, she could reframe it as a natural part of the ebb and flow of social interaction. When David notices a bodily sensation, instead of immediately assuming the worst, he could remind himself that these sensations are often benign and that his body can heal and self-regulate.

Over time, individuals can consistently challenge confirmation bias and practice cognitive reappraisal to weaken the grip of anxious thoughts and develop a more balanced and realistic perspective. This process is not always easy and may require the support of a therapist or counselor, particularly for individuals with more severe or entrenched anxiety.

Confirmation bias is a powerful cognitive mechanism that can contribute to the maintenance and exacerbation of anxiety. By constantly seeking evidence to support anxious beliefs and discounting evidence that challenges them, individuals can become trapped in a cycle of anxious thoughts and feelings. However, by becoming aware of this bias and actively working to counteract it through strategies such as seeking disconfirming evidence and practicing cognitive reappraisal, individuals can break free from the grip of anxiety and develop a more resilient and adaptive mindset.

**Embracing Cognitive Behavioral Therapy (CBT) for Anxiety**

Cognitive Behavioral Therapy (CBT) is a well-established and widely used therapeutic approach for managing anxiety disorders. CBT offers a structured, goal-oriented framework that helps individuals understand the complex interplay between their thoughts, emotions, and behaviors. It provides practical tools for modifying these components to reduce anxiety symptoms and improve overall well-being.

At its core, CBT operates on the principle that our thoughts, feelings, and behaviors are interconnected and mutually influential. In other words, how we think about ourselves, others, and the world around us directly impacts our emotional state and informs our actions. Conversely, our behaviors and emotions can also shape our thoughts and beliefs over time.

In the context of anxiety, CBT posits that anxious thoughts and beliefs, such as overestimating the likelihood or severity of adverse outcomes, underestimating one's ability to cope, or catastrophizing about potential dangers, can lead to intense feelings of fear, worry, and unease. These anxious feelings, in turn, often lead to maladaptive behaviors, such as avoidance, safety-seeking, or excessive reassurance-seeking, which can reinforce and maintain the anxiety cycle.

For example, let's consider the case of Maria, a young woman who struggles with panic disorder. Maria's anxiety is characterized by recurrent panic attacks, accompanied by intense physical symptoms such as rapid heartbeat, sweating, and trembling, as well as fear of losing control or "going crazy."

From a CBT perspective, Maria's panic attacks are fueled by catastrophic misinterpretations of her bodily sensations. When she notices her heart racing or her palms sweating, she automatically thinks, "I'm having a heart attack!" or "I'm losing control!" These thoughts trigger intense feelings of fear and panic, which further amplify her physical symptoms, creating a vicious cycle.

In response to these panic attacks, Maria starts to avoid situations that she fears might trigger an attack, such as crowded places, public transportation, or being alone. She also engages in safety behaviors, like always carrying a water bottle or sitting near the exit in case she needs to escape. While these behaviors provide short-term relief from anxiety, they ultimately reinforce Maria's belief that the situations are dangerous and that she cannot cope with her anxiety.

CBT interventions for Maria would focus on helping her identify and challenge her catastrophic thoughts about her bodily sensations. Through cognitive restructuring, Maria would learn to question the evidence for her automatic thoughts and generate alternative, more realistic interpretations. For example, she might challenge the thought "I'm having a heart attack" by reminding herself that she has had numerous medical check-ups, indicating her heart is healthy and that rapid heartbeat is a common and harmless symptom of anxiety.

Maria would also learn relaxation techniques, such as deep breathing or progressive muscle relaxation, to help calm her body's physiological response to anxiety. Notably, she would be encouraged to gradually confront the situations she fears, starting with less challenging scenarios and building up to more difficult ones. This exposure therapy helps Maria learn experientially that her feared consequences are unlikely to occur and that she can tolerate and manage her anxiety in these situations.

Throughout this process, Maria's therapist would emphasize the importance of consistently practicing these new skills and perspectives, even in the face of setbacks or challenges. CBT is not a quick fix but rather a set of tools and strategies that require ongoing effort and application to yield lasting results.

Another example of how CBT can be applied to anxiety is in the case of Tom, a middle-aged father who struggles with generalized anxiety disorder (GAD). Tom's anxiety manifests as constant, uncontrollable worry about a wide range of topics, from his job performance to his children's safety to potential health issues. His worries are accompanied by restlessness, difficulty concentrating, muscle tension, and sleep disturbances.

From a CBT standpoint, Tom's chronic worry is maintained by his belief that worrying serves a protective function, helping him anticipate and prepare for potential dangers. He also holds perfectionist standards, believing he must control every aspect of his life to avoid adverse outcomes. These beliefs lead him to engage in unproductive problem-solving, such as mentally rehearsing worst-case scenarios or seeking excessive reassurance from others.

In CBT, Tom would learn to recognize and label his worries as unhelpful and unrealistic rather than seeing them as important or necessary. He would practice "worry postponement," setting aside dedicated worry time each day and learning to delay engaging with worries that arise outside of this time. He would also learn to differentiate between productive and unproductive worry, focusing his problem-solving efforts on issues that are within his control and practicing acceptance of uncertainties that he cannot change.

To address his perfectionist tendencies, Tom would work on setting more realistic expectations for himself and others and developing self-compassion for his mistakes or limitations. He would also practice delegating responsibilities and tolerating minor discomforts or inconveniences rather than striving for constant control.

Like Maria, Tom would be encouraged to face his fears and worries through gradual exposure, testing his catastrophic predictions in real-world situations. For example, he might practice letting a work project be "good enough" rather than perfect or allow his children to engage in age-appropriate risks while tolerating his own anxiety about their safety.

These examples illustrate the core principles and strategies of CBT for anxiety, including cognitive restructuring, behavioral modification, relaxation techniques, and exposure therapy. By targeting the thoughts, emotions, and behaviors that maintain anxiety, CBT helps individuals develop a more balanced, realistic perspective on their fears and worries and equips them with practical tools for managing anxiety in their daily lives.

Importantly, CBT is not a one-size-fits-all approach. It is a collaborative process tailored to each individual's unique needs and goals. Therapists work closely with clients to develop a shared understanding of their anxiety and to create a personalized treatment plan that builds on their strengths and addresses their specific challenges.

Moreover, CBT is not limited to individual therapy but can also be delivered in group settings, through self-help books or online programs, or in combination with medication for more severe or complex cases of anxiety. The flexibility and adaptability of CBT make it a valuable resource for a wide range of individuals struggling with anxiety, from mild to severe cases.

Cognitive Behavioral Therapy offers a comprehensive, evidence-based framework for understanding and treating anxiety disorders. CBT helps individuals develop a more realistic, adaptive perspective on their fears and worries by targeting the interconnected components of thoughts, emotions, and behaviors. It equips them with practical tools for managing anxiety in their daily lives. Through a collaborative, goal-oriented process, CBT empowers individuals to take an active role in their recovery and build the skills and resilience needed to thrive in life's challenges.

### Navigating the Landscape of Perception and Reality in Anxiety

Navigating the complex landscape of perception and reality is a crucial aspect of managing anxiety. This journey involves deeply understanding how our thoughts, beliefs, and experiences shape our emotional responses and behaviors. By cultivating self-awareness, individuals can recognize the patterns of thinking and behavior contributing to their anxiety and take steps to modify them more adaptively.

One of the key steps in this process is learning to identify cognitive distortions, which are inaccurate or exaggerated thoughts that can fuel anxiety. These distortions can take many forms, such as catastrophizing (assuming the worst-case scenario will occur), overgeneralization (drawing broad conclusions based on a single event), or emotional reasoning (assuming that one's feelings reflect reality). By becoming attuned to these distortions, individuals can start to catch them in the moment and question their validity.

This questioning process, known as cognitive restructuring, involves examining the evidence for and against one's anxious thoughts and considering alternative, more balanced perspectives. Through this process, individuals can start to chip away at the false beliefs and assumptions that underlie their anxiety, gradually replacing them with more realistic and adaptive thoughts.

For example, a person who tends to catastrophize about their health might have the automatic thought, "This headache means I have a brain tumor." Through cognitive restructuring, they might challenge this thought by considering the actual likelihood of a brain tumor, the many other potential causes of headaches, and the fact that they have had similar headaches in the past that turned out to be harmless. By repeatedly practicing this kind of balanced thinking, the individual can start to weaken the grip of their catastrophic thoughts and reduce their overall level of health anxiety.

In addition to modifying anxious thoughts, navigating the landscape of anxiety also involves understanding and changing behavioral responses to anxiety. Many individuals with anxiety engage in avoidance behaviors, such as steering clear of feared situations or objects, or safety behaviors, such as always carrying a cell phone in case of emergency. While these behaviors can provide short-term relief from anxiety, they can maintain and worsen anxiety in the long run by preventing individuals from learning that their fears are unlikely to come true and that they can cope with their anxiety.

Exposure therapy is a key behavioral intervention in CBT that involves gradually confronting feared situations, sensations, or objects in a safe and controlled way. Through repeated exposure, individuals learn that their feared consequences do not occur or are not as bad as they thought and that they can tolerate and manage their anxiety. Over time, this learning process helps to reduce the intensity and frequency of anxious responses. It expands the individual's range of comfortable activities and experiences.

For instance, a person with a phobia of dogs might start by looking at pictures of dogs. Then, watching videos of friendly dogs. Maybe observing a dog from a distance in a park, gradually getting closer to a calm, leashed dog. By progressing through these stages at a manageable pace, the individual can start to retrain their brain to view dogs as safe and neutral rather than threatening.

Throughout the process of navigating anxiety, it is essential to cultivate self-compassion and patience. Changing long-standing patterns of anxious thinking and behavior is a gradual process that requires ongoing effort and practice. There will inevitably be setbacks and challenges along the way, and it is important to view these as opportunities for learning and growth rather than signs of failure.

Moreover, the journey of managing anxiety is not linear but rather a continuous process of self-discovery and adaptation. As individuals navigate new life stages, stressors, and experiences, they may encounter new triggers for anxiety or find that old coping strategies no longer work as well. By remaining curious, flexible, and committed to personal growth, individuals can continue to deepen their self-awareness and expand their repertoire of coping skills.

Ultimately, navigating the landscape of perception and reality in anxiety is a deeply personal and empowering journey. By learning to recognize and modify the thoughts, beliefs, and behaviors that fuel anxiety, individuals can gradually reclaim a sense of control and mastery over their emotional experiences. They can start to view anxiety not as an enemy to be eliminated but as a natural and manageable part of the human experience, one that can be softened and transformed through the power of self-understanding and intentional change.

In this way, the journey of managing anxiety becomes not just a process of symptom reduction but a path of personal growth and transformation. As individuals learn to relate to their anxiety with greater wisdom, compassion, and skill, they open up new possibilities for living with greater freedom, resilience, and joy. While the path may be challenging at times, the rewards of this journey - a deeper sense of self-awareness, a more balanced perspective on life, and a greater capacity for facing challenges with courage and grace—are truly invaluable.

# Week 3 Self-Help Guide

## *Mastering Anxiety with Cognitive Behavioral Therapy*

Welcome to Week Three of your journey through understanding and managing anxiety. This week, we delve into Cognitive Behavioral Therapy (CBT). This highly effective psychological treatment has been extensively researched and proven to help reduce symptoms of anxiety. CBT explores relationships among a person's thoughts, feelings, and behaviors. By examining these interactions, CBT helps change unhelpful thinking patterns and thus positively influences emotions and actions.

Throughout this week, you will engage in a series of exercises designed to enhance your awareness of the thoughts contributing to your anxiety and systematically address and modify these thoughts. Each day is structured to gradually build your skills in identifying, challenging, and altering anxiety-provoking thoughts using CBT principles. You will learn to:

- **Identify and record triggers and anxious thoughts**, helping you to recognize the patterns that exacerbate your anxiety.
- **Challenge these thoughts and beliefs**, using techniques to dispute irrational or unhelpful thoughts and to replace them with more balanced, constructive thinking.
- **Engage in gradual exposure exercises**, where you will safely confront the situations that trigger your anxiety, which is crucial in reducing the power these triggers have over you.

- **Reflect on your progress and set personal goals**, ensuring that you continue to apply these new skills and extend them into your everyday life.

CBT is a skill-building approach. Like learning any new skill, it requires practice and patience. This week, you are encouraged to approach each task with an open mind and a commitment to engage fully with the exercises. The activities and reflections are designed to challenge your existing thought patterns and foster a new understanding of your ability to effectively manage and reduce anxiety.

Safety and comfort are paramount. Please remember to approach each exercise within your own limits and consider having support from a friend or family member when trying new activities, especially those involving exposure to anxiety-provoking situations.

By the end of this week, you should have a toolkit of strategies to help you manage your anxiety more effectively. These tools are not only useful for immediate relief but are also stepping stones toward long-term change. With continued practice, the skills you develop this week can significantly improve your quality of life, enhancing your resilience against anxiety and equipping you with the confidence to face new challenges.

# Week 3 Day 1

## ABCD-CBT

**Objective:** To identify and dispute irrational thoughts and beliefs that contribute to anxiety and emotional distress by dissecting these thought patterns and replacing them with more realistic and positive alternatives.

**Information:** The ABCD–CBT technique is a cognitive-behavioral tool that helps individuals identify and effectively manage the thoughts and feelings that lead to emotional distress. It is rooted in Cognitive Behavioral Therapy (CBT) principles, which posits that our thoughts, feelings, and behaviors are interconnected and that negative thought patterns can lead to emotional and behavioral difficulties.

**Components of the ABCD–CBT Technique:**

- **A – Activating Event:** This event or situation initially triggers the emotional response. It can be anything from a specific incident, like receiving criticism at work, to a more general problem, such as dealing with a chronic illness.
- **B – Beliefs/Thoughts:** These are the automatic thoughts that occur in response to the activating event. These thoughts are often rapid, reflexive interpretations of the event and are influenced by deeper beliefs and values.
- **C – Consequences:** This refers to the emotional and behavioral reactions that follow the beliefs and thoughts. The consequences can vary widely depending on the individual's thoughts. They

can include feelings such as sadness, anger, or anxiety and behaviors like avoidance, confrontation, or withdrawal.

- **D – Disputation:** This step involves challenging the automatic thoughts and beliefs to alter them. The disputation process encourages questioning the validity and utility of the thoughts and replacing them with more rational, balanced ones.

**How It Works:** The ABCD–CBT technique operates on the premise that altering one's thoughts can change the following emotional and behavioral reactions. This method encourages individuals to critically evaluate their thoughts and consider if they are distorted or unhelpful. By disputing these thoughts, individuals can develop a more realistic outlook, leading to healthier emotional responses and more adaptive behaviors.

**Benefits of the ABCD–CBT Technique:**

- **Improved Self-Awareness:** Regularly using the ABCD–CBT technique increases awareness of the automatic thought processes that influence emotions and behaviors.
- **Enhanced Emotional Regulation:** Individuals can better manage their emotional responses to various situations by understanding and restructuring negative thoughts.
- **Behavioral Change:** As thoughts become more positive and balanced, behaviors that stem from negative thoughts (such as avoidance or aggression) can be altered, leading to more effective coping strategies in challenging situations.
- **Reduction in Stress and Anxiety:** This technique helps break the cycle of negative thinking that often escalates stress and anxiety, providing a practical tool for managing day-to-day pressures.

**Implementing the Technique:** To effectively implement the ABCD–

CBT technique, it is crucial to practice it regularly. This could involve daily reflections where individuals identify events that trigger strong emotional responses and then work through the ABCD steps. Over time, this practice can significantly improve how individuals perceive and react to the challenges in their lives, fostering a greater sense of control and well-being.

## Instructions:

1. **Activating Event (A):** Identify an event or situation that triggered a negative emotional or behavioral response. This could be anything from a stressful encounter at work to a disagreement with a friend.

2. **Beliefs and Thoughts (B):** Write down the automatic thoughts or beliefs in response to the activating event. Be as specific as possible about what went through your mind.

3. **Consequences (C):** Describe the emotional and behavioral consequences that followed your beliefs and thoughts. This might include feelings like anxiety, sadness, or anger and behaviors such as withdrawal, argumentation, or procrastination.

4. **Disputation (D):** Challenge the irrational or negative thoughts identified in the Beliefs and Thoughts section. Ask yourself:
   - What evidence supports these thoughts?
   - What evidence contradicts these thoughts?
   - Are there alternative, more positive ways to view the situation?
   - How might someone else perceive this situation?
   - How does holding onto these thoughts benefit me, and what could be the outcome of thinking differently?

## Task: Create & Fill in an ABCD Worksheet:

- **A (Activating Event):** Describe a specific event.

- **B (Beliefs/Thoughts):** List the immediate thoughts associated with the event.
- **C (Consequences):** Note the emotional and behavioral outcomes.
- **D (Disputation):** Provide evidence against the irrational beliefs and suggest rational alternatives.

For example:

- **A:** I have an important exam approaching.
- **B:** "I'm going to fail! This is unbearable. I can't stand it. I'll never be able to prepare for it, not with life as it is now. I'm useless. Why am I bothering?"
- **C:** Anxious, can't sleep or focus on anything.
- **D:** The belief that I will fail is an assumption, not a fact. I have passed exams before under challenging conditions. It is not true that I am useless; I have strengths in other areas. Stress is normal, but I can manage it with proper planning and preparation.

**Reflection:** After completing the ABCD worksheet, reflect on the process:

- How did it feel to dissect your thoughts this way?
- Did challenging your beliefs change how you felt about the event?
- Can you see a pattern in how certain events trigger specific irrational thoughts?

**Integration:** Continue to use the ABCD method regularly as new stressful situations arise. Incorporate this technique into your daily routine to gradually improve your emotional responses and reduce the intensity of negative feelings. By practicing this method, you aim to develop healthier thought patterns and a more balanced perspective on life's challenges.

# Week 3 Day 2

## Identifying and Challenging Distorted Thoughts

**Objective:** Today's session focuses on identifying and challenging distorted thoughts that stem from traumatic experiences and anxiety triggers. By examining these thoughts, you will learn to apply cognitive reappraisal techniques to reduce their impact on your emotions and behaviors.

**Instructions:**

1. **Identifying Distorted Thoughts:**
   - **Trauma-Influenced Thoughts:**
     - Write down three thoughts or beliefs about yourself and three about the world that have been influenced by your traumatic experiences.
     - Examples might include feelings of distrust toward others or beliefs about personal vulnerability.
   - **Anxiety-Provoking Thoughts:**
     - Note three anxiety-provoking thoughts about yourself and three regarding specific situations that trigger your anxiety.
     - These could include thoughts like "I can't handle going to crowded places" or "I'm always going to react this way."
2. **Processing and Challenging Thoughts:**
   - **Trauma-Influenced Thoughts:**
     - Reflect on how your traumatic experiences might

skew these thoughts. Consider both the evidence supporting these beliefs and arguments against them.

- Ask yourself if these beliefs are absolute or if there are exceptions that indicate a more balanced view of yourself and the world.

    ○ **Anxiety-Provoking Thoughts:**

- Reflect on how these thoughts contribute to your feelings of anxiety.

- Choose one of the anxiety-provoking thoughts. Challenge this thought by considering alternative perspectives and gathering evidence that contradicts it.

3. **Cognitive Reappraisal:**

    ○ For both sets of thoughts (trauma-influenced and anxiety-provoking), engage in cognitive reappraisal by assessing the validity of these thoughts and considering more rational, balanced alternatives.

    ○ Reflect on how changing your perspective on these thoughts affects your emotional response. Does recognizing and challenging these distortions reduce the intensity of your anxiety or alter your feelings related to trauma?

**Reflection:** After completing this exercise, take some time to journal about the process:

- How did it feel to confront these thoughts?
- What did you learn about the way trauma and anxiety influence your thinking?
- Have your feelings changed after challenging these thoughts?

**Integration:**

- Practice this technique daily when different thoughts arise. Make it a habit to question and reassess thoughts that bring discomfort or distress.

- This continuous practice will help build mental resilience and decrease the automatic acceptance of negative or distorted thought patterns.

By systematically challenging distorted thoughts influenced by trauma and anxiety, you will gradually decrease their power over your emotions and actions, leading to more balanced thinking and reduced anxiety.

# Week 3 Day 3

## Understanding Anxiety-Driven Behaviors

**Objective:** To identify and analyze behaviors that you engage in response to anxiety. To understand these behaviors and their triggers and begin to see how they may perpetuate your anxiety over time. To explore ways to modify them for better coping.

**Instructions:**

1. **Identify Anxiety-Driven Behavior:**
   - Reflect on a specific behavior you typically resort to when feeling anxious. This could be anything like avoidance (e.g., avoiding social gatherings), seeking reassurance (e.g., repeatedly asking others for validation), or compulsive checking (e.g., checking locks or appliances repeatedly).
   - Write down this behavior as clearly and specifically as possible.

2. **Document Triggers:**
   - Identify and document what triggers this behavior. Consider specific situations, thoughts, or feelings that precede the behavior. For example, attending a social event may trigger avoidance behaviors, or feelings of inadequacy may lead to seeking reassurance.
   - Record these triggers in detail to understand the conditions under which your anxiety-driven behavior is most likely to occur.

3. **Analyze the Behavior:**

- Reflect on how this behavior responds to your anxious thoughts and feelings. Try to connect the dots between the feeling of anxiety and your behavioral response. How does this behavior serve as a coping mechanism for your anxiety?
- Consider the short-term relief this behavior might provide versus its long-term impact on your life and mental health. How might this behavior be maintaining or even exacerbating your anxiety over time?

**Reflection:** After you have identified and analyzed your anxiety-driven behavior, take some time to reflect on what you have learned:

- How does recognizing these behaviors change your understanding of your anxiety?
- In what ways might you begin to change or replace this behavior with more adaptive coping mechanisms?

**Integration:**

- How did it feel to confront these thoughts?
- What did you learn about the way trauma and anxiety influence your thinking?
- Have your feelings changed after challenging these thoughts?

This process aims to foster a deeper understanding of how certain behaviors are linked to your anxiety and to encourage the development of healthier coping strategies that reduce anxiety rather than maintain it.

# Week 3 Day 4

## *Exploring Anxiety Triggers*

**Objective:** Today's focus is on identifying and understanding the specific triggers that lead to feelings of anxiety. You will explore the thoughts and physical sensations accompanying these triggers and reflect on their deeper connections to your underlying fears and beliefs. This awareness can guide you in developing more adaptive responses to these triggers.

**Instructions:**

1. **Identify Anxiety Triggers:**
   - Throughout the day, stay alert to moments when you feel anxious. As soon as you notice anxiety setting in, pause and document the immediate trigger. This could be a specific situation, interaction, thought, or environmental factor.
   - Write the trigger as soon as possible to ensure accuracy in capturing the event or thought that initiated the anxiety.
1. **Note Thoughts and Physical Sensations:**
   - Alongside identifying the trigger, record any thoughts going through your mind. These thoughts are often predictive or evaluative, such as fearing the outcome of an event or doubting your ability to cope.
   - Also, note the physical sensations associated with the anxiety. This might include a racing heart, sweating, trembling, or feeling tight in your chest. These bodily responses

are important as they can provide clues to the intensity and nature of your anxiety.

1. **Processing the Information:**
   - Reflect on how the identified triggers are connected to deeper fears and beliefs. For example, if a work meeting triggers anxiety, is it linked to a fear of judgment or a belief that you are not competent?
   - Analyze these connections to understand the underlying patterns of your anxiety. Recognizing these patterns is crucial in addressing the root causes of your anxiety rather than just the symptoms.

1. **Develop Adaptive Responses:**
   - Based on your reflection, consider healthier or more adaptive ways to respond to these triggers. This might involve challenging negative thoughts with evidence-based reasoning, using relaxation techniques to manage physical responses, or seeking alternative perspectives.
   - Plan specific actions or responses for future occurrences of similar triggers. For instance, if presenting at meetings is a trigger, you might prepare more thoroughly or practice relaxation techniques beforehand.

**Reflection:** Review your notes and reflections at the end of the day. Consider the effectiveness of your responses and whether they helped reduce your anxiety. Reflect on any insights gained about your anxiety triggers and how they relate to deeper fears or beliefs. How can these insights inform your approach to managing anxiety moving forward?

**Integration:** Continue to use this technique of identifying triggers and associated thoughts and sensations in your daily life. Over time, this practice can help you become more adept at recognizing and managing anxiety promptly. As you become more familiar with your triggers, begin integrating more proactive strategies into your routine to manage anxiety, such as mindfulness, preemptive relaxation, or cognitive restructuring exercises.

By actively exploring and understanding the triggers of your anxiety, you gain valuable insights into your emotional responses and learn effective strategies to manage and reduce anxiety in your everyday life.

# Week 3 Day 5

## *Breaking the Cycle of Anxious Thinking*

Anxiety often stems from our deepest fears and insecurities, particularly those revolving around our adequacies and self-worth. It can manifest as a pervasive whisper that we are not good enough, not capable enough, or simply not up to the tasks life throws our way. These thoughts do not exist in isolation; they are deeply interwoven with our experiences and our perceptions of ourselves in the world.

This week focuses on identifying and breaking the cycle of anxious thinking that may lead you to imagine the worst outcomes in various situations. Such patterns are not just habits of thought; they also reflect how we see ourselves—often less as agents of our own lives and more as subjects to forces beyond our control. This negative self-perception can significantly impact how we interact with the world, leading to a cycle of anxiety that reinforces these negative thoughts.

However, the reality is often much more positive than our anxieties would have us believe. By confronting these patterns directly, we can dismantle the distorted beliefs that fuel our fears. This involves challenging the automatic thoughts that lead us to expect failure and underestimating our abilities. Through this week's exercises, you will be encouraged to explore these anxious thoughts and the underlying beliefs that sustain them. You will learn to apply reality testing to assess the likelihood of feared outcomes and reflect on past successes and abilities that contradict your fears.

The aim is to gradually shift your perspective from self-doubt and insecurity to resilience and self-confidence. This shift is crucial for reducing anxiety and fostering a sense of control and competence in your interactions with the world around you. You can replace the anxious thinking cycle with a more balanced and positive outlook through diligent practice and self-reflection.

**Objective:** Today's exercise aims to address and modify the cycle of anxious thinking, often rooted in deep-seated feelings of inadequacy and low self-worth. You will explore these underlying insecurities and challenge your perceptions through reality testing, focusing on recognizing and affirming your abilities, successes, and capabilities.

**Instructions:**

1. **Identifying Anxious Thoughts:**
   - Throughout the day, be vigilant about moments when your thoughts spiral into worst-case scenarios or when you are overwhelmed by excessive worry.
   - Document each instance, noting the specific thoughts, the context in which they occurred, and your initial emotional response. This step is crucial for building awareness of the patterns of your anxious thinking.

1. **Explore Underlying Insecurities:**
   - For each recorded instance, delve deeper into the personal insecurities or feelings of inadequacy that may be driving these thoughts. Are these thoughts related to fears of failure, not feeling equipped to handle particular situations, or perhaps feelings of not measuring up to others?
   - Reflect on how these insecurities shape your view of yourself and your world.

1. **Reality Testing and Affirmation:**
   - Challenge these anxious thoughts by engaging in reality testing. Assess the likelihood of the feared outcomes occurring and consider the real-world consequences.

- Counter negative self-perceptions by listing examples of your abilities, past successes, and moments when you effectively managed similar situations. This evidence will help you construct a more positive and realistic view of your capabilities.

1. **Redirecting Thoughts:**
   - Practice actively redirecting spiraling or excessively worried thoughts toward more balanced and constructive perspectives. Use the evidence from your reality testing to dispute irrational fears and replace them with affirmations of your strengths and successes.

**Reflection:** At the end of the day, review the instances of anxious thinking you noted and the alternative thoughts you used to challenge them. Reflect on how this process affected your anxiety levels and your overall mood.

Consider the changes in your perceptions of yourself and your abilities. How does acknowledging your strengths alter your feelings of anxiety?

**Integration:** Integrate this practice into your daily routine, continually noting and challenging anxious thoughts as they arise. Over time, this will help you break the cycle of anxious thinking and build a stronger, more resilient self-concept.

As you become more comfortable with this technique, extend it to more challenging or stressful situations to strengthen your coping skills.

By confronting and reshaping the anxious thoughts stemming from feelings of inadequacy, you can gradually transform how you perceive challenges and your ability to handle them, fostering a healthier, more confident approach to life's uncertainties.

# Week 3 Day 6

## Gradual Exposure to Anxiety-Provoking Situations

**Introduction:** Gradual exposure is a therapeutic technique used to manage and reduce anxiety associated with specific situations. By slowly and safely exposing yourself to situations that provoke anxiety, you can begin to diminish the fear response and increase your comfort level over time. It is essential to approach this exercise cautiously, ensuring your safety and comfort are not compromised.

**Caution:** Always prioritize your safety and well-being. Do not put yourself in harm's way or push yourself too far outside your comfort zone. Having a supportive friend or family member with you is advisable when engaging in gradual exposure, especially for the first few times or when tackling more challenging situations.

**Objective:** To develop and implement a controlled plan for gradually exposing yourself to a situation that typically induces mild to moderate anxiety and to reflect on the emotional and cognitive changes that occur through this process.

**Instructions:**

1. **Select an Anxiety-Provoking Situation:**
   - Identify a situation that consistently triggers mild to moderate anxiety. This should be manageable and pose no real danger to your physical or emotional well-being.

- Examples might include making a phone call, attending a social event, or driving in light traffic.

1. **Develop a Gradual Exposure Plan:**
   - Outline a step-by-step approach to expose yourself to the anxiety-provoking situation. Start with the least anxiety-inducing aspect of the situation and gradually build up to more challenging aspects.
   - Determine practical steps and set realistic goals for each exposure. For instance, if you are anxious about social gatherings, you might start by attending a short event with a close friend and gradually increase the duration or attend gatherings where you know fewer people.

1. **Implement the Exposure:**
   - Engage in the planned exposure while keeping your safety and emotional well-being in mind. Use coping strategies such as deep breathing or positive self-talk to manage anxiety during the exposure.
   - Have a support person available, either accompanying you or aware of your activity, so they can offer assistance or encouragement if needed.

1. **Reflect on the Experience:**
   - After completing the exposure, reflect on your emotional and cognitive responses. Note any changes in your anxiety levels before, during, and after the exposure.
   - Consider how your perception of the situation might have shifted. Were there aspects that were less challenging than expected? How did your coping strategies influence your experience?

**Integration:** Based on your reflections, adjust your exposure plan for future practices. Gradually increase the challenge as your comfort level improves.

Continue to practice exposure regularly, noting progress and any new insights into managing your anxiety.

**Conclusion:** Gradual exposure can be a powerful method for reducing anxiety related to specific situations. By carefully planning and executing exposure exercises and reflecting on your experiences, you can gradually desensitize yourself to previously daunting situations, leading to greater confidence and reduced anxiety. Always proceed cautiously and utilize support systems to ensure safe and beneficial experiences.

# Week 3 Day 7

## *Reflecting on Progress and Setting Goals*

**Objective:** Today, you'll take a moment to pause and reflect on the progress you've made over the past week. This is a crucial step in recognizing your achievements and the effectiveness of your strategies. Based on this reflection, you'll set new goals and intentions for the upcoming week, focusing on continuing your journey toward better anxiety management.

**Instructions:**

1. **Review Progress:**
   - Reflect on the past week and note the techniques and exercises you implemented to manage your anxiety. Consider each day's activities and the strategies you used.
   - Identify specific instances where you noticed improvements in your anxiety management. This could include successful gradual exposure sessions, effective use of coping strategies during high anxiety moments, or more controlled responses to previously triggering situations.
1. **Assess Insights and Changes:**
   - Identify key insights you have gained about your anxiety and your responses. What have you learned about your triggers, thought patterns, or emotional responses?
   - Note any positive changes in your behavior or feelings. Have you noticed a reduction in anxiety levels? Are there situations that you now find more manageable?

1. **Set Goals for the Upcoming Week:**
   - Based on your reflections and the progress you've made, set specific, achievable goals for the next week. Consider aspects of your anxiety management that you wish to improve or continue developing.
   - Choose new coping strategies you want to try. This might involve integrating mindfulness exercises, testing new cognitive restructuring techniques, or expanding your gradual exposure to more challenging situations.
   - Plan to continue practicing exposure in situations where you've seen progress, aiming to increase your comfort level and reduce anxiety further.
1. **Plan Implementation:**
   - Outline how you will integrate these goals into your daily routine. Be specific about when and how to practice these strategies to ensure consistency and effectiveness.
   - Consider any potential challenges and plan how you will address them. This might include scheduling specific times for practice, enlisting support from friends or family, or setting reminders.

**Reflection:** Reflect on the value of setting weekly goals and how this helps manage your anxiety. How do planning and goal setting influence your motivation and your ability to cope with anxiety?

Consider the benefits of regular reflection and adjustment of your goals based on your ongoing experiences and needs.

**Integration:** Make goal setting and weekly reflection a regular routine. This practice can provide structure and direction in your continued efforts to manage anxiety, allowing you to systematically build on your successes and address improvement areas.

**Conclusion:** Reflecting on your progress and setting informed goals are critical steps toward better anxiety management. By acknowledging your achievements and setting clear, focused goals, you enhance your ability to navigate anxiety confidently and resiliently. Continue to build on this foundation, adapting your strategies as you grow and learn about your mental health needs.

# Week 3 Tracking Progress

As you wrap up this week's CBT exercises, reflect on your growth. Return to the bridge illustration and mark your current position. Rate your anxiety level on the 0-10 scale, considering how your perspective and coping strategies may have shifted. Celebrate your dedication to this journey.

**Instructions**:

1. Take a moment to reflect on your progress and experiences.
2. Refer to the bridge illustration below.
3. Consider where you currently stand on your journey.
4. Place a mark on the bridge representing your current position.
5. Next, rate where your average anxiety level has been over this week.
6. Record your anxiety rating on the provided 0-10 scale, with 0 being no anxiety and 10 being the most intense anxiety you've experienced.
7. Reflect and journal.

**Reflection**: After marking your bridge position and anxiety rating, reflect on your progress. Examine skills learned, challenges faced, and changes in thoughts and behaviors. Journal your insights and observations. Identify successes, challenges, and areas requiring more attention. Determine if you need to slow down, revisit previous weeks or skills, or seek professional help to maintain progress. Assess your

overall progress and consider if professional support is needed or how it's contributing to your journey.

| 0 | 1 | 2 | 3 | 4 | 5 | 6 | 7 | 8 | 9 | 10 |

No
Anxiety

Moderate
Anxiety

High
Anxiety

# 8

# *Cognitive Distortions*

Cognitive distortions are a central theme in cognitive psychology and significantly shape our mental well-being. These distortions are habitual and often unconscious ways of thinking that are frequently inaccurate, negative, and irrational. They can influence our perceptions, emotions, and behaviors, usually acting as unseen forces that color our experiences and interpretations of the world.

Research has shown that cognitive distortions are a common feature of various mental health issues, including anxiety disorders, depression, and stress-related conditions. They can contribute to developing and maintaining these problems by perpetuating negative thought patterns, reinforcing maladaptive beliefs, and influencing unhelpful behaviors.

However, it's important to recognize that cognitive distortions are not always negative. Positive distortions, such as optimism bias (the tendency to overestimate the likelihood of positive outcomes) or the illusion of control (the belief that we have more control over events than we do), can sometimes serve adaptive functions. These positive distortions can provide us with hope, motivation, and resilience in the face of challenges, helping us to persevere and maintain a sense of agency in difficult circumstances.

Nevertheless, when positive distortions become excessive or unrealistic, they can also have detrimental effects. Overconfidence in our abilities or an exaggerated sense of control can lead to risky behaviors, poor decision-making, and eventual disappointment when reality fails to meet our expectations. It's crucial to balance maintaining a positive outlook and staying grounded in reality.

On the other hand, negative cognitive distortions are more commonly problematic and are often the focus of therapeutic interventions. These distortions tend to skew our thinking to pessimism, self-doubt, and helplessness, making us feel overwhelmed, anxious, or depressed even when the reality of our situation is not as dire as we perceive it to be.

Cognitive distortions can take many forms, but some of the most common ones include:

All-or-Nothing Thinking (also known as Black-and-White Thinking): This distortion involves seeing things in absolute, binary categories with no middle ground or shades of gray. People with this distortion often think in terms of "always" or "never," "good" or "bad," "success" or "failure." For example, a student might think, "If I don't get an A on this exam, I'm a complete failure." This thinking can lead to intense pressure, perfectionism, and self-judgment.

Overgeneralization: This distortion involves taking a single negative event or experience and extrapolating it into a never-ending pattern of defeat or disappointment. It's characterized by the use of words like "always," "never," "every," or "all." For instance, after a relationship ends, someone might conclude, "I'll never find love again" or "All my relationships are doomed to fail." Overgeneralization can lead to hopelessness and a negative outlook on the future.

Mental Filter (also known as Selective Abstraction): This distortion involves focusing exclusively on the negative aspects of a situation while filtering out or ignoring any positive elements. It's like looking at the world through dark-tinted glasses, where everything appears gloomy and pessimistic. For example, an employee might receive mostly positive feedback in a performance review but fixate on a single piece of constructive criticism, concluding that they are a terrible worker. This distortion can fuel low self-esteem, anxiety, and depression.

Disqualifying the Positive: Similar to the mental filter, this distortion involves rejecting, dismissing, or minimizing positive experiences, accomplishments, or qualities. People with this distortion might receive compliments or praise but insist that they "don't count" for some reason, such as being easy or insignificant. They might attribute positive outcomes to external factors like luck or chance rather than their efforts or abilities. This distortion can maintain a negative self-image and prevent people from recognizing and appreciating their strengths and successes.

Jumping to Conclusions: Jumping to conclusions can fuel anxiety, self-doubt, and avoidance behaviors. This distortion involves making negative interpretations or predictions without sufficient evidence or facts to support them. It often manifests in two ways:

Mind-Reading: Assuming that others are thinking negatively about or reacting negatively to us without concrete evidence. For example, suppose a friend doesn't respond to a text message immediately. In that case, someone might conclude, "They must be angry at me" or "They don't like me anymore," without considering alternative explanations.

Fortune-Telling: Predicting that things will turn out badly or anticipating the worst-case scenario, often without any basis in reality. For instance, someone might worry, "I'm going to fail this interview," or "I'll never be able to handle this challenge," even before attempting the task.

These are just a few cognitive distortions that can impact our thinking and well-being. You will find a comprehensive list of cognitive distortions, detailed descriptions, and examples in the appendix of this book.

Identifying cognitive distortions will assist in managing our mental health and promoting emotional well-being. By recognizing these negative thinking patterns as they occur, we can begin to challenge and reframe them, gradually replacing them with more balanced, realistic, and adaptive thoughts. This process of cognitive restructuring is a cornerstone of Cognitive Behavioral Therapy (CBT), a highly effective and evidence-based approach to treating a wide range of mental health issues.

As discussed in the first and second weeks of this book, cognitive restructuring involves several key steps:

1. Identifying negative automatic thoughts: These are the spontaneous, emotionally charged thoughts that pop into our minds in response to certain triggers or situations. They are often brief, unexamined, and tied to cognitive distortions.
2. Evaluating the validity of these thoughts: This step involves examining the evidence for and against the negative thoughts, considering alternative explanations, and assessing the reasonableness and helpfulness of the thoughts.
3. Replacing the negative thoughts with more accurate and adaptive ones: Based on the evaluation process, we can develop more balanced and realistic thoughts that consider the full context of the situation and our strengths and resources.

By becoming aware of our cognitive distortions and actively working to restructure our thinking, we can break free from negative thought cycles and develop a more resilient and positive mindset.

However, cognitive restructuring is not just about changing our thoughts in isolation. Engaging in behavioral interventions that reinforce our new, more balanced thinking patterns is essential to transform our mental habits and promote lasting change. This might involve:

- Gradually facing feared situations or challenges rather than avoiding them based on distorted predictions or assumptions.
- Scheduling enjoyable activities and self-care practices, even when we don't feel like it, to combat distortions like mental filtering or disqualifying the positive.
- Practicing assertiveness and setting healthy boundaries to counteract distortions related to people-pleasing or self-sacrifice.

- Engaging in problem-solving and goal-setting to build self-efficacy and challenge distortions of helplessness or hopelessness.

By aligning our behaviors with restructured thoughts, we create a positive feedback loop that reinforces healthy thinking patterns and builds emotional resilience. We also gather evidence and experiences that directly challenge our cognitive distortions, making it easier to recognize and refute them in the future.

Throughout the next seven days, we will explore a range of practical strategies and techniques for identifying and overcoming cognitive distortions. Each day will focus on a specific evidence-based approach, providing you with a diverse toolkit of skills to foster more balanced, realistic, and adaptive thinking patterns.

These strategies will include:

- Thought Records: A structured way to identify, evaluate, and respond to negative automatic thoughts and cognitive distortions.
- Examining the Evidence: A technique for objectively assessing the accuracy and validity of our thoughts by looking at the facts and data.
- Reframing: The practice of considering alternative perspectives or interpretations of a situation to counteract mental filtering or jumping to conclusions.
- Behavioral Experiments: Designing and carrying out specific actions or tasks to test the validity of our assumptions and predictions, gather new evidence, and challenge cognitive distortions experientially.
- Self-Compassion: Cultivating a kind, understanding, and forgiving attitude toward ourselves to combat distortions related to self-criticism, perfectionism, or shame.
- Cognitive Defusion: Learning to observe and detach from our thoughts, recognizing them as mental events rather than absolute truths, and reducing their emotional impact and power over us.

- Gratitude and Positive Reframing: Deliberately focusing on the positive aspects of our experiences to balance out negative biases and build emotional resilience.

As you work through these strategies over the coming week, remember that overcoming cognitive distortions is a process, not a one-time event. It requires consistent practice, patience, and self-compassion. You may find some techniques more helpful or resonant than others, and that's perfectly normal. The key is experimenting with different approaches, finding what works best for you, and gradually integrating these skills into your daily life and thinking habits.

It's also important to recognize that changing long-standing thinking and behavior patterns is not always easy. There may be times when you feel discouraged, frustrated, or doubtful about your progress. Try to be kind and understanding with yourself in these moments, remembering that growth and change are rarely linear. Every step you take, no matter how small, is a meaningful victory worth celebrating.

If you find yourself struggling with persistent or severe cognitive distortions that significantly impact your daily functioning or well-being, don't hesitate to seek professional support. A trained mental health professional, such as a licensed therapist or counselor, can provide individualized guidance, support, and additional strategies tailored to your unique needs and experiences.

As you embark on this journey of self-discovery and growth, remember you are not alone. Cognitive distortions are a common human experience, and many people have successfully learned to recognize, challenge, and overcome them. By committing to this process and practicing the strategies outlined in this chapter, you are committing to improved mental health, emotional resilience, and overall well-being.

In the coming chapters, we will continue to build on the foundation of cognitive restructuring, exploring additional topics and techniques that can support your anxiety-free journey. We will delve into the power of self-compassion, the benefits of mindfulness and acceptance-based approaches, and the importance of values and committed action in creating a life aligned with your deepest aspirations.

Remember, the path to mental wellness is an ongoing journey, not a destination. With each day and each practice, you are strengthening your ability to navigate life's challenges with greater clarity, resilience, and self-understanding. Trust in the process, be patient with yourself, and celebrate every step forward, knowing you are worth the effort and investment in your well-being.

# Week 4 Self-Help Guide

*Cognitive Distortions:*

*Understanding and Overcoming Negative Thinking Patterns*

Misaligned and negative thinking can cause and perpetuate anxiety. Learning about negative thinking patterns and skewed world views are powerful tools for managing anxiousness. Over the next week you will learn these tools, and as you implement them, you will see firsthand the effectiveness at redirecting thoughts and reducing anxiety.

# Week 4 Day 1

## Cognitive Restructuring with Thought Records

**Objective**: Develop the skill of identifying and challenging cognitive distortions using thought records to promote balanced thinking and emotional well-being.

**Information**: Thought records are a powerful tool in cognitive restructuring, a process that involves identifying negative automatic thoughts, recognizing the cognitive distortions they contain, and developing more balanced and realistic thinking patterns. By systematically examining our thoughts and the evidence for and against them, we can gain a clearer understanding of how our thinking influences our emotions and behaviors. Thought records help us break free from the cycle of negative thinking and develop a more adaptive and flexible mindset.

**Instructions**:

1. Notice and record distressing emotions:
   - When you experience a distressing emotion, such as anxiety, sadness, or anger, take a moment to pause and reflect on the situation.
   - In a journal or thought record worksheet, write down the date, time, and a brief description of the situation that triggered the emotion.
   - Rate the intensity of the emotion on a scale from 0 to 100.
2. Identify automatic thoughts:
   - Reflect on the thoughts that accompanied the distressing

emotion. These are often automatic, negative thoughts that pop into your mind without conscious effort.

- ○ Write down these automatic thoughts in your thought record, using the exact words that crossed your mind.
- ○ If you had multiple thoughts, focus on the one that seemed most significant or distressing.

3. Recognize cognitive distortions:
   - ○ Examine your automatic thoughts and try to identify any cognitive distortions they contain. Refer to the list of common cognitive distortions provided in the appendix.
   - ○ Label the specific distortions you notice, such as all-or-nothing thinking, overgeneralization, mental filtering, or catastrophizing.
   - ○ Remember that automatic thoughts often contain multiple distortions, so identify as many as you can.

4. Challenge the distortions:
   - ○ For each distortion you identified, challenge the thought by examining the evidence for and against it. Ask yourself:
     - ■ What facts support this thought? What facts contradict it?
     - ■ Are there alternative explanations or perspectives I haven't considered?
     - ■ What would I tell a friend who had this thought?
     - ■ Is this thought helpful or beneficial to me?
   - ○ Write down the evidence and alternative perspectives in your thought record.

5. Develop balanced thoughts:
   - ○ Based on the evidence you gathered and the alternative perspectives you considered, develop a more balanced and realistic thought that takes into account the full reality of the situation.
   - ○ The balanced thought should be a fair and accurate representation of the situation, rather than an extreme or distorted view.

- Write down the balanced thought in your thought record.
6. Reassess your emotions:
    - After developing a balanced thought, take a moment to reassess your emotional state. Rate the intensity of your emotion again on the same scale from 0 to 100.
    - Notice any changes in your emotional intensity or the emergence of new, more adaptive emotions.
    - Reflect on how the process of challenging distortions and developing balanced thoughts impacted your emotional state.
7. Practice regularly:
    - Make thought records a regular part of your self-reflection and personal growth practice. Set aside time each day to complete a thought record, even if you haven't experienced significant distress.
    - The more you practice identifying and challenging distortions, the more naturally balanced thinking will come to you.
    - Remember that cognitive restructuring is a skill that improves with practice, so be patient and consistent in your efforts.

**Reflection**: After completing a thought record, take a moment to reflect on your experience. Consider how the process of identifying and challenging cognitive distortions impacted your emotional state and outlook on the situation. Notice any shifts in your perspective or the intensity of your emotions. Reflect on the benefits of balanced thinking and how it can contribute to your overall well-being and resilience.

**Integration**: Integrate thought records into your daily life as a tool for self-awareness and personal growth. Use them regularly to examine your thoughts and emotions, especially in situations that trigger distress or negative thinking patterns. As you become more skilled in identifying and challenging distortions, notice how your thinking becomes more balanced and flexible over time. Remember that thought records are not just a tool for managing distress but also a means of cultivating a more resilient and adaptive mindset.

# Week 4 Day 2

## Examining the Evidence

**Objective**: Develop the skill of evaluating the validity of automatic thoughts by examining the evidence, promoting a more balanced and realistic perspective.

**Information**: Cognitive distortions often lead us to accept negative thoughts as truth without questioning their accuracy or validity. By examining the evidence, we can objectively assess the credibility of our thoughts and challenge the distortions that contribute to emotional distress. This process involves treating our thoughts as hypotheses to be tested rather than absolute facts. By gathering and evaluating evidence that supports and contradicts our thoughts, we can develop a more balanced and realistic understanding of the situation.

**Instructions**:

1. Identify the automatic thought:
    - When you notice a negative automatic thought, write it down in a clear and specific statement.
    - For example, "I'm a failure because I made a mistake at work."
2. Treat the thought as a hypothesis:
    - Approach the thought as a hypothesis to be tested rather than a proven fact.
    - Remind yourself that thoughts are not necessarily reality and that it's important to examine the evidence objectively.
3. List evidence that supports the thought:

- Write down any evidence that seems to support the automatic thought.
  - Be specific and honest, including concrete examples and observations.
  - For example, "I missed a deadline on an important project."
4. List evidence that contradicts the thought:
  - Write down evidence that contradicts or challenges the automatic thought.
  - Consider past experiences, alternative explanations, and input from trusted others.
  - For example, "I have met many deadlines in the past and received positive feedback from my supervisor."
5. Evaluate the quality and relevance of the evidence:
  - Assess the quality and relevance of the evidence you listed.
  - Consider factors such as the reliability of the source, the context of the situation, and the overall pattern of evidence.
  - For example, "The missed deadline was an isolated incident, and I have a track record of meeting expectations."
6. Develop a balanced and realistic evaluation:
  - Based on your examination of the evidence, develop a more balanced and realistic evaluation of the situation.
  - Incorporate the evidence that contradicts the automatic thought and consider alternative perspectives.
  - For example, "While I made a mistake, it doesn't define me as a failure. I have a history of success and can learn from this experience."
7. Practice regularly:
  - Make examining the evidence a regular practice whenever you identify negative automatic thoughts.
  - Set aside time each day to evaluate your thoughts objectively, even if they don't seem particularly distressing.
  - The more you practice, the more natural it will become to challenge distortions and maintain a balanced perspective.

**Reflection**: After examining the evidence for an automatic thought, take a moment to reflect on the process. Consider the following questions: Did you find that your initial thought was based more on emotion than facts? How did evaluating the evidence impact your perspective on the situation? What insights did you gain about the relationship between your thoughts and emotions?

**Integration**: Integrate the practice of examining the evidence into your daily life. Make it a habit to question the validity of your automatic thoughts regularly. When you notice a negative thought, pause and ask yourself, "What is the evidence for and against this thought?" By consistently evaluating your thoughts against reality, you'll develop a more balanced and resilient mindset over time. Remember that examining the evidence is a skill that requires practice and patience, but it can significantly improve your emotional well-being and cognitive flexibility.

# Week 4 Day 3

## *Reframing*

**Objective**: Reframe negative situations in a more balanced, realistic, or neutral perspective to reduce the impact of cognitive distortions and alleviate emotional distress.

**Information**: Reframing is a powerful cognitive technique that involves examining a situation from various angles and exploring alternative interpretations. By challenging our initial negative perceptions and considering different viewpoints, we can develop a more balanced and realistic understanding of the situation. This process helps to minimize the influence of cognitive distortions, which are exaggerated or irrational thought patterns that contribute to emotional distress.

**Instructions**:

1. Identify a specific situation that you have been interpreting negatively. Write down your initial thoughts and beliefs about the situation in detail.
2. Recognize the cognitive distortions that may be influencing your perception. Common distortions include all-or-nothing thinking, overgeneralization, mental filtering, disqualifying the positive, jumping to conclusions, magnification, emotional reasoning, should statements, labeling, and personalization.
3. Challenge your initial negative interpretation by asking yourself questions such as: Is this the only way to view the situation? What evidence supports or contradicts my interpretation? Are there any alternative explanations or perspectives?

4. Brainstorm at least three alternative ways of viewing the situation. Consider perspectives that are more positive, neutral, or simply different from your initial view. Write down these alternative interpretations.

5. Evaluate the evidence for each perspective. Examine the facts and reality of the situation objectively. Consider which interpretation is most consistent with the available evidence and reality.

6. Generate a balanced and realistic perspective by combining the most accurate and helpful elements from your initial view and the alternative interpretations. This new perspective should take into account the full context of the situation and avoid extreme or irrational thinking.

7. Adopt this balanced and realistic perspective as your new frame of reference. Write down your new interpretation of the situation and the evidence supporting it.

8. Reassess your emotional response to the situation based on your new perspective. Notice any changes in your feelings, such as reduced anxiety, frustration, or sadness.

**Reflection**: After completing the reframing process, take a moment to reflect on your experience. Consider the following questions: How did reframing impact your emotional response to the situation? Did adopting a different perspective help alleviate distress? What insights did you gain about your thought patterns and their influence on your emotions? How can you apply this reframing technique to other areas of your life?

**Integration**: Make reframing a regular practice in your daily life. Start by applying the technique to minor daily stressors and gradually work up to more significant challenges. Consistently practice reframing in various situations to develop cognitive flexibility and resilience. Over time, reframing will become a natural habit, allowing you to approach situations with a more balanced and adaptive mindset. Remember that reframing is a skill that improves with practice, so be patient and persistent in your efforts.

# Week 4 Day 4

## *Behavioral Experiments*

**Objective**: Gather evidence about the accuracy of automatic thoughts and beliefs through carefully designed behavioral experiments, allowing for the development of more balanced and realistic thinking patterns.

**Information**: Behavioral experiments are a powerful cognitive-behavioral technique that involves testing the validity of our thoughts and beliefs through deliberate action and observation. By engaging in specific behaviors and evaluating the outcomes, we can gather objective evidence that either supports or challenges our automatic thoughts. This process helps to counteract cognitive distortions, which are inaccurate or exaggerated interpretations of reality that contribute to emotional distress. Behavioral experiments enable us to break free from the cycle of negative thinking by providing concrete evidence that our thoughts may not be entirely accurate or helpful.

**Instructions**:

1. Identify a specific negative automatic thought or belief that you want to test. Write down the thought in detail, along with the emotions and behaviors it typically triggers. For example, "If I speak up in the meeting, everyone will think my ideas are stupid, and I'll feel embarrassed."

2. Develop a clear and specific behavioral experiment to test the validity of this thought. Design the experiment to be as realistic and representative of the actual situation as possible. Consider the following steps: a. Define the specific behavior you will

engage in during the experiment. In this case, it might involve speaking up and sharing your ideas in the next meeting. b. Identify the predicted negative outcome based on your automatic thought. Be specific about what you expect to happen. For example, "I predict that people will laugh at my ideas, and I will feel humiliated." c. Establish a way to measure or observe the actual outcomes of the experiment. This might involve paying attention to verbal and nonverbal reactions, asking for feedback, or reflecting on your own emotional response.

3. Carry out the behavioral experiment as planned. Engage in the specific behavior you identified and observe the results closely. Record the actual outcomes, including any reactions from others and your own thoughts and emotions during and after the experiment.

4. Evaluate the evidence gathered from the experiment. Compare the actual outcomes to your predicted negative outcome. Consider the following questions: a. Were the actual results consistent with your automatic thought, or were they different? b. Did you observe any evidence that challenges your initial belief? c. Were there any positive or neutral outcomes that you hadn't anticipated?

5. Use the evidence from the experiment to develop a more balanced and realistic thought. Based on the actual results, create a new, alternative thought that takes into account the full reality of the situation. For example, "Although I felt nervous, my ideas were well-received, and several people expressed interest in discussing them further. Speaking up wasn't as bad as I predicted."

6. Repeat the process with other automatic thoughts and beliefs. Continue to design and conduct behavioral experiments to test the accuracy of your thoughts across different situations.

**Reflection**: After completing each behavioral experiment, take time to reflect on the insights gained. Consider what you learned about the accuracy of your automatic thoughts and the impact of acting on them. Reflect on how the experiment challenged your assumptions and whether it provided evidence for a more balanced perspective. Evaluate the emotional and behavioral changes that resulted from testing your thoughts against reality.

**Integration**: Make behavioral experiments a regular part of your cognitive-behavioral practice. Incorporate this technique into your daily life, starting with smaller, less challenging situations and gradually progressing to more significant ones. Consistently test your automatic thoughts and beliefs through action and observation, allowing the evidence to shape more accurate and helpful thinking patterns. Over time, behavioral experiments will become a valuable tool in your toolkit for managing cognitive distortions and promoting emotional well-being. Remember to approach each experiment with curiosity and an open mind, and celebrate the insights and progress you make along the way.

# Week 4 Day 5

## Self-Compassion Practice

**Objective**: Develop self-compassion as a coping strategy to counteract negative self-talk, cognitive distortions, and self-criticism, promoting emotional well-being and resilience.

**Information**: Self-compassion is the practice of treating ourselves with kindness, understanding, and forgiveness, particularly during times of difficulty, personal shortcomings, or perceived inadequacies. It involves recognizing that challenges and imperfections are a shared human experience and that we deserve compassion and understanding, just as we would extend to a good friend. Self-compassion acts as a powerful antidote to negative self-talk and cognitive distortions, which often fuel feelings of self-doubt, guilt, or inadequacy. By cultivating self-compassion, we can develop greater emotional resilience, reduce the impact of negative thinking patterns, and foster a more balanced and supportive inner dialogue.

**Instructions**:

1. Develop awareness of negative self-talk and cognitive distortions:
   - Pay attention to your inner dialogue and thoughts, especially in situations that trigger self-criticism or negative self-evaluation.
   - Notice when you engage in cognitive distortions, such as all-or-nothing thinking, overgeneralization, or labeling yourself harshly.

- Acknowledge the presence of these negative thoughts without judgment or self-condemnation.
2. Recognize the universality of human struggles and imperfections:
    - Remind yourself that everyone faces challenges, makes mistakes, and experiences setbacks.
    - Acknowledge that feelings of inadequacy, self-doubt, or frustration are a common part of the human experience.
    - Understand that you are not alone in your struggles and that others can relate to your difficulties.
3. Treat yourself with kindness and understanding:
    - Imagine how you would respond to a good friend who is going through a similar situation or experiencing self-doubt.
    - Speak to yourself using the same compassionate, understanding, and supportive language you would use with a friend.
    - Use gentle and encouraging words that validate your emotions and experiences while offering comfort and reassurance.
4. Engage in self-compassion exercises:
    - Write a supportive letter to yourself, expressing understanding, kindness, and encouragement, as if you were writing to a dear friend.
    - Practice a loving-kindness meditation, directing feelings of warmth, care, and compassion towards yourself.
    - Place your hand on your heart and offer yourself words of comfort, such as "I am here for you" or "I accept myself as I am."
    - Engage in self-care activities that nurture your physical, emotional, and mental well-being.
5. Challenge negative self-talk and cognitive distortions:
    - When you notice negative self-talk or cognitive distortions, gently question the accuracy and helpfulness of these thoughts.

- Ask yourself if you would speak to a friend in the same way or if there are alternative, more compassionate perspectives.
- Reframe negative thoughts in a more balanced, understanding, and self-supportive manner.

6. Practice self-compassion regularly:
   - Make self-compassion a daily practice, even in small moments throughout the day.
   - Set aside dedicated time for self-compassion exercises, such as writing or meditation.
   - Incorporate self-compassion into your self-care routine and prioritize activities that promote self-kindness and understanding.

**Reflection**: After practicing self-compassion, take a moment to reflect on your experience. Notice how treating yourself with compassion and understanding affects your emotional state, self-talk, and overall well-being. Consider the following questions: Does self-compassion help soften the impact of negative thoughts and cognitive distortions? How does it influence your ability to cope with challenges or setbacks? What shifts do you notice in your inner dialogue and self-perception when you practice self-compassion?

**Integration**: Make self-compassion an integral part of your daily life and emotional self-care. Consistently practice self-compassion exercises, such as self-supportive writing or loving-kindness meditations. Look for opportunities to apply self-compassion in various situations, especially when facing difficulties or self-criticism. Over time, self-compassion will become a natural and automatic response to negative self-talk and cognitive distortions, fostering greater emotional resilience and a more supportive internal environment. Remember to be patient and gentle with yourself as you cultivate self-compassion, acknowledging that it is an ongoing practice and journey of self-discovery and growth.

# Week 4 Day 6

## *Cognitive Defusion Practice*

**Objective**: Develop the skill of cognitive defusion to detach from negative thoughts, reduce their emotional impact, and promote a more flexible and adaptive mindset.

**Information**: Cognitive defusion is a technique that helps create distance between ourselves and our thoughts, allowing us to observe them as mental events rather than absolute truths or facts. By learning to detach from negative thoughts, we can reduce their emotional impact and the power they hold over our well-being. Cognitive defusion enables us to recognize that thoughts are simply products of our mind and do not necessarily reflect reality. This understanding empowers us to respond to thoughts more flexibly and adaptively, rather than getting caught up in their content or automatically believing them.

**Instructions**:

1. Identify negative thoughts:
   - Pay attention to your internal dialogue and notice when negative thoughts arise.
   - These thoughts may involve self-criticism, worry, rumination, or pessimistic predictions.
   - Remember that having negative thoughts is a common human experience and does not define your worth or reality.
2. Label thoughts as thoughts:

- When you catch a negative thought, mentally label it as a thought rather than a fact.
- Use phrases like "I'm having the thought that..." or "I'm noticing the thought that..." to create distance between yourself and the thought.
- For example, instead of saying "I'm a failure," say "I'm having the thought that I'm a failure."

3. Observe thoughts without judgment:
   - Practice observing your thoughts as if you were an impartial witness, without trying to change, suppress, or engage with them.
   - Imagine your thoughts as leaves floating down a stream, clouds passing in the sky, or cars driving by on a road.
   - Allow the thoughts to come and go without getting attached to their content or letting them dictate your emotions or actions.

4. Use defusion techniques:
   - If a thought feels particularly sticky or persistent, try using a defusion technique to create further distance:
     - Repeat the thought in a silly voice, such as a cartoon character or a robot.
     - Sing the thought to the tune of a familiar song, like "Happy Birthday" or "Row, Row, Row Your Boat."
     - Visualize the thought as words on a screen, and imagine the screen gradually fading or the words becoming jumbled.
   - Experiment with different defusion techniques to find what works best for you in various situations.

5. Refocus on the present moment:
   - After observing and defusing from a negative thought, gently redirect your attention to the present moment and your current activities.
   - Engage your senses by noticing what you can see, hear, feel, smell, or taste in your immediate environment.

- If needed, take a few deep breaths to ground yourself and anchor your attention in the present.

6. Practice regularly:
    - Make cognitive defusion a regular practice, using it whenever you notice yourself getting caught up in negative thinking patterns.
    - Set aside dedicated time each day to practice observing and defusing from thoughts, even when you're not experiencing significant distress.
    - Remember that cognitive defusion is a skill that improves with practice, so be patient and consistent in your efforts.

**Reflection**: After practicing cognitive defusion, take a moment to reflect on your experience. Consider how creating distance from negative thoughts affects their emotional impact and your ability to respond to them flexibly. Notice any shifts in your perspective or reactivity to thoughts. Reflect on the benefits of seeing thoughts as mental events rather than facts, and how this understanding can support your overall well-being.

**Integration**: Integrate cognitive defusion into your daily life by making it a habitual response to negative thinking patterns. Practice observing and defusing from thoughts in various contexts, such as work, relationships, or personal challenges. Notice how this practice influences your emotional resilience and ability to engage with life more fully. Remember that cognitive defusion is not about eliminating negative thoughts entirely but rather developing a new relationship with them that allows for greater flexibility and adaptability.

# Week 4 Day 7

## Gratitude and Positive Reframing

**Objective**: Cultivate gratitude and practice positive reframing to counteract cognitive distortions.

**Information**: Gratitude and positive reframing help shift our focus from the negative aspects of a situation to the positive. This can help balance out the impact of cognitive distortions.

**Instructions**:

1. Each day, write down three things you are grateful for. These can be small, everyday things or more significant aspects of your life.
2. When faced with a challenging situation, try to find something positive or a potential opportunity for growth within the difficulty.
3. Reframe negative self-talk into more positive, supportive statements. For example, instead of "I can't handle this," try "This is difficult, but I'm learning and growing."
4. At the end of each day, reflect on any positive experiences, accomplishments, or moments of joy, no matter how small.

**Reflection**: Reflect on how gratitude and positive reframing affect your overall outlook and emotional well-being. Do you notice a shift in your thinking patterns?

**Integration**: Make gratitude and positive reframing a daily practice.

The more you focus on the positive aspects of life, the less power cognitive distortions will hold over your thinking.

Remember, overcoming cognitive distortions is a journey that takes consistent practice. Be patient with yourself and celebrate each step forward. With time and dedication, you can develop more balanced, realistic thinking patterns that support your mental health and well-being.

As you work through these strategies, remember to refer to the cognitive restructuring and behavioral techniques discussed in the first and second weeks. Integrating thought records, examining evidence, and behavioral activation into your daily routine will complement the specific strategies outlined in this chapter, creating a comprehensive approach to managing cognitive distortions.

If you find yourself struggling with persistent or severe cognitive distortions, don't hesitate to seek professional support. A trained therapist can provide additional guidance and support as you work to develop healthier thinking patterns.

The next chapter will delve into self-compassion, exploring how cultivating a kind and understanding relationship with ourselves can promote emotional resilience and well-being.

# Week 4 Tracking

Week 4 has provided insights into defense mechanisms. Take a moment to contemplate your progress. Identify your position on the bridge and rate your anxiety level on the 0-10 scale. Recognize the awareness you've gained and the steps you've taken toward understanding your anxiety.

**Instructions**:

1. Take a moment to reflect on your progress and experiences.
2. Refer to the bridge illustration below.
3. Consider where you currently stand on your journey.
4. Place a mark on the bridge representing your current position.
5. Next, rate where your average anxiety level has been over this week.
6. Record your anxiety rating on the provided 0-10 scale, with 0 being no anxiety and 10 being the most intense anxiety you've experienced.
7. Reflect and journal.

**Reflection**: After marking your bridge position and anxiety rating, reflect on your progress. Examine skills learned, challenges faced, and changes in thoughts and behaviors. Journal your insights and observations. Identify successes, challenges, and areas requiring more attention. Determine if you need to slow down, revisit previous weeks or skills, or seek professional help to maintain progress. Assess your overall progress and consider if professional support is needed or how it's contributing to your journey.

| 0 | 1 | 2 | 3 | 4 | 5 | 6 | 7 | 8 | 9 | 10 |

No
Anxiety

Moderate
Anxiety

High
Anxiety

# 9

# *Defense Mechanisms*

Defense mechanisms are unconscious psychological strategies employed by individuals to cope with anxiety, stress, and uncomfortable emotions. These mechanisms protect the mind from feelings that are too difficult or overwhelming to confront consciously. Although defense mechanisms can temporarily relieve distress, excessive or inappropriate reliance on them may lead to complications.

These strategies operate unconsciously, meaning people are often unaware of their use. They are automatic and involuntary, activating in response to perceived threats or stressors. Defense mechanisms vary widely, ranging from denial and repression to intellectualization and sublimation, each functioning uniquely to help the individual manage anxiety and maintain emotional equilibrium.

Defense mechanisms play a crucial role in managing anxiety by helping individuals avoid or minimize distressing thoughts, feelings, and situations. When confronted with a stressful event or overwhelming emotion, these mechanisms automatically activate to protect the ego or sense of self. They reduce the intensity of anxiety by redirecting attention away from the source of distress or by altering the individual's perception of the situation.

For example, a person who experiences anxiety about public speaking might use rationalization to lessen their worry. They may reassure themselves with thoughts like, "Everyone gets nervous about public speaking; it's not a big deal," or "I've done this before and survived. I can handle it again." Through rationalization, the individual temporarily reduces their anxiety, feeling more capable of managing the challenging situation.

However, while defense mechanisms can provide short-term relief, they can become problematic if used excessively or inappropriately. An overreliance on defense mechanisms might prevent individuals from confronting the underlying causes of their anxiety, leading to mal-adaptive behavioral patterns. For instance, consistent use of avoidance might cause someone to miss out on important growth opportunities, potentially increasing their anxiety over time.

Cognitive-behavioral therapy (CBT) is a well-established and highly effective treatment approach for anxiety disorders. CBT focuses on helping individuals identify and change negative patterns of thinking and behavior that contribute to their anxiety. Understanding defense mechanisms is crucial in this context because these strategies can some-times interfere with the therapeutic process.

Defense mechanisms can prevent individuals from fully engaging with their thoughts and emotions, which is necessary to make positive CBT changes. For example, someone who uses denial as a defense mechanism may struggle to acknowledge the severity of their anxiety symptoms, making it difficult for them to fully participate in treat-ment. Similarly, someone who relies on intellectualization may focus excessively on the theoretical aspects of therapy while avoiding the emotional work necessary for progress.

By helping clients become aware of their defense mechanisms, CBT therapists can guide them toward more adaptive coping strategies and facilitate long-term anxiety relief. Through the process of cogni-tive restructuring, clients learn to identify and challenge the negative thoughts and beliefs that underlie their anxiety. They also learn to tolerate and manage uncomfortable emotions rather than relying on defense mechanisms to avoid them.

Incorporating an understanding of defense mechanisms into CBT can enhance the effectiveness of treatment by addressing the unconscious barriers to change. By working collaboratively with clients to explore and modify their defense mechanisms, therapists can help them develop more flexible and adaptive ways of coping with anxiety. Ultimately, this integration of psychodynamic concepts with cognitive-behavioral techniques can lead to more comprehensive and lasting anxiety relief.

### Historical and Theoretical Foundations of Defense Mechanisms

The concept of defense mechanisms has its roots in psychoanalytic theory, developed by Sigmund Freud in the late 19th and early 20th centuries. Freud proposed that the human psyche consists of three elements: the id, the ego, and the superego. The id represents our primitive unconscious desires, the superego embodies our internalized moral standards and values, and the ego serves as a mediator between the id's demands and the superego's constraints, helping individuals navigate the challenges of reality.

Freud believed that when the ego confronts anxiety-provoking thoughts, feelings, or experiences, it employs various defense mechanisms to protect itself from the resultant emotional distress. These mechanisms operate on an unconscious level, distorting reality to allow the individual to maintain psychological equilibrium. Freud identified several key defense mechanisms, including repression, denial, projection, and sublimation, which have become cornerstones of psychoanalytic theory.

Over time, understanding defense mechanisms has evolved and expanded beyond Freud's original formulations. Anna Freud, Sigmund Freud's daughter, made significant contributions to the study of defense mechanisms in her book "The Ego and the Mechanisms of Defense" (1936). She elaborated on her father's ideas, providing a more comprehensive and systematic analysis of the various defense mechanisms and their roles in personality development.

Subsequent psychoanalytic thinkers, such as Melanie Klein and

Otto Kernberg, further refined and expanded upon the concept of defense mechanisms. They explored how these mechanisms function in different personality structures and psychopathologies, deepening our understanding of their clinical implications.

As psychology evolved, the study of defense mechanisms extended beyond psychoanalysis. Researchers in cognitive psychology, developmental psychology, and neuroscience have explored how defense mechanisms influence our perceptions, thoughts, and behaviors. For instance, cognitive psychologists have examined how defense mechanisms can lead to biases in information processing and decision-making, while developmental psychologists have looked at their role in shaping attachment patterns and interpersonal relationships.

In recent years, there has been a growing recognition of the importance of integrating insights from various theoretical perspectives to develop a more comprehensive understanding of defense mechanisms. Contemporary researchers and clinicians draw upon psychoanalytic, cognitive-behavioral, and neurobiological frameworks to explore the complex interplay between unconscious defense mechanisms and conscious coping strategies. This integrative approach has led to new therapeutic interventions aimed at helping individuals identify and modify their maladaptive defense mechanisms, enhancing their ability to cope with emotional distress.

## The Dual Nature of Defense Mechanisms

Defense mechanisms serve both protective and potentially problematic functions in managing anxiety. While they can offer temporary relief from overwhelming feelings, they can also lead to long-term issues if used excessively or inappropriately.

*Positive Aspects of Defense Mechanisms.* Defense mechanisms can serve a vital protective function by shielding the ego, or sense of self, from anxiety that feels too intense to handle. In situations of stress, these unconscious strategies help reduce the immediate emotional impact, preventing the individual from becoming overwhelmed. This protective function is particularly crucial during times of crisis or trauma when the mind needs to cope with a sudden influx of distressing emotions.

In some cases, defense mechanisms provide a temporary buffer, allowing individuals time to adapt to challenging circumstances gradually. By partially shielding the ego from the full intensity of a stressor, these mechanisms help people maintain their emotional equilibrium while they develop more effective coping strategies. For example, sublimation involves channeling anxious or aggressive energies into socially acceptable activities, such as sports, art, or work, offering a distraction and a productive outlet for their feelings.

Humor is another defense mechanism that can have positive effects. By finding the light-hearted or absurd aspects of a stressful situation, individuals can temporarily distance themselves from their anxiety and gain a new perspective. Humor also serves a social function by helping to diffuse tense or uncomfortable situations and fostering a sense of connection with others.

*Negative Aspects of Defense Mechanisms.* However, while defense mechanisms can provide temporary relief, they can also cause complications if used excessively or inappropriately. One of the main drawbacks is that they can distort an individual's perception of reality. By unconsciously altering or avoiding certain aspects of a situation, defense mechanisms can prevent people from fully understanding and addressing the sources of their anxiety.

For instance, someone who relies heavily on denial might refuse to acknowledge the severity of their anxiety symptoms, thus avoiding necessary treatment. Similarly, an individual who uses rationalization to justify their avoidance of anxiety-provoking situations might miss out on important opportunities for personal growth and development.

Overuse of defense mechanisms can also perpetuate maladaptive patterns of behavior that maintain or exacerbate anxiety over time. When individuals consistently rely on these mechanisms to cope with distress, they may fail to develop more effective problem-solving and emotion-regulation skills. This can lead to a vicious cycle in which anxiety is temporarily alleviated but never fully resolved, causing it to resurface in the future.

Furthermore, some defense mechanisms can actively contribute to interpersonal problems and increase anxiety. For example, individuals who frequently use projection may attribute their unwanted thoughts or feelings to others, leading to misunderstandings and conflicts in their relationships.

## Overview of Key Defense Mechanisms

As we delve into the world of defense mechanisms, it is essential to understand some of the most commonly employed strategies that individuals use to cope with anxiety. Each defense mechanism has its unique characteristics and can manifest in various ways in daily life and the context of anxiety disorders.

*Repression* is a defense mechanism that involves unconsciously pushing distressing thoughts, feelings, or memories out of conscious awareness. This can be considered a mental "pushing away" of content that feels too threatening or overwhelming to confront. For instance, someone who has experienced a traumatic event might use repression to avoid consciously remembering or dealing with the painful emotions associated with the trauma. In anxiety disorders, repression might manifest as a general sense of unease or tension without a clear understanding of the underlying causes.

*Denial* involves refusing to acknowledge reality, particularly when it is anxiety-provoking. This differs from repression, which pushes distressing content out of awareness; denial involves a more active rejection of reality. For example, someone who receives a concerning medical diagnosis might use denial to avoid the emotional impact, perhaps insisting, "This can't be happening to me" or "The doctors must have made a mistake." In the context of anxiety disorders, denial can prevent individuals from recognizing the severity of their symptoms and seeking appropriate treatment.

*Projection* is when an individual unconsciously attributes unacceptable thoughts, feelings, or impulses to another person or group. Individuals avoid taking responsibility for their emotions and behaviors by externalizing these internal conflicts. For instance, someone insecure about their abilities might accuse a coworker of incompetence, projecting their feelings of inadequacy. In anxiety disorders, projection can lead to distorted perceptions of others' intentions or behaviors, exacerbating interpersonal difficulties.

*Displacement* involves redirecting intense emotions, such as anger or anxiety, from their source to a less threatening target. This allows individuals to express their emotions without confronting the person or situation causing the distress directly. For example, someone anxious about an upcoming job interview might displace their anxiety onto a family member by snapping at them over a minor issue. In anxiety disorders, displacement can result in strained relationships and a failure to address the true sources of anxiety.

*Rationalization* involves creating logical explanations or excuses to justify one's thoughts, feelings, or behaviors. This defense mechanism allows individuals to avoid confronting the underlying emotions driving their actions. Someone afraid of flying, for example, might rationalize their avoidance by claiming they prefer to "take their time and enjoy the scenery" during travel. In anxiety disorders, rationalization can prevent individuals from acknowledging and addressing the irrational fears contributing to their anxiety.

*Sublimation* is considered a more adaptive defense mechanism involving channeling anxious or aggressive energies into socially acceptable activities, such as sports, art, or work. This not only provides a constructive outlet for these feelings but also helps individuals reduce their anxiety while developing new skills and interests.

As we've seen, defense mechanisms can take many forms and serve various functions in managing anxiety. While some defense mechanisms, like sublimation, can be adaptive in certain contexts, others, such as denial and projection, can lead to long-term problems if used excessively or inappropriately. By gaining a deeper understanding of these key defense mechanisms, individuals can begin to recognize how they may be unconsciously coping with anxiety and work towards developing more effective strategies for managing their emotions.

## Identifying Defense Mechanisms

As we continue our exploration of defense mechanisms, it is crucial to understand how to identify these unconscious strategies in ourselves and others. Developing self-awareness is key to recognizing when we are using defense mechanisms to cope with anxiety. By becoming more attuned to our thoughts, feelings, and behaviors, we can start to notice patterns and signs that may indicate the use of defense mechanisms.

One common sign of using defense mechanisms is a sense of disconnection or emotional numbness. When we rely heavily on strategies like repression or denial, we may feel detached from our true emotions and experiences. We might go through daily life without fully engaging with our feelings or the world around us.

Another sign is a tendency to avoid or minimize the impact of stressful situations. For instance, someone who uses rationalization may consistently make excuses or find ways to justify their avoidance of anxiety-provoking situations. This could include downplaying the significance of stressful events or dismissing emotional responses.

Identifying defense mechanisms in ourselves can be challenging, as these strategies operate unconsciously. We may not always be aware of how we are coping with anxiety, particularly if we have been using certain defense mechanisms for a long time. This is where the role of a therapist can be invaluable. A skilled therapist, particularly one trained in cognitive-behavioral therapy (CBT), can help us identify the defense mechanisms we are using and explore the underlying emotions and beliefs driving our behavior.

In therapy, we may be asked to reflect on our thoughts, feelings, and experiences more deeply than we are used to. Our therapist may gently challenge us to consider alternative perspectives or to confront the emotions we have been avoiding. Through this process of self-exploration and insight-building, we recognize the patterns of defense mechanisms used and develop a greater understanding of our emotional landscape.

Our therapist may also help us identify defense mechanisms by pointing out inconsistencies or contradictions in our thoughts and behaviors. For example, if we consistently rationalize our avoidance of social situations, our therapist may help us see how this behavior is perpetuating our anxiety rather than helping us overcome it. By gently challenging our defenses and helping us develop more adaptive coping strategies, our therapist can support us in managing our anxiety in a healthier, more effective way.

It's important to remember that using defense mechanisms is a normal and natural part of the human experience. We all rely on these strategies to some extent to cope with life's stresses and challenges. However, when defense mechanisms are used excessively or inappropriately, they can prevent us from fully engaging with our emotions and experiences, leading to long-term problems with anxiety and personal growth.

By cultivating self-awareness and working with a supportive therapist, we can learn to identify the defense mechanisms we are using and develop more adaptive ways of coping with anxiety. This process of self-discovery and insight-building can be challenging at times, but it is necessary to foster greater emotional resilience and well-being.

### Defense Mechanisms and Cognitive Behavioral Therapy (CBT)

Understanding the relationship between defense mechanisms and cognitive behavioral therapy (CBT) is essential. These unconscious strategies are closely linked to the cognitive distortions that often fuel anxiety. Cognitive distortions are inaccurate or exaggerated thoughts that can intensify anxious feelings and behaviors. Examples include catastrophizing, assuming the worst will happen, and overgeneralization, which involves drawing broad conclusions based on a single event. These distorted thoughts often lead individuals to rely on defense mechanisms to cope with anxiety.

In CBT, the process of cognitive restructuring helps individuals identify and challenge both cognitive distortions and the defense mechanisms that contribute to their anxiety. This approach starts with increasing awareness of one's thoughts and behaviors and the emotions that drive them. Therapists guide individuals to examine specific situations that trigger anxious feelings, encouraging them to identify the automatic thoughts and beliefs that emerge in response.

Once a defense mechanism is identified, the next step is to evaluate the evidence for and against it. For instance, someone using rationalization to avoid social situations might be encouraged to assess the likelihood and consequences of the outcomes they fear. Evaluating the realistic probabilities of these fears can help individuals develop a more balanced perspective.

The process continues with developing alternative, more adaptive responses to anxiety-provoking situations. Instead of relying on defense mechanisms to avoid or minimize emotions, individuals learn to face their fears gradually and tolerate the discomfort that arises. This might involve practicing relaxation techniques such as deep breathing or progressive muscle relaxation to manage the physical symptoms of anxiety at the moment.

Behavioral therapy is another crucial element in addressing defense mechanisms in CBT. A key behavioral technique is exposure therapy, which involves gradually confronting feared situations or emotions in a controlled and safe manner. This method helps individuals realize that their feared consequences are unlikely and they can handle the anxiety that arises. For example, someone who avoids social interactions due to anxiety might start by imagining themselves in social settings, then progress to interacting in small groups, and eventually engage in larger social gatherings.

Another important behavioral technique is behavioral activation, which encourages individuals to engage in activities that foster a sense of achievement and pleasure. When anxiety leads to withdrawal from enjoyable activities, reintroducing these activities can help break the cycle of avoidance and isolation that perpetuates anxiety.

Throughout CBT, therapists also teach various relaxation techniques to help individuals manage the physical symptoms of anxiety. These techniques, including mindfulness meditation, allow individuals to relax their bodies and quiet their minds, reducing overall stress and tension.

As individuals progress in CBT and begin to modify their defense mechanisms and cognitive distortions, they often experience reduced anxiety and increased confidence and resilience. While the journey of change can be challenging, the skills developed in CBT provide lasting benefits, enabling individuals to manage their anxiety more effectively and enjoy a greater sense of peace and fulfillment in their lives.

This chapter has explored the complex world of defense mechanisms and their role in managing anxiety. We have seen how these unconscious strategies can serve both positive and negative functions, protecting us from overwhelming emotions in the short term and perpetuating maladaptive patterns of behavior if relied upon too heavily.

We have delved into some of the most common defense mechanisms, such as repression, denial, projection, displacement, rationalization, and sublimation, and examined how they can manifest in daily life and the context of anxiety disorders. We have also emphasized the importance of developing self-awareness in recognizing these defense mechanisms and highlighted the valuable role a therapist can play in helping individuals identify and challenge these unconscious strategies.

Furthermore, we have explored the connection between defense mechanisms and cognitive behavioral therapy (CBT), one of the most effective evidence-based treatments for anxiety disorders. We have seen how the process of cognitive restructuring can help individuals identify and challenge the cognitive distortions and defense mechanisms that underlie their anxiety and how behavioral interventions, such as exposure therapy and behavioral activation, can promote more adaptive coping strategies and long-term anxiety relief.

As we conclude this chapter, it is essential to underscore the importance of understanding and addressing defense mechanisms in the treatment of anxiety disorders. While these unconscious strategies can provide temporary relief from distress, they can also hinder personal growth and perpetuate the cycle of anxiety if not addressed. By developing a greater awareness of our emotional landscape and learning to confront our fears in a safe and controlled way, we can begin to break free from the grip of anxiety and cultivate a greater sense of resilience and well-being.

The journey of self-discovery and personal growth is ongoing and not always easy. It requires courage, vulnerability, and a willingness to face discomfort in the service of long-term healing. However, the rewards of this journey are immeasurable. As we learn to manage our anxiety in healthier, more effective ways, we open ourselves up to a greater sense of peace, fulfillment, and connection in our lives.

To support you on this journey, we have developed a 7-day self-help homework guide that will allow you to practice the concepts and strategies covered in this chapter. Each day, you will be introduced to a new exercise or reflection that will help you deepen your understanding of defense mechanisms and develop more adaptive coping strategies for managing anxiety.

Whether working with a therapist or embarking on this journey of self-discovery, know that you are not alone. The path to greater emotional well-being is one that countless individuals have walked before you, and a wealth of support and resources are available to guide you along the way.

As you move forward, remember to be kind and compassionate with yourself. Change takes time, and there will inevitably be challenges and setbacks along the way. However, with each step you take and each insight you gain, you are moving closer to a life of greater freedom, authenticity, and joy.

So, let us now turn our attention to the 7-day self-help homework guide, where you can put the concepts and strategies covered in this chapter into practice. Remember, this journey is yours to navigate at your own pace and in your way. Trust in the process, and know that you have the strength and resilience to overcome the challenges you face and cultivate a life of greater peace and fulfillment.

# Week 5 Self-Help Guide

## *Defense Mechanisms*

The following 7-day self-help homework guide is designed to help you better understand and manage your defense mechanisms. Each day focuses on self-discovery and personal growth, providing exercises and reflections to guide you. As you progress through the guide, remember to be patient and compassionate with yourself, and don't hesitate to seek professional support if needed. By combining the insights gained from this guide with the expertise of a mental health professional, you can work towards developing healthier coping strategies and greater emotional resilience.

Before embarking on the 7-day self-help homework guide, it is essential to acknowledge the limitations of self-help approaches in addressing defense mechanisms. While this guide provides valuable insights and strategies for personal growth, overcoming deeply ingrained defense mechanisms may require the support of a trained mental health professional. Attempting to challenge these mechanisms without proper guidance could lead to increased anxiety or emotional distress.

# Week 5 Day 1

## Getting to Know Defense Mechanisms

**Objective:** Today focuses on understanding and identifying your most commonly used defense mechanisms. By becoming aware of these psychological strategies, you can see how they influence your reactions and behaviors, particularly in stressful or anxiety-inducing situations.

**Information:** Defense mechanisms are unconscious psychological strategies that people use to protect themselves from anxiety and the perception of internal or external stresses or threats. They can serve useful purposes but might also hinder personal growth and effective handling of reality if overused or misapplied. Recognizing these can provide crucial insights into your emotional and mental health.

**Instructions:**

1. **Review the List of Defense Mechanisms:**
   - Start by reviewing the comprehensive list of defense mechanisms provided in the appendix of *ANXIETY FREE*. Read each definition carefully and consider examples of how each might manifest in everyday situations.
2. **Self-Reflection:**
   - Reflect on recent events or interactions where you felt stressed, anxious, or upset. Write these down and try to identify any defense mechanisms you employed. Were you rationalizing your actions? Denying any facts? Projecting

feelings onto others? Suppressing uncomfortable emotions?

- It might help to think about the feedback you've received from others about your reactions in certain situations or recurring themes in conflicts or challenges.

3. **Recording and Analysis:**
   - Create a chart or journal section to note the defense mechanisms you identify with. Rank them based on how frequently you believe you use them, with one being the most frequent.
   - For each top-ranked defense mechanism, write a brief example of how it has shown up in your life. This could be during work interactions, personal relationships, or stress handling.

4. **Develop Awareness:**
   - As you go about your day, remember moments when you might use these mechanisms. Awareness of these patterns can sometimes reduce automatic use and help you handle situations more authentically.

**Reflection:** At the end of the day, take some time to reflect on this exercise. Were there any surprises about the defense mechanisms you use? How do you feel about how these mechanisms affect your behavior and emotions? Reflecting on these questions can deepen your understanding and give you clearer direction on potential areas for personal growth.

**Integration:** Incorporate this newfound awareness into your daily interactions and observations. By recognizing when you are using defense mechanisms, you can begin to choose how you respond to stress and anxiety more consciously. This can lead to more honest interactions and effective personal coping strategies, enhancing emotional intelligence and resilience.

This exercise is a stepping stone towards greater self-awareness and healthier emotional management, making it a valuable addition to your toolbox for managing anxiety.

# Week 5 Day 2

*Identifying Your Defense Mechanisms*

**Objective**: The objective of today's exercise is to help you become more aware of the defense mechanisms you commonly use to cope with anxiety and stress.

**Information**: Recognizing your defense mechanisms is the first step in understanding how they may influence your thoughts, emotions, and behaviors. By increasing self-awareness, you can begin to make conscious choices about how you respond to anxiety-provoking situations.

**Instructions:**

1. Take some time to reflect on situations that typically trigger feelings of anxiety for you. These might include social interactions, work or school-related pressures, or personal challenges.
2. As you reflect on these situations, pay attention to your thoughts, emotions, and behaviors. Ask yourself: How do I typically respond when I feel anxious? Do I try to avoid or escape the situation? Do I minimize or deny my feelings? Do I blame others or become defensive?
3. Write down the defense mechanisms you identify in your responses. Refer to the list of common defense mechanisms discussed in the chapter (repression, denial, projection, displacement, rationalization, sublimation) as a guide.
4. For each defense mechanism you identify, write down a specific example of how you have used it in the past to cope with anxiety.

**Reflection**: Reflect on the defense mechanisms you have identified. How have they helped you cope with anxiety in the short term? How might they be limiting your personal growth or perpetuating anxiety in the long run?

**Integration**: As you go about your day, try to notice when you are using defense mechanisms to cope with anxiety. Practice observing your thoughts and emotions without judgment, and consider alternative ways of responding that align with your values and goals.

# Week 5 Day 3-5

## *Overcoming Self-Identified Defense Mechanisms*

**Objective**: The objective of the exercises for days 3, 4, and 5 is to practice confronting situations or emotions that you typically avoid due to anxiety.

**Information**: Now that you have consulted the list of cognitive distortions in the appendix and identified the defense mechanisms that are most prominent in your life, it's time to take steps to address and overcome them. This process can be applied to any defense mechanism you have identified, helping you to understand better the situations that trigger these defenses, the reasons behind their use, and strategies to move past them.

**Instructions:**

### Step 1: Identify Triggering Situations

Reflect on the situations or experiences that activate your chosen defense mechanism. These triggers can be external, such as specific people, places, or events, or internal, such as particular thoughts, emotions, or physical sensations. Take some time to write down these triggering situations in detail, being as specific as possible.

For example, if you have identified rationalization as a prominent defense mechanism, you might note situations such as receiving constructive criticism at work or confronting a difficult relationship issue.

## Step 2: Understand the Purpose of the Defense Mechanism

Next, examine the defense mechanism's function in these triggering situations. Defense mechanisms are unconscious strategies that we use to protect ourselves from painful or overwhelming emotions, such as anxiety, fear, or shame. By understanding the emotional discomfort your defense mechanism is trying to shield you from, you can develop greater self-awareness and compassion.

Ask yourself: What uncomfortable emotions or thoughts arise in these triggering situations? How does the defense mechanism help me cope with or avoid these feelings in the short term? What are the potential long-term consequences of relying on this defense?

## Step 3: Challenge the Defense Mechanism

Once you understand the situations that trigger your defense mechanism and the emotional discomfort it is trying to protect you from, you can start to challenge the defense directly. This involves questioning the accuracy and usefulness of the thoughts and beliefs that underlie the defense and considering alternative perspectives.

For example, suppose you use projection to cope with feelings of insecurity or self-doubt. In that case, you might challenge this defense by asking yourself: Is there evidence to support my belief that others are judging me negatively? Are there alternative explanations for their behavior? How might my insecurities be coloring my perception of the situation?

## Step 4: Practice Self-Compassion

Challenging long-standing defense mechanisms can be a difficult and emotionally demanding process. It is important to approach this work with self-compassion and understanding. Remember that defense mechanisms develop as a way of coping with painful experiences or emotions and that learning to let go of them is a gradual process.

Practice treating yourself with kindness and patience as you navigate this process. Acknowledge the discomfort when you confront your defenses and remind yourself that this discomfort is a natural part of growth and change.

## Step 5: Develop Alternative Coping Strategies

As you work to let go of your defense mechanisms, replacing them with healthier and more adaptive coping strategies is important. These might include:

- Mindfulness practices, such as deep breathing or meditation, help you stay present and grounded in the face of difficult emotions.
- Cognitive reframing techniques, such as questioning the evidence for your thoughts or considering alternative perspectives, help you develop a more balanced and realistic outlook.
- Assertive communication skills are needed to help you express your needs and boundaries directly and respectfully.
- Seeking support from trusted friends, family members, or a therapist to help you process your experiences and emotions in a safe and validating environment.

## Step 6: Practice and Integrate

Overcoming defense mechanisms is an ongoing process that requires practice and integration. Look for opportunities to apply your new coping strategies in real-life situations, and be patient with yourself as you learn and grow.

Keep a journal to track your progress and reflections, and celebrate your successes, no matter how small they may seem. Remember that every step toward greater self-awareness and emotional resilience is valuable.

As you continue to practice and integrate these strategies into your life, you may find that your reliance on defense mechanisms gradually diminishes, replaced by a greater sense of authenticity, adaptability, and emotional well-being. Trust in the process, and know that you have the strength and wisdom within you to overcome any obstacle on your path to growth and healing.

# Week 5 Day 6

## Practicing Self-Compassion

**Objective**: The objective of today's exercise is to practice self-compassion to counter the negative self-talk and self-judgment that can fuel anxiety and defensive reactions.

**Information:** Self-compassion involves treating yourself with the same kindness, understanding, and acceptance that you would offer to a good friend. By developing a more compassionate and forgiving relationship with yourself, you can reduce the shame and self-criticism that often underlie anxiety and defensive behavior.

**Instructions:**

1. Take a few moments to reflect on your inner self-talk, particularly in situations that trigger anxiety or self-doubt. Notice any harsh, critical, or judgmental statements that you make to yourself.
2. For each self-critical statement, imagine what you might say to a good friend experiencing a similar struggle. Write down these compassionate responses.
3. Practice redirecting your self-talk to be more compassionate and understanding. Use the statements you generated in step 2 as a guide.
4. Engage in a self-compassion meditation or exercise, such as the "Self-Compassion Break" developed by Dr. Kristin Neff. This involves acknowledging your suffering, recognizing that suffering is a part of the human experience, and offering yourself kindness and support.

**Reflection**: Reflect on how self-criticism and self-judgment may have been contributing to your anxiety and defensive reactions. What shifts do you notice in your thoughts, feelings, and behaviors when you practice self-compassion instead?

**Integration:** Look for opportunities to practice self-compassion in your daily life, particularly in situations that trigger anxiety or self-doubt. Remember that developing self-compassion is a skill that requires ongoing practice and commitment.

# Week 5 Day 7

*Developing a Personalized Coping Plan*

**Objective:** Today's exercise aims to develop a personalized plan for coping with anxiety that incorporates the insights and strategies you have learned throughout this 7-day self-help guide.

**Information:** Developing a personalized coping plan can help you feel more prepared and empowered to manage anxiety in healthy and adaptive ways. By identifying your specific triggers, defense mechanisms, and coping strategies, you can create a roadmap for navigating anxiety-provoking situations with greater self-awareness and resilience.

**Instructions:**

1. Review the insights and reflections you have gathered throughout this 7-day self-help guide. Identify the defense mechanisms you use most frequently and the underlying emotions and beliefs that drive these defenses.
2. Create a list of your top anxiety triggers, such as specific situations, people, or internal experiences that tend to provoke anxiety for you.
3. For each trigger, brainstorm healthy coping strategies that you can use to manage your anxiety in the moment. These might include relaxation techniques, cognitive reframing, self-compassion, or seeking support from others.
4. Develop a step-by-step action plan for implementing these coping strategies in real-life situations. Be specific and concrete

as possible, and include any resources or support you need to follow through on your plan.

5. Create a visual reminder of your personalized coping plan, such as a poster or a small card you can carry. Place this reminder where you see it regularly, such as in your bedroom or office.

**Reflection**: Reflect on how having a personalized coping plan may help you feel more confident and prepared to manage anxiety healthily. What challenges or obstacles do you anticipate in implementing your plan, and how can you address these proactively?

**Integration**: Commit to implementing your personalized coping plan in your daily life. Remember that developing new habits and skills takes time and practice, and be patient and compassionate with yourself as you navigate this process. Consider sharing your plan with a trusted friend, family member, or therapist who can provide support and accountability.

# Week 5 Tracking Progress

As you complete this week's exploration of cognitive distortions, assess your progress. Look at the bridge illustration and place a mark representing your current position. Rate your anxiety level on the 0-10 scale, acknowledging the work you've done to identify and challenge distorted thoughts.

**Instructions**:

1. Take a moment to reflect on your progress and experiences.
2. Refer to the bridge illustration below.
3. Consider where you currently stand on your journey.
4. Place a mark on the bridge representing your current position.
5. Next, rate where your average anxiety level has been over this week.
6. Record your anxiety rating on the provided 0-10 scale, with 0 being no anxiety and 10 being the most intense anxiety you've experienced.
7. Reflect and journal.

**Reflection**: After marking your bridge position and anxiety rating, reflect on your progress. Examine skills learned, challenges faced, and changes in thoughts and behaviors. Journal your insights and observations. Identify successes, challenges, and areas requiring more attention. Determine if you need to slow down, revisit previous weeks or skills, or seek professional help to maintain progress. Assess your overall progress and consider if professional support is needed or how it's contributing to your journey.

| 0 | 1 | 2 | 3 | 4 | 5 | 6 | 7 | 8 | 9 | 10 |
|---|---|---|---|---|---|---|---|---|---|----|

No
Anxiety

Moderate
Anxiety

High
Anxiety

## 10

# *Acceptance and Commitment Therapy for Anxiety Management*

Anxiety can feel like a relentless adversary, its tendrils reaching into every corner of our lives, coloring our thoughts and constricting our actions. We may find ourselves locked in a constant battle, desperately trying to banish anxious thoughts and quell uneasy feelings. But what if the key to finding peace lies not in eliminating anxiety but in learning to coexist with it? This is the core premise of Acceptance and Commitment Therapy, or ACT.

ACT represents a paradigm shift in the way we approach anxiety and other psychological challenges. Unlike traditional therapeutic approaches that often focus on eliminating or controlling unwanted thoughts and feelings, ACT suggests a different path: creating a new relationship with our thoughts and feelings, characterized by acceptance and mindfulness rather than struggle and avoidance.

At its core, ACT is rooted in the understanding that pain is an inevitable part of life, but suffering is optional. Pain is the physical or emotional discomfort we feel while suffering, resulting from our attempt to control, avoid, or eliminate that pain. When faced with anxiety, our natural instinct is often to push it away, distract ourselves, or numb the feeling. However, the more we struggle against our anxiety, the more we tend to suffer.

ACT invites us to consider a different approach that involves accepting difficult emotions and thoughts while redirecting our energy toward what matters most to us. This process is not about passively resigning ourselves to a life of suffering but instead learning to coexist with these experiences in a way that allows us to move forward and live a meaningful life.

Imagine a person in a tug-of-war with their anxiety, represented by a monster. The more the person pulls, trying to control the monster, the more the monster pulls back. The struggle exhausts the person, draining their energy and attention. Ultimately, even if they temporarily subdue the monster, they're left depleted and no closer to their values or goals.

ACT suggests a different approach: dropping the rope. By learning to accept the presence of the monster (anxiety) and making room for it, we can redirect our energy toward what matters most to us. This is not about giving up or giving in but recognizing that the struggle itself causes much of our suffering.

The principles of ACT work together to help us develop psychological flexibility—the ability to be present, open up to our experiences, and take action guided by our values, even with complex thoughts and feelings. By cultivating these skills, we can start to loosen the grip of anxiety and build a life of vitality and meaning.

It's important to note that ACT is not about eliminating anxiety altogether. Anxiety is a normal, even adaptive, part of the human experience. It can alert us to potential threats, motivate us to take action, and help us navigate the complexities of life. The goal of ACT is not to eliminate anxiety but to change our relationship with it so that we can live full, meaningful lives, even with anxiety as a passenger.

At the heart of ACT are six core principles: acceptance, cognitive defusion, being present, self as context, values, and committed action. By cultivating these principles, we learn to relate to our anxiety in a new way, one that allows us to step back from the whirlwind of anxious thoughts and redirect our energy toward what truly matters to us.

Acceptance involves making space for all our difficult and uncomfortable experiences without trying to change, suppress, or avoid them. It's about acknowledging the presence of anxiety without getting caught up in a struggle to control it. Acceptance doesn't mean passively resigning ourselves to a life of anxiety. We simply make room for anxiety as part of our current experience without letting it dictate our actions.

Cognitive defusion involves learning to see thoughts for what they are—just thoughts, not necessarily truths or facts. ACT teaches us to step back and observe these thoughts with curiosity rather than getting tangled up in them. We can reduce their power over us by creating distance between ourselves and our thoughts.

Being present means connecting with the here and now rather than getting lost in worries about the future or regrets about the past. Through practices like mindfulness, ACT encourages us to anchor ourselves in the present moment, tuning into our senses and observing our thoughts and feelings without getting caught up in them.

Self as context is the idea that a part of us is separate from our thoughts, feelings, and experiences—a transcendent sense of self that remains constant even as our internal experiences shift and change. By connecting with this sense of self, we can find a stable foundation to observe and accept our anxiety.

Values are the compass that guides us toward a rich and meaningful life. ACT helps us clarify our values and use them as a guide for our actions. We can find purpose and direction by aligning our actions with our values, even in the face of anxiety.

Committed action is about translating our values into concrete behaviors. It's about taking effective action toward the life we want to live, even in the presence of difficult thoughts and feelings. ACT encourages us to practice willingness—the willingness to feel our anxiety and take action anyway, gradually expanding our comfort zone.

One of the most powerful tools in the ACT toolkit is the concept of willingness. Willingness means being open to experiencing whatever thoughts and feelings arise without trying to control or eliminate them. It's about making room for anxiety rather than trying to push it away.

Let's consider an example of how someone might systematically apply the principles of ACT to address anxiety around public speaking:

Imagine that Sarah has been asked to present at her company's annual conference. Standing up in front of a large audience fills her with dread. Her mind starts generating a stream of anxious thoughts: "I'm going to freeze up," "Everyone will see how nervous I am," and "I'm going to make a fool of myself."

Rather than trying to suppress these thoughts, Sarah practices acceptance. She acknowledges the presence of anxious thoughts and feelings without trying to change them. She recognizes that these are just thoughts, not necessarily truths, practicing cognitive defusion.

When Sarah gets lost in worries about the future, she practices returning her attention to the present moment, focusing on her breath and tuning into her senses. She connects with a sense of self that is larger than her anxiety, recognizing that she is more than her thoughts and feelings.

Sarah reflects on her values—what truly matters to her. She realizes she values being a contributing team member and wants to share her knowledge with her colleagues. With her values in mind, Sarah commits to taking action. She practices willingness—the willingness to feel her anxiety and give the presentation anyway.

She starts by practicing her presentation in front of a mirror, then in front of a trusted friend. Finally, the day of the conference arrives. As Sarah stands up to give her presentation, she feels the familiar flutter of anxiety. But rather than trying to eliminate the anxiety, she makes room for it, acknowledging its presence and then focusing on what matters—sharing her knowledge with her colleagues.

After the presentation, Sarah takes a moment to reflect. The anxiety was still there, but it didn't control her. She was able to be anxious and still do what mattered to her. She faced her fear, stayed true to her values, and took committed action.

This example illustrates the power of willingness in ACT. It's not about eliminating anxiety but about changing our relationship to it. It's about making room for the full range of our human experience while still moving forward in the direction of our values.

Of course, practicing willingness is easier said than done. It takes courage, self-compassion, and a willingness to be uncomfortable. But with practice, we can start to loosen the grip of anxiety and reclaim our lives.

The systematic application of the six principles of ACT—acceptance, cognitive defusion, being present, self as context, values, and committed action—can provide a robust framework for this practice. By learning to accept our thoughts and feelings, defuse our anxious thoughts, connect with the present moment, view ourselves in context, clarify our values, and take committed action, we can develop the psychological flexibility to navigate life's challenges with greater ease and purpose.

ACT is not a quick fix for anxiety. It's a practice, a way of relating to our thoughts and feelings that requires patience, self-compassion, and a willingness to step out of our comfort zone. But by embracing the principles of acceptance, mindfulness, and values-guided action, we can start to loosen the grip of anxiety and build a life of meaning and vitality.

This approach has been backed by a growing body of research, showing that ACT can be effective in reducing symptoms of anxiety and improving overall well-being and quality of life. But ACT is more than just a set of techniques—it's a way of relating to the full spectrum of human experience, the joys and the sorrows, the ease and the struggles.

In the face of anxiety, it's easy to feel like we're at the mercy of our thoughts and feelings. But ACT reminds us that we have a choice. We can choose to get caught up in the struggle, or we can choose to take a step back, make room for our anxiety, and redirect our energy toward what truly matters. It's a practice that requires courage, self-compassion, and a willingness to be present with discomfort. But it's also a path toward a life of greater meaning, connection, and vitality.

As we navigate the challenges of anxiety, may we remember the words of psychologist Steven Hayes, one of the pioneers of ACT: "The goal of life is not to be without any anxiety. The goal is to be able to have anxiety and still do what matters in life." By embracing acceptance and committing to values-guided action, we can start to do just that—to carry our anxiety with grace and to step forward into the life we want to live.

# Week 6 Self-Help Guide

This seven-day journey will guide you through the transformative principles of Acceptance and Commitment Therapy (ACT) and how to apply them to your experience with anxiety. Each day focuses on a key aspect of ACT, including mindfulness, acceptance, values clarification, and committed action. You'll learn new skills, engage in practical exercises, and reflect on your experiences to develop a healthier relationship with anxious thoughts and feelings. The goal is not to eliminate anxiety but to cultivate the flexibility and resilience needed to navigate life's challenges while staying true to your values. Approach this process with self-compassion and openness, and be willing to step outside your comfort zone. By engaging fully in this journey, you'll build a foundation for a more meaningful and fulfilling life, even when anxiety is present.

# Week 6 Day 1

## Introduction to Acceptance and Mindfulness

**Objective**: Gain a deeper understanding of the role acceptance and mindfulness play in managing anxiety from an Acceptance and Commitment Therapy (ACT) perspective.

**Information**: ACT offers a unique approach to managing anxiety by focusing on acceptance and mindfulness rather than control and avoidance. Trying to control or eliminate anxious thoughts and feelings often leads to more distress and struggle. Instead, ACT encourages us to accept these experiences as a natural part of life and to focus on the present moment with openness and curiosity.

Acceptance involves making room for difficult thoughts and feelings without trying to change or suppress them. It's about acknowledging their presence without getting caught up in a struggle to control them. Mindfulness, on the other hand, is the practice of being fully present in the moment with a non-judgmental and compassionate attitude. It allows us to observe our thoughts and feelings without getting tangled up in them.

By combining acceptance and mindfulness, we can develop a new relationship with anxiety characterized by greater flexibility and resilience. Rather than being controlled by our anxious thoughts and feelings, we can learn to coexist with them while still engaging in meaningful activities and pursuing our values.

**Instructions**:

1. Take a moment to reflect on your typical response to anxious thoughts and feelings. Do you tend to try to control, avoid, or suppress them? How effective have these strategies been in the long run?

2. Now, consider an alternative approach based on acceptance and mindfulness. Imagine acknowledging the presence of anxiety without trying to fight against it. Picture yourself observing your anxious thoughts and feelings with curiosity and compassion, without getting caught up in them.

3. Practice a basic mindfulness exercise to cultivate present-moment awareness and non-judgmental observation. Find a quiet, comfortable space where you can sit undisturbed for a few minutes.

   ○ Close your eyes and bring your attention to your breath. Notice the sensation of the air moving in and out of your body.

   ○ When you notice your mind wandering (which is natural and expected), gently redirect your attention back to your breath without judgment.

   ○ If anxious thoughts or feelings arise, simply acknowledge their presence without trying to change them. Imagine them as passing clouds in the sky, and gently return your focus to your breath.

   ○ Continue this practice for 5-10 minutes, or longer if you feel comfortable.

4. After the mindfulness exercise, take a few moments to reflect on your experience. What did you notice about your thoughts and feelings during the practice? Did you find it challenging to accept and observe them without getting caught up in them?

**Reflection**: In your journal, write about your experience with the mindfulness exercise and any insights you gained about your relationship with anxious thoughts and feelings. Consider how practicing acceptance and mindfulness might support you in managing anxiety differently. What challenges do you anticipate in applying these concepts, and how might you address them?

**Integration**: Throughout your day, look for opportunities to practice acceptance and mindfulness in response to anxious thoughts and feelings. Notice when you're getting caught up in a struggle to control or avoid anxiety, and experiment with acknowledging its presence with openness and curiosity instead. Remember, developing these skills takes time and practice. Be patient and compassionate with yourself as you explore this new way of relating to anxiety.

# Week 6 Day 2

## Gaining Freedom from Anxious Thoughts through Cognitive Defusion

**Objective**: Learn and practice cognitive defusion techniques to create distance from anxious thoughts and reduce their impact on emotional well-being.

**Information**: Cognitive fusion is the process of becoming entangled with our thoughts, treating them as literal truths rather than mental events. When we're fused with anxious thoughts, we may feel controlled by them and experience increased distress. Cognitive defusion, on the other hand, involves learning to observe thoughts as temporary mental events rather than facts. By creating distance from anxious thoughts, we can reduce their emotional impact and respond to them more flexibly.

Cognitive defusion techniques help us step back from our thoughts and view them from a different perspective. These techniques can include labeling thoughts (e.g., "I'm having the thought that..."), visualizing thoughts as passing clouds or leaves on a stream, or repeating a thought until it loses its meaning. The goal is not to eliminate or suppress anxious thoughts but to change our relationship with them, allowing us to respond more effectively.

**Instructions**:

1. Identify a specific anxious thought that frequently troubles you, such as "I'm going to fail" or "Something terrible will happen."

2. Practice a cognitive defusion technique with this thought:
    ○ Labeling: Preface the thought with "I'm having the thought that..." (e.g., "I'm having the thought that I'm going to fail"). Notice how this creates some distance between you and the thought.
    ○ Visualization: Imagine the thought as a cloud passing through the sky or a leaf floating down a stream. Observe it without trying to hold onto it or push it away.
    ○ Repetition: Repeat the thought out loud or in your mind for 30 seconds. Notice how the meaning and emotional impact of the thought may change as you repeat it.
3. Reflect on your experience with the cognitive defusion technique. Did you notice any changes in your relationship with the thought or your emotional response to it?
4. Practice applying cognitive defusion to other anxious thoughts that arise throughout your day. Notice how it affects your perspective and emotional well-being.

**Reflection**: In your journal, write about your experience with cognitive defusion. What techniques did you find most helpful? How did defusion affect your relationship with anxious thoughts? What challenges did you encounter, and how might you address them?

**Integration**: Make cognitive defusion a regular practice in your life. Whenever you notice yourself getting caught up in anxious thoughts, take a step back and apply a defusion technique. Remember that the goal is not to eliminate the thoughts but to change your relationship with them, allowing you to respond more flexibly and effectively.

# Week 6 Day 3

## Discovering Your Core Values for a Meaningful Life

**Objective**: Identify and clarify personal values across different life domains to create a foundation for meaningful action and decision-making.

**Information**: Values are the qualities that matter most to us, the principles that guide our actions and give our lives meaning and purpose. In ACT, clarifying our values is essential because they provide a compass for navigating life's challenges and making decisions that align with what's truly important to us.

Values are different from goals in that they are ongoing qualities we strive to embody, rather than specific outcomes we aim to achieve. For example, "being a loving and supportive partner" is a value, while "getting married" is a goal. By clarifying our values, we can make choices and take actions that are consistent with our deepest priorities, even in the face of difficult thoughts and feelings.

**Instructions**:

1. Reflect on the different domains of your life, such as relationships, career, personal growth, health and well-being, spirituality, and community.
2. For each domain, consider the qualities that matter most to you. What kind of person do you want to be in each area of your

life? What principles do you want to guide your actions and decisions?

3. Make a list of your core values in each domain. Be specific and focus on the qualities you want to embody, rather than specific outcomes you want to achieve.

4. Review your list of values and identify any common themes or overarching principles that emerge. These may represent your deepest, most fundamental values.

5. Reflect on how well your current actions and choices align with your identified values. Are there areas where you're living consistently with your values? Are there areas where you'd like to make changes to be more values-aligned?

**Reflection**: In your journal, write about your experience of clarifying your values. What insights did you gain about what matters most to you? How did it feel to identify your core values? What challenges or obstacles do you anticipate in living consistently with your values?

**Integration**: Make your values a regular touchpoint in your life. Review your list of values often and consider how you can embody them in your daily choices and actions. When faced with difficult decisions or challenges, ask yourself, "What choice would be most consistent with my values?" Use your values as a guide for setting goals and making meaningful changes in your life.

# Week 6 Day 4

## Translating Values into Meaningful Goals and Actions

**Objective**: Set specific, actionable goals that align with your core values and break them down into manageable steps to create a roadmap for values-consistent living.

**Information**: While values provide a broad direction for our lives, goals are the specific, achievable milestones that help us move in that direction. In ACT, setting values-aligned goals is crucial because it allows us to translate our values into concrete actions and make meaningful progress in the areas that matter most to us.

When setting goals, it's important to make them SMART: Specific, Measurable, Achievable, Relevant, and Time-bound. This means clearly defining what you want to accomplish, how you'll know when you've achieved it, ensuring it's realistic and aligned with your values, and setting a timeline for completion.

It's also important to break down larger goals into smaller, manageable steps. This makes the goal feel less overwhelming and allows you to take action even in the presence of difficult thoughts and feelings. By consistently taking small steps in a values-aligned direction, you can create significant change over time.

**Instructions**:

1. Review your list of core values from Day 3. Choose one value that feels particularly important to you right now.
2. Brainstorm a specific, achievable goal that aligns with this value. Make sure the goal is SMART: Specific, Measurable, Achievable, Relevant, and Time-bound.
3. Break the goal down into smaller, manageable steps. Identify the specific actions you can take to move closer to your goal, even in the presence of anxiety or other challenges.
4. Create a timeline for your goal and small steps. When will you start taking action? How often will you work on your goal? When do you aim to achieve the goal?
5. Reflect on potential obstacles or barriers to achieving your goal. What difficult thoughts or feelings might arise? What practical challenges might you face? Brainstorm strategies for addressing these obstacles.

**Reflection**: In your journal, write about your experience of setting values-aligned goals. What goal did you choose, and how does it align with your core values? What steps did you identify to move closer to your goal? What obstacles do you anticipate, and how might you address them?

**Integration**: Make your values-aligned goals a regular focus in your life. Take consistent action on the small steps you identified, even in the presence of difficult thoughts and feelings. Celebrate your progress along the way and adjust your goals as needed. Remember that the process of moving in a values-aligned direction is just as important as achieving the end result.

# Week 6 Day 5

## Cultivating Commitment and Resilience through Committed Action

**Objective**: Develop a detailed plan for taking committed action toward your values-aligned goals and cultivate the resilience to persist in the face of challenges and setbacks.

**Information**: Committed action is the process of consistently taking values-aligned action, even in the presence of difficult thoughts, feelings, or circumstances. It involves making a choice to move in a meaningful direction, regardless of the internal or external barriers that may arise.

Committed action is different from avoidance or control strategies because it's not about trying to eliminate or suppress difficult experiences. Instead, it's about making room for those experiences while still taking effective action toward what matters most. This requires a willingness to be uncomfortable at times and to persist in the face of challenges and setbacks.

Developing a detailed action plan can support committed action by providing a roadmap for values-aligned behavior. This plan should include specific steps, timelines, and strategies for addressing potential obstacles. It's also important to build in flexibility and self-compassion, acknowledging that setbacks and course corrections are a normal part of the process.

**Instructions**:

1. Review the values-aligned goal you set on Day 4 and the small steps you identified to move toward that goal.
2. Create a detailed action plan for the coming week. For each day, identify the specific actions you'll take to move closer to your goal. Be as specific and concrete as possible.
3. For each action, anticipate potential obstacles or challenges that may arise. These could be internal (difficult thoughts or feelings) or external (practical barriers). Brainstorm strategies for addressing these obstacles.
4. Identify any resources or support you may need to follow through on your plan. This could include practical support, emotional support, or skills you need to develop.
5. Make a commitment to following through on your action plan, even in the presence of difficult thoughts and feelings. Recognize that discomfort is a normal part of the process and that you have the resilience to persist.

**Reflection**: In your journal, write about your experience of creating a committed action plan. What actions did you identify for the coming week? What obstacles do you anticipate, and how will you address them? What supports or resources will you draw on to follow through on your plan?

**Integration**: Put your committed action plan into practice. Each day, follow through on the actions you identified, even if difficult thoughts or feelings arise. If you encounter setbacks or challenges, use your strategies for addressing obstacles and adjust your plan as needed. Remember to celebrate your successes along the way and to approach the process with self-compassion and flexibility.

# Week 6 Day 6

## Nurturing Self-Compassion and Acceptance in the Face of Anxiety

**Objective**: Cultivate self-compassion and acceptance to support yourself through the challenges of anxiety and the process of committed action.

**Information**: Self-compassion is the practice of treating ourselves with kindness, care, and understanding, especially in the face of difficult experiences. It involves recognizing that challenges and setbacks are a normal part of the human experience and that we all deserve compassion and support.

In the context of ACT, self-compassion is an essential component of acceptance. When we're struggling with anxiety or other difficult experiences, self-compassion allows us to be present with those experiences with kindness and understanding rather than judgment or resistance. This supports the process of acceptance by creating a more gentle and nurturing internal environment.

Self-compassion is also crucial for maintaining committed action. When we encounter setbacks or challenges in pursuing our values-aligned goals, self-compassion allows us to respond with understanding and encouragement rather than harsh self-criticism. This helps us maintain motivation and persist in the face of difficulty.

**Instructions**:

1. Reflect on your recent experiences with anxiety and the process of committed action. Notice any self-critical or judgmental thoughts that arise.
2. Practice a self-compassion exercise, such as:
   ○ Placing a hand on your heart and offering yourself kind, supportive words, such as "This is difficult, and I'm here for you" or "You're doing your best, and that's enough."
   ○ Imagine what you might say to a dear friend who was struggling with anxiety. Offer those same words of compassion and understanding to yourself.
   ○ Write a compassionate letter to yourself, acknowledging your struggles and expressing support and understanding.
3. Identify a recent situation where you struggled with anxiety or encountered a setback in your committed action. Apply self-compassion to that situation, acknowledging the difficulty and responding with kindness and understanding.
4. Reflect on how self-compassion affects your experience of anxiety and your ability to engage in committed action. Does it create a more supportive internal environment? Does it help you maintain motivation and persistence?

**Reflection**: In your journal, write about your experience of practicing self-compassion. What self-compassion exercises did you find most helpful? How did self-compassion affect your experience of anxiety and your ability to engage in committed action? What challenges or resistances to self-compassion did you notice?

**Integration**: Make self-compassion a regular practice in your life, especially in the face of anxiety and the challenges of committed action. Whenever you notice self-critical or judgmental thoughts arising, respond with kindness and understanding. Use self-compassion to support the process of acceptance and to maintain your commitment to values-aligned action.

# Week 6 Day 7

## Integrating ACT Principles into Your Life for Lasting Change

**Objective**: Review and integrate the key principles of ACT into a cohesive approach to managing anxiety and living a meaningful life aligned with your values.

**Information**: Over the past six days, you've explored the core principles of ACT, including acceptance, mindfulness, cognitive defusion, values, committed action, and self-compassion. Each of these principles offers a unique perspective and set of tools for relating to difficult thoughts and feelings more effectively and pursuing what matters most.

Acceptance allows us to make room for anxiety and other challenging experiences, rather than getting caught up in a struggle to eliminate them. Mindfulness helps us stay present and aware of our experiences without getting lost in them. Cognitive defusion enables us to step back from anxious thoughts and view them as temporary mental events rather than literal truths.

Values provide a compass for our lives, guiding us in the direction of what's truly important to us. Committed action is the process of consistently taking values-aligned steps, even in the presence of difficult internal and external barriers. And self-compassion supports us through this process, providing a nurturing and understanding relationship with ourselves.

By integrating these principles into a cohesive approach, we can develop greater psychological flexibility - the ability to be present, open up, and do what matters, even in the face of anxiety and other challenges. This is an ongoing process of practice and growth, requiring patience, persistence, and a willingness to learn.

**Instructions**:

1. Review the key principles and practices of ACT from the past six days. Reflect on what you've learned about acceptance, mindfulness, cognitive defusion, values, committed action, and self-compassion.
2. Consider how these principles and practices interact and support each other. For example, how does acceptance support committed action? How does self-compassion facilitate the process of cognitive defusion?
3. Identify the principles and practices that resonate most with you and that you find most helpful in managing anxiety and pursuing a meaningful life. Make a plan for continuing to practice and integrate these into your daily life.
4. Anticipate challenges or obstacles that may arise as you continue to apply ACT principles. Brainstorm strategies for addressing these challenges, drawing on the skills and perspectives you've developed.
5. Set an intention for your ongoing practice and growth with ACT. What kind of relationship do you want to have with your thoughts and feelings? What kind of life do you want to build, guided by your values?

**Reflection**: In your journal, write about your key takeaways from this seven-day exploration of ACT. What insights have you gained about managing anxiety and living a meaningful life? What principles and practices do you find most helpful? What intentions are you setting for your ongoing practice and growth?

**Integration**: Make the principles and practices of ACT a regular part of your life. Continue to practice acceptance, mindfulness, cognitive defusion, values clarification, committed action, and self-compassion. Notice how these practices impact your relationship with anxiety and your ability to pursue what matters most to you. Remember that this is an ongoing journey of learning and growth, requiring patience, persistence, and self-compassion.

# *Week 6 Tracking Progress*

With the completion of Week 6's ACT exercises, it's time to gauge your progress. Consider your position on the bridge and place a mark signifying where you stand. Rate your anxiety level on the 0-10 scale, reflecting on your acceptance and commitment to values-aligned actions.

**Instructions**:

1. Take a moment to reflect on your progress and experiences.
2. Refer to the bridge illustration below.
3. Consider where you currently stand on your journey.
4. Place a mark on the bridge representing your current position.
5. Next, rate where your average anxiety level has been over this week.
6. Record your anxiety rating on the provided 0-10 scale, with 0 being no anxiety and 10 being the most intense anxiety you've experienced.
7. Reflect and journal.

**Reflection**: After marking your bridge position and anxiety rating, reflect on your progress. Examine skills learned, challenges faced, and changes in thoughts and behaviors. Journal your insights and observations. Identify successes, challenges, and areas requiring more attention. Determine if you need to slow down, revisit previous weeks or skills, or seek professional help to maintain progress. Assess your overall progress and consider if professional support is needed or how it's contributing to your journey.

| 0 | 1 | 2 | 3 | 4 | 5 | 6 | 7 | 8 | 9 | 10 |
|---|---|---|---|---|---|---|---|---|---|----|

No
Anxiety

Moderate
Anxiety

High
Anxiety

# 11

# *Embracing Transpersonal and Buddhist Psychology*

Anxiety has become a widespread issue in modern society, affecting millions of individuals worldwide. The fast-paced, high-pressure environments that characterize contemporary life, along with the uncertainties and challenges of a rapidly changing world, have contributed to a significant increase in the prevalence of anxiety disorders. Traditional Western approaches to treating anxiety, such as cognitive-behavioral therapy and pharmacotherapy, have proven helpful for many individuals. However, they may not always provide a comprehensive solution to the complex and multifaceted nature of anxiety.

The limitations of traditional Western approaches lie in their primary focus on symptom reduction and behavioral modification, often neglecting the deeper existential and spiritual dimensions of human experience. These approaches may not fully address the underlying causes of anxiety, such as a lack of meaning and purpose, a disconnection from one's authentic self, or a fundamental misunderstanding of the nature of reality. As a result, individuals may find themselves trapped in a cycle of recurring anxiety, even after undergoing treatment.

Recently, there has been growing interest in the potential of transpersonal and Buddhist psychologies in addressing anxiety. These approaches offer a unique perspective on the human condition, acknowledging the inherent interconnectedness of all beings and the potential for personal transformation and spiritual growth. By integrating the insights and practices of these ancient wisdom traditions with the scientific rigor of modern psychology, we may develop more holistic and practical approaches to managing anxiety.

Transpersonal psychology emerged in the 1960s as a response to the limitations of mainstream psychology. It recognizes the importance of transcendent experiences and the exploration of higher states of consciousness for healing and personal growth. Transpersonal psychology emphasizes the development of a more expansive sense of self that goes beyond the narrow confines of the ego and embraces a deeper connection to the universe as a whole. By cultivating this sense of interconnectedness and purpose, individuals may be better equipped to navigate the challenges and uncertainties of life with greater resilience and stability.

Buddhist psychology, rooted in the teachings of the Buddha over 2,500 years ago, offers a profound understanding of the nature of suffering and the path to liberation. Central to Buddhist thought is that suffering arises from our attachments and aversions, our constant struggle to control and manipulate reality to fit our desires and expectations. By learning to let go of these attachments and cultivate mindfulness, self-compassion, and equanimity, we can free ourselves from the grip of anxiety and find a deeper sense of peace and well-being.

The integration of transpersonal and Buddhist principles into the treatment of anxiety holds promise for those seeking a more comprehensive and transformative approach to healing. By addressing the spiritual and existential dimensions of human experience, these approaches can help individuals manage their symptoms and cultivate a greater sense of meaning, purpose, and connection in their lives.

## Historical Roots and Context

To fully appreciate the potential of transpersonal and Buddhist psychologies in addressing anxiety, it is essential to understand their historical roots and the context in which they emerged.

The origins of transpersonal psychology can be traced back to the late 1960s, when it emerged as a response to the limitations of mainstream psychology, primarily focused on studying behavior and cognition. The term "transpersonal" was coined by Stanislav Grof and Abraham Maslow, who sought to expand the boundaries of psychological inquiry to include the spiritual and transcendent dimensions of human experience.

At its core, transpersonal psychology is concerned with exploring higher states of consciousness and realizing human potential. It recognizes that the human psyche is not limited to the individual ego but encompasses a broader range of experiences, including mystical states, peak experiences, and a sense of unity with the cosmos. By integrating the insights of various spiritual traditions, such as Buddhism, Hinduism, and Taoism, with the methods of modern psychology, transpersonal psychology seeks to provide a more comprehensive understanding of the human condition.

Key figures in the development of transpersonal psychology include Abraham Maslow, known for his hierarchy of needs and the concept of self-actualization; Stanislav Grof, a pioneer in the field of consciousness research and the therapeutic use of non-ordinary states of consciousness; and Ken Wilber, who developed an integrative framework for understanding the evolution of consciousness and the interconnectedness of all beings.

On the other hand, Buddhist psychology is rooted in the teachings of Siddhartha Gautama, who became known as the Buddha or "awakened one" after attaining enlightenment in the 6th century BCE. The Buddha's insights into the nature of suffering and the path to liberation have profoundly impacted the development of Eastern thought and have recently gained increasing recognition in the West.

At the heart of the Buddha's teachings are the Four Noble Truths, which outline the fundamental nature of human suffering and how it can be overcome. The First Noble Truth acknowledges the pervasiveness of suffering in human life. At the same time, the Second Noble Truth identifies the cause of suffering as our attachments and cravings. The Third Noble Truth asserts that it is possible to end suffering, and the Fourth Noble Truth outlines the path to liberation, known as the Eightfold Path.

The Eightfold Path consists of eight practices or disciplines to help individuals cultivate wisdom, compassion, and mindfulness. These include right view, right intention, right speech, right action, right livelihood, right effort, right mindfulness, and right concentration. By integrating these practices into daily life, individuals can transform their relationship with their thoughts, emotions, and experiences, leading to greater peace and well-being.

In recent decades, there has been a growing interest in the West in the insights and practices of Eastern philosophies, particularly Buddhism. This interest has been fueled in part by the limitations of traditional Western approaches to mental health, which have often focused on symptom reduction rather than the cultivation of well-being and human potential.

As a result, there has been a growing movement to integrate Buddhist principles into Western psychological practices. This integration has taken many forms, from the development of mindfulness-based interventions for anxiety and depression to the incorporation of Buddhist concepts such as non-attachment and self-compassion into psychotherapy.

One key figure in this movement was Jon Kabat-Zinn, who developed the Mindfulness-Based Stress Reduction (MBSR) program in the late 1970s. MBSR has since become one of the most widely studied and applied mindfulness interventions, with numerous studies demonstrating its effectiveness in reducing symptoms of anxiety, depression, and chronic pain.

Other notable figures in the integration of Buddhist principles into Western psychology include Marsha Linehan, who developed

Dialectical Behavior Therapy (DBT) as a treatment for borderline personality disorder; Mark Epstein, a psychiatrist who has written extensively on the integration of Buddhist and psychoanalytic thought; and Tara Brach, a clinical psychologist and meditation teacher who has popularized the practice of self-compassion.

As the convergence of Eastern philosophies and Western psychology continues to evolve, we can expect to see further innovations in the treatment of anxiety and other mental health challenges. By drawing on the wisdom of these ancient traditions and integrating them with the scientific rigor of modern psychology, we may be able to develop more holistic and effective approaches to healing and personal transformation.

## The Nature of Suffering

To understand how transpersonal and Buddhist psychologies can help address anxiety, it is crucial to explore the nature of suffering and its root causes. Gaining insight into the universal experience of suffering and the factors that contribute to its perpetuation can help develop a more compassionate and effective approach to managing anxiety.

One of the fundamental insights of Buddhist psychology is the recognition that suffering is a universal human experience. We encounter challenges, setbacks, and losses regardless of our background, circumstances, or achievements. This understanding is encapsulated in the First Noble Truth, which acknowledges that suffering, or dukkha, is an inherent part of the human condition.

The concept of dukkha encompasses not only physical pain and emotional distress but also the pervasive sense of dissatisfaction and unease that often underlies our daily experiences. It is the nagging feeling that something is missing or not quite right, even in the midst of apparent success or happiness. Acknowledging the universality of suffering allows us to approach our struggles with greater compassion and understanding.

Buddhist psychology identifies three primary root causes of suffering:

attachments and cravings, aversion and avoidance, and ignorance and delusion.

Attachments and cravings refer to our tendency to cling to people, objects, and experiences that we believe will bring us happiness or fulfillment. Whether it is a relationship, a job, or a material possession, we often pin our hopes and expectations on external factors, believing that they will provide us with lasting satisfaction. However, the impermanent nature of all things means that these attachments are ultimately a source of suffering as we inevitably face loss, change, and disappointment.

Aversion and avoidance, on the other hand, refer to our tendency to resist or flee from unpleasant experiences, such as physical pain, emotional discomfort, or difficult life circumstances. By attempting to avoid or suppress these experiences, we often create additional suffering for ourselves as we become trapped in a cycle of fear, anxiety, and resistance.

Ignorance and delusion refer to our fundamental misunderstanding of the nature of reality. We often operate under the illusion that we are separate, isolated beings, disconnected from the world. This sense of separateness can lead to feelings of alienation, loneliness, and anxiety as we struggle to find our place in the world. Additionally, our delusions about the permanence and stability of things can cause us to cling to unrealistic expectations and resist the natural flow of change.

Attachments and expectations play a significant role in the development and maintenance of anxiety. When we become overly attached to specific outcomes or circumstances, we often experience a heightened sense of fear and unease as we worry about the possibility of loss or disappointment.

The desire for control and certainty is a common manifestation of attachment in the context of anxiety. We may feel a strong need to control our environment, relationships, or future, believing that if we can just plan and prepare enough, we can avoid potential pitfalls and ensure a positive outcome. However, this desire for control is ultimately an illusion, as life is inherently unpredictable and uncertain.

The more we try to hold on to a sense of control, the more anxious and stressed we become.

The fear of losing what we have or not getting what we want is another way in which attachments can fuel anxiety. We may worry about losing a job, a relationship, or a cherished possession, or we may feel anxious about not achieving a desired goal or outcome. These fears can lead to constant unease and apprehension as we try to protect ourselves from potential loss or failure.

Recognizing the role of attachments and expectations in anxiety allows us to develop a more flexible and adaptable approach to life. Instead of clinging to specific outcomes or circumstances, we can learn to embrace uncertainty and change, trusting in our resilience and ability to navigate challenges as they arise. This shift in perspective is at the heart of both transpersonal and Buddhist approaches to managing anxiety, as we will explore in the following sections.

Thank you for the reminder. I will review the writing rules and ensure adherence to them as we continue with the next section.

## The Path to Liberation

Transpersonal and Buddhist psychologies offer a path to liberation from anxiety by cultivating mindfulness, letting go of attachments, and developing self-compassion. These practices can play a crucial role in reducing anxiety and promoting emotional well-being.

Mindfulness is a fundamental practice in both transpersonal and Buddhist traditions. It involves cultivating present-moment awareness and non-judgmental observation of one's thoughts, emotions, and sensations. By learning to anchor our attention in the present moment, we can break free from the cycle of rumination and worry that often fuels anxiety.

At its core, mindfulness involves paying attention to our experience in a curious, open, and accepting way. Rather than getting caught up in our thoughts or judgments about what is happening, we simply observe our experience as it unfolds, moment by moment. This practice can help us develop greater clarity, perspective, and emotional balance.

Research has consistently shown that mindfulness practice can be a powerful tool for reducing anxiety and promoting emotional well-being. By cultivating present-moment awareness, we can learn to respond to stressful situations with greater flexibility and resilience rather than getting trapped in patterns of anxious reactivity. Additionally, mindfulness can help us develop greater self-awareness and self-acceptance, further reducing anxiety and promoting overall well-being.

Letting go of attachments is another key aspect of the path to liberation. As we have seen, attachments and cravings are a fundamental cause of suffering according to Buddhist psychology. By learning to let go of our attachments and cultivate a more open and flexible relationship with life, we can begin to free ourselves from the grip of anxiety.

One key insight of Buddhist psychology is the recognition of the impermanence of all things. Everything in life is transitional. Thoughts and emotions about our relationships and circumstances are always in flux and constantly changing. By acknowledging this fundamental reality, we can begin to let go of our attempts to control or hold onto things and instead learn to flow with the natural unfolding of life.

Practicing non-attachment to outcomes is another important aspect of letting go. Often, our anxiety is fueled by our fixation on specific results or outcomes, such as achieving a particular goal or maintaining a certain relationship. By learning to let go of our attachment to these outcomes and instead focusing on the process of living and engaging with life, we can reduce our anxiety and find greater peace and contentment.

Cultivating equanimity in the face of change is a way to practice letting go. Equanimity involves maintaining a balanced and composed mind, even in challenging circumstances. By developing this quality of mind, we can learn to ride the waves of change with greater ease and grace rather than getting tossed about by our anxieties and fears.

Self-compassion is another key practice in both transpersonal and Buddhist psychologies. It involves cultivating kindness, understanding, and acceptance toward oneself. By learning to relate to ourselves with greater compassion, we can reduce the impact of anxiety and promote emotional healing and growth.

One of the dangers of anxiety is that it often goes hand in hand with self-judgment and self-criticism. We may berate ourselves for feeling anxious or criticize ourselves for being unable to control our thoughts or emotions. However, this kind of self-judgment only serves to exacerbate our anxiety and maintain the cycle of suffering.

In contrast, self-compassion involves treating ourselves with the same kindness and understanding that we would extend to a close friend or loved one. By learning to relate to ourselves with greater gentleness and care, we can create a sense of emotional safety and support that can be deeply healing in the face of anxiety.

Many techniques for cultivating self-compassion include loving-kindness meditation, self-compassion journaling, and self-care practices. By incorporating these techniques into our daily lives, we can transform our relationship with ourselves and develop greater emotional resilience and well-being.

Ultimately, the path to liberation from anxiety involves a fundamental shift in our relationship with ourselves, others, and the world around us. By cultivating mindfulness, letting go of attachments, and developing self-compassion, we can break free from the patterns of suffering that keep us trapped in anxiety and find a greater sense of peace, purpose, and connection.

## Integrating Transpersonal and Buddhist Principles into Daily Life

Integrating transpersonal and Buddhist principles into daily life involves applying these insights to everyday experiences. This integration can help transform our relationship with anxiety and cultivate greater emotional well-being and resilience.

Establishing a regular meditation practice is one of the most powerful ways to integrate these principles. As explored in Week 1 of this book, mindfulness meditation can be a transformative tool for reducing anxiety and promoting emotional balance. Setting aside time daily to cultivate present-moment awareness and non-judgmental observation of thoughts and emotions can help develop a more grounded and centered approach to life.

In addition to formal meditation practice, applying the principles of non-attachment and self-compassion in everyday situations is crucial. This involves bringing greater awareness and intentionality to our interactions with ourselves, others, and the world around us.

One way to apply the principle of non-attachment is by recognizing and letting go of attachments as they arise. We may notice ourselves getting caught up in specific desires, expectations, or outcomes throughout the day. By bringing mindful awareness to these attachments without judgment, we can loosen their grip and cultivate a more open and flexible relationship to life. This might involve simply acknowledging the presence of an attachment and gently redirecting our attention back to the present moment.

Applying the principle of self-compassion involves treating ourselves with kindness and understanding, particularly during challenging times. When we experience anxiety or other forms of emotional distress, it can be easy to fall into patterns of self-criticism and self-judgment. However, by intentionally cultivating a more compassionate and supportive inner dialogue, we can begin to soothe and comfort ourselves in moments of difficulty. This might involve offering ourselves encouragement, reminding ourselves of our inherent worthiness and value, or simply holding our pain with tenderness and care.

Cultivating a sense of connection and purpose is another way to integrate transpersonal and Buddhist principles into daily life. This involves recognizing our fundamental interconnectedness with others and the world and engaging in activities aligning with our deepest values and aspirations.

One way to cultivate a sense of connection is by actively recognizing our interdependence with others and the natural world. This might involve practicing gratitude for how we are supported and sustained by the people and resources around us or engaging in acts of kindness and compassion toward others. By nurturing a sense of connection and belongingness, we can ease the feelings of isolation and separation that often fuel anxiety.

Engaging in meaningful activities that align with our values and beliefs is another way to cultivate a sense of purpose and direction in life. This might involve volunteering for a cause we care about, pursuing a creative passion, or dedicating time to learning and personal growth. By actively shaping our lives around what matters most, we can develop a greater sense of meaning and fulfillment, even in the face of life's challenges and uncertainties.

Integrating transpersonal and Buddhist principles into daily life is an ongoing learning, growth, and self-discovery process. By bringing greater awareness, compassion, and intentionality to our everyday experiences, we can transform our relationship with anxiety and unlock our potential for emotional well-being and resilience. Through regular practice and a commitment to living in alignment with our deepest values, we can chart a path toward greater peace, purpose, and connection in all areas of our lives.

Throughout this chapter, we have explored the rich insights and practices offered by transpersonal and Buddhist psychologies for addressing anxiety and cultivating emotional well-being. By delving into the historical roots of these traditions, examining the nature of suffering and its causes, and outlining a path toward greater freedom and resilience, we have laid the groundwork for a more holistic and transformative approach to anxiety management.

The potential of transpersonal and Buddhist psychologies in transforming our relationship with anxiety is significant. These traditions offer a profound shift in perspective, inviting us to move beyond symptom management and toward a deeper understanding of the human condition. By recognizing the universality of suffering, the role of attachments and expectations in perpetuating anxiety, and the power of mindfulness, non-attachment, and self-compassion in promoting healing and growth, we can develop a more liberating and empowering relationship with our anxious experiences.

It is important to recognize that the journey toward greater peace and well-being is not always straightforward. Integrating transpersonal and Buddhist principles into our lives requires patience, persistence, and a deep commitment to self-exploration and growth. We may encounter setbacks, challenges, and moments of doubt. Approaching these experiences with self-compassion and a willingness to learn and adapt, we can continue to make progress and deepen our understanding.

As we conclude this chapter, I encourage you, the reader, to continue exploring and integrating these principles into your own life. Whether through establishing a regular meditation practice, applying the principles of non-attachment and self-compassion in your daily interactions, or cultivating a greater sense of connection and purpose, there are countless ways to bring these insights to bear on your own journey with anxiety. By staying curious, open, and committed to your own growth and healing, you can transform your relationship with anxiety and unlock your potential for emotional freedom and resilience.

As we move forward, we focus on a series of self-help homework processes and skills that can further support you in integrating transpersonal and Buddhist principles into your daily life. Over the next seven days, we will explore a range of practices and exercises designed to help you deepen your mindfulness, self-compassion, and sense of connection and develop a more grounded and centered approach to anxiety management. By engaging with these practices and making them a regular part of your routine, you can continue to build on the insights and skills you have gained throughout this chapter and take concrete steps toward greater peace, purpose, and well-being in all areas of your life.

The journey through transpersonal and Buddhist approaches to managing anxiety is one of profound transformation and growth. By embracing the wisdom of these ancient traditions and integrating them with the scientific rigor of modern psychology, we can chart a path toward greater emotional freedom, resilience, and well-being. As we navigate life's challenges with mindfulness, compassion, and a deep sense of connection to ourselves and the world around us, we open ourselves to the possibility of profound healing and transformation.

Remember, the path to greater peace and well-being is an ongoing process of learning, growth, and self-discovery. By staying committed to your journey and remaining open to the insights and practices offered by transpersonal and Buddhist psychologies, you can continue to deepen your understanding of yourself and your relationship to anxiety and develop the skills and resilience needed to thrive in life's challenges.

As you embark on the next phase of your journey, trust in your own inner wisdom and the transformative power of these practices. With patience, persistence, and a willingness to embrace the ups and downs of the path, you can unlock your fullest potential for emotional freedom, resilience, and well-being and discover a greater sense of peace, purpose, and connection in all areas of your life.

# Week 7 Self-Help Guide

Congratulations on completing the chapter on the transpersonal and Buddhist psychology approaches to managing anxiety. You have learned valuable insights and practices that can help you cultivate a more grounded, compassionate, and resilient relationship with your anxious experiences.

We have created a seven-day self-help homework guide to help you integrate these principles into your daily life. Each day, you will focus on a specific practice or theme drawn from the wisdom of transpersonal and Buddhist psychologies. These practices are designed to help you deepen your mindfulness, self-compassion, and sense of connection and to develop a more flexible and adaptive approach to navigating life's challenges.

As you work through this guide, remember that change is a process, and it is common to encounter obstacles or setbacks. Be patient and compassionate with yourself, and trust in the transformative power of these practices. With consistent effort and an open heart, you can gradually shift your relationship with anxiety and cultivate a greater sense of peace, purpose, and well-being.

It is important to note that while these practices can be deeply supportive, they are not intended as a substitute for professional treatment. If you are experiencing severe or persistent anxiety, or if you have a history of trauma or mental health concerns, it is strongly recommended that you seek the guidance of a qualified mental health professional. A skilled therapist can help you navigate the challenges of anxiety and provide personalized support and guidance tailored to your unique needs and circumstances.

Remember, seeking help is a sign of strength and self-care. By combining the wisdom of transpersonal and Buddhist psychologies with the support of a compassionate therapeutic relationship, you can create a strong foundation for healing and transformation.

As you embark on this seven-day journey, approach each practice with curiosity, openness, and self-compassion. Trust in the wisdom of your experience, and allow yourself to be guided by the insights and practices that resonate most deeply with you. With patience, persistence, and a commitment to your own growth and well-being, you can cultivate a more peaceful, purposeful, and connected life one day at a time.

# Week 7 Day 1

## The River Visualization

**Objective:** To cultivate the ability to observe and allow anxiety to exist without being swept away by its turbulent current, fostering a sense of presence, adaptability, and resilience in the face of challenging emotions.

**Information:** Transpersonal and Buddhist psychologies emphasize the importance of developing a non-reactive, observant relationship with our inner experiences, including difficult emotions like anxiety. By practicing mindfulness and visualization, we can learn to deal with our anxiety more skillfully and compassionately without getting caught up in its narrative or overwhelmed by its intensity. This visualization exercise, titled "The River," draws on the Buddhist concept of "non-self" (anatta) and the transpersonal notion of expanding our sense of identity beyond our individual ego to include a more interconnected and fluid understanding of ourselves and our experiences.

**Instructions:**

1. Find a quiet, comfortable place to sit or lie down without disturbance.
2. Close your eyes and take a few deep, cleansing breaths, allowing your body to relax and settle.
3. Visualize yourself standing in a turbulent river, with fast-moving water swirling around you. Notice the power and intensity of the current and how it feels to be caught in its midst.
4. Observe your response to being in the river. Are you trying to

fight against the current or hold onto a log or rock for stability? Are you being swept downstream, feeling out of control? Take a moment to be with this experience without judgment.

5. Now, imagine yourself slowly and deliberately moving toward the shoreline. With each step, feel yourself gaining greater stability and control until you reach the shallow water or the riverbank.

6. Once you have reached a place of safety, take a few deep breaths and allow your body to relax. Feel the solid ground beneath you and the sense of being anchored and present.

7. From this new vantage point, observe the river and its turbulent waters. Notice its power, its movement, and its inherent nature. Recognize that, like anxiety, the river is a natural force that arises and passes away without solidity or permanence.

8. As you watch the river, cultivate a sense of respect and appreciation for its energy and purpose. Just as the river plays a vital role in the ecosystem, our anxious experiences can also serve a purpose, alerting us to potential dangers or areas of our lives that need attention.

9. Embrace the paradox of being separate from the river yet still connected to it. In the same way, our anxiety is a part of our experience, but it does not define who we are. We can learn to observe and be with our anxiety without being swept away by its current.

10. When you feel ready, take a few deep breaths and slowly open your eyes, bringing this sense of perspective and presence with you as you move through your day.

**Reflection:** Take some time to journal about your experience with this visualization practice. What did you notice about your relationship with the river and anxious experiences? What insights or challenges arose for you during the visualization? Consider how you can apply this newfound perspective to your daily life, particularly when facing anxious or challenging situations.

**Integration:** When you notice anxiety arising throughout your day, remember the image of the river and your ability to observe it from the shore. Practice bringing a sense of perspective and presence to your experience without getting caught up in your anxiety story. Over time, this practice can help you cultivate a more spacious and resilient relationship with your inner experiences, grounded in the wisdom of transpersonal and Buddhist psychologies.

# Week 7 Day 2

## Cultivating Self-Compassion

**Objective:** To develop a more compassionate and understanding relationship with oneself, particularly during times of anxiety or distress.

**Information:** Self-compassion involves treating oneself with kindness, care, and understanding, especially in difficult emotions or challenging situations. Research has shown that self-compassion can help reduce anxiety, increase resilience, and promote overall well-being. By learning to relate to ourselves with greater gentleness and compassion, we can create a sense of emotional safety and support that can be deeply healing in the face of anxiety.

**Instructions:**

1. Take a few moments to bring to mind a current source of anxiety or distress in your life.
2. Notice any self-critical or judgmental thoughts that arise in relation to this situation.
3. Place a hand on your heart or another comforting place, and take a few deep breaths.
4. Silently repeat the following phrases to yourself: "This is a moment of suffering. Suffering is a part of life. May I be kind to myself at this moment. May I give myself the compassion I need."
5. Continue repeating these phrases, allowing their meaning to sink in and infuse your experience with a sense of warmth and care.
6. If your mind wanders or you notice self-critical thoughts arising,

gently redirect your attention back to the phrases and the feeling of compassion for yourself.

7. When you feel ready, take a few deep breaths and slowly open your eyes, bringing this sense of self-compassion with you as you move through your day.

**Reflection:** Take some time to journal about your experience with this self-compassion practice. What did your body and mind notice as you repeated the phrases? How did it feel to offer yourself compassion in a moment of difficulty? Consider any barriers or resistance that may have arisen and how you might work with these obstacles moving forward.

**Integration:** Look for opportunities to practice self-compassion throughout your day, especially when you notice feelings of anxiety or self-criticism arising. Remember that self-compassion is a skill that can be cultivated with practice and patience. By making self-compassion a regular part of your daily routine, you can transform your relationship with yourself and your anxious experiences, creating a greater sense of emotional resilience and well-being.

# Week 7 Day 3

## Recognizing Impermanence

**Objective:** To develop a greater understanding and acceptance of the impermanent nature of life as a way to reduce attachment and anxiety.

**Information:** One of the core insights of Buddhist psychology is the recognition that all things are impermanent and subject to change. By deeply understanding and accepting this truth, we can relinquish our attachments and expectations and cultivate a more flexible and resilient approach to life's challenges. This practice invites us to explore the impermanent nature of our experiences and use this understanding to soften our resistance to change and uncertainty.

**Instructions:**

1. Take a few moments to settle into a comfortable position and bring your attention to your breath.
2. Reflect on the following prompts, allowing each one to sink in before moving on to the next:
   - Think of a cherished possession. Recognize that it will eventually break, be lost, or fade away.
   - Bring to mind a close relationship. Acknowledge that it will inevitably change and that all relationships end through separation or death.
   - Consider your own body and mind. Notice how your thoughts, emotions, and physical sensations constantly shift and change.

3. Allow yourself to sit with the truth of impermanence without judgment or resistance.

4. If you notice any feelings of anxiety, fear, or sadness arising, acknowledge them with kindness and compassion.

5. Reflect on how understanding impermanence can help you let go of attachment and cultivate greater resilience in the face of change.

6. When you feel ready, take a few deep breaths and slowly open your eyes, bringing this understanding of impermanence with you as you move through your day.

**Reflection:** Take some time to journal about your experience with this impermanence practice. What insights or challenges arose for you as you contemplated the impermanent nature of things? How might recognizing impermanence help you to release anxiety and attachment in your daily life? Consider any resistance or discomfort that may have arisen and how you might work with these feelings moving forward.

**Integration:** Throughout your day, look for opportunities to recognize and acknowledge the impermanent nature of life. Notice how this awareness can help you to hold your experiences more lightly and respond to challenges with greater flexibility and grace. Accepting impermanence is a practice, and it is natural to feel resistance or discomfort at times. By bringing mindfulness and compassion to your experiences, you can gradually deepen your understanding and acceptance of impermanence. Use this wisdom to navigate life's ups and downs with greater ease.

# Week 7 Day 4

## Cultivating Equanimity

**Objective:** To develop a more balanced and even-minded approach to life's ups and downs as a way to reduce anxiety and increase resilience.

**Information:** Equanimity is a state of mental calmness and composure characterized by the ability to meet life's joys and sorrows with an open and accepting presence. By cultivating equanimity, we can learn to ride the waves of change with greater ease and skill rather than getting tossed about by our anxious reactions. This practice invites us to explore the possibility of meeting life's experiences with balance and steadiness, even in challenging circumstances.

**Instructions:**

1. Find a comfortable seated position, and take a few deep breaths to settle your mind and body.
2. Bring to mind a recent situation that triggered feelings of anxiety or distress.
3. Notice any sensations of tension or tightness in your body and any anxious or fearful thoughts in your mind.
4. Silently repeat the following phrases to yourself: "Anxiety is rising. It is a natural part of life. It will eventually pass away. May I meet this moment with poise and balance."
5. Continue repeating these phrases, allowing their meaning to infuse your experience with a sense of calm and stability.
6. If your mind wanders or you notice yourself getting caught up in

anxious thoughts, gently redirect your attention to the phrases and the feeling of calmness.

7. When you feel ready, take a few deep breaths and slowly open your eyes, bringing this sense of balance and steadiness with you as you move through your day.

**Reflection:** Take time to journal about your experience with this equanimity practice. What did your body and mind notice as you repeated the phrases? How did it feel to bring balance and acceptance to your anxious experience? Consider any challenges or insights that arose and how you might continue cultivating serenity in your daily life.

**Integration:** As you move through your day, notice when you feel knocked off balance by difficult emotions or challenging situations. Experiment with bringing a sense of calmness to these moments, reminding yourself that all experiences eventually pass and that you can meet them with an open and accepting presence. Remember that cultivating equanimity is a practice, and it is natural to feel unsteady or reactive sometimes. By bringing mindfulness and compassion to your experiences, you can gradually develop a greater sense of balance and resilience in life's ups and downs.

# Week 7 Day 5

*Exploring Interconnectedness*

**Objective:** To cultivate a deeper sense of connection and belonging as a way to reduce feelings of isolation and anxiety.

**Information:** Transpersonal psychology recognizes that all beings are fundamentally interconnected and that our individual well-being is intimately tied to the well-being of others and the world around us. By exploring and nurturing this sense of interconnectedness, we can begin to ease the feelings of separation and loneliness that often fuel anxiety. This practice invites us to reflect on how we are connected to and supported by the people and world around us and to cultivate a greater sense of belonging and purpose.

**Instructions:**

1. Find a comfortable position, and take a few moments to settle into your body and breathe.
2. Bring to mind someone you care about deeply - a friend, family member, or loved one.
3. Reflect on how your life is connected to and supported by this person. Consider the love, care, and kindness they have shown you and their positive impact on your life.
4. Expand your awareness to consider the many other people who have positively touched your life - teachers, mentors, colleagues, neighbors, and even strangers who have shown you kindness or support.
5. Allow yourself to rest in this feeling of connection and support,

knowing you are part of a larger web of interdependence and care.

6. If you notice feelings of isolation or loneliness, acknowledge them with kindness and compassion and gently redirect your attention to the sense of connection and belonging.

7. When you feel ready, take a few deep breaths and slowly open your eyes, carrying this sense of interconnectedness with you as you move through your day.

**Reflection:** Take some time to journal about your experience with this interconnectedness practice. What feelings or insights arose as you reflected on your connections with others? How might nurturing a sense of interconnectedness help ease feelings of isolation or anxiety in your daily life? Consider any barriers or resistance that may have arisen and how you might work with these obstacles moving forward.

**Integration:** Look for opportunities to recognize and appreciate your connections with others throughout your day. Offer small gestures of kindness and care, and notice how these actions contribute to a greater sense of belonging and purpose. Remember that cultivating a sense of interconnectedness is a practice; sometimes, it is natural to feel disconnected or isolated. By bringing awareness and compassion to your experiences, you can gradually deepen your understanding and embodiment of interconnectedness. Use this understanding to navigate feelings of anxiety and loneliness with greater ease and grace.

# Week 7 Day 6

## Practicing Non-Attachment

**Objective:** To develop a more flexible and open relationship to life's experiences by practicing non-attachment to specific outcomes or expectations.

**Information:** Attachment to particular outcomes or desires is a common source of anxiety and suffering. By practicing non-attachment, we can learn to engage with life more fully and freely without getting caught up in the need for things to be a certain way. This practice invites us to explore our relationship to attachment and expectation and to experiment with letting go of our fixed ideas about how things "should" be.

**Instructions:**

1. Consider a current situation or experience you feel particularly attached to or invested in.
2. Notice any feelings of anxiety, tension, or grasping that arise in relation to this situation.
3. Take a few deep breaths, and silently repeat the following phrases to yourself: "I am letting go of my attachment to a specific outcome. I trust in my ability to handle whatever unfolds. I am open to the mystery and uncertainty of life."
4. Continue repeating these phrases, allowing yourself to soften and release your grip on your desired outcome.
5. If you notice any resistance or discomfort, acknowledge it with

kindness and compassion and gently redirect your attention to the phrases and the sensation of letting go.

6. When you feel ready, take a few deep breaths and slowly open your eyes, carrying this sense of openness and flexibility as you move through your day.

**Reflection:** Take some time to journal about your experience with this non-attachment practice. What did you notice in your body and mind as you worked with your attachment? What challenges or insights arose? Consider how practicing non-attachment might support you in navigating anxiety and uncertainty in your daily life.

**Integration:** As you move through your day, notice when you feel pulled into attachment or grasping. Experiment with meeting these moments with a spirit of openness and curiosity, reminding yourself that you can meet life's unfolding with flexibility and grace. Remember that practicing non-attachment is a process, and it is natural to feel resistance or discomfort. By bringing awareness and compassion to your experiences, you can gradually develop a greater sense of ease and freedom in your relationship to life's ups and downs.

# Week 7 Day 7

## Aligning with Values

**Objective:** To reduce anxiety and increase a sense of meaning and purpose by connecting with and acting in alignment with one's deepest values.

**Information:** When we feel disconnected from our core values and beliefs, we may experience a sense of anxiety or emptiness. By clarifying what matters most to us and aligning our actions with these values, we can cultivate a greater sense of meaning, purpose, and fulfillment. This practice invites us to reflect on our deepest values and explore how we might bring them more fully into our daily lives.

**Instructions:**

1. Take a few moments to reflect on your deepest values and priorities. What qualities or principles do you most want to embody in your life? What activities or relationships bring you the greatest sense of joy and meaning?
2. Choose one value that resonates particularly with you today, and identify one small action you can take to express or honor this value.
3. As you engage in this action, bring your full attention and presence to the experience. Notice any feelings of ease, joy, or connection that arise.
4. If you notice any anxiety or resistance, acknowledge them with kindness and compassion and gently redirect your attention to the value you seek to embody.

5. Take a moment to appreciate yourself for taking this step and your commitment to living in alignment with your values.
6. When you feel ready, take a few deep breaths and slowly open your eyes, carrying this sense of purpose and intentionality with you as you move through your day.

**Reflection:** Take some time to journal about your experience with this values alignment practice. What value did you choose to focus on, and how did you express it through action? What impact did this have on your sense of well-being and purpose? Consider any barriers or challenges that may have arisen and how you might work with these obstacles moving forward.

**Integration:** Look for opportunities to align your choices and actions with your core values throughout your day. Notice how this practice can help anchor you in a sense of meaning and purpose, even in the face of anxiety or uncertainty. Remember that aligning with our values is a lifelong process and natural to feel.

# Week 7 Tracking Progress

As you conclude this week's focus on transpersonal psychology, take a moment to assess your journey. Visualize the bridge and mark your current position. Rate your anxiety level on the 0-10 scale, considering the insights you've gained about your spiritual and transcendent experiences.

**Instructions**:

1. Take a moment to reflect on your progress and experiences.
2. Refer to the bridge illustration below.
3. Consider where you currently stand on your journey.
4. Place a mark on the bridge representing your current position.
5. Next, rate where your average anxiety level has been over this week.
6. Record your anxiety rating on the provided 0-10 scale, with 0 being no anxiety and 10 being the most intense anxiety you've experienced.
7. Reflect and journal.

**Reflection**: After marking your bridge position and anxiety rating, reflect on your progress. Examine skills learned, challenges faced, and changes in thoughts and behaviors. Journal your insights and observations. Identify successes, challenges, and areas requiring more attention. Determine if you need to slow down, revisit previous weeks or skills, or seek professional help to maintain progress. Assess your overall progress and consider if professional support is needed or how it's contributing to your journey.

| 0 | 1 | 2 | 3 | 4 | 5 | 6 | 7 | 8 | 9 | 10 |

No
Anxiety

Moderate
Anxiety

High
Anxiety

---

## 12

# Solution-Focused Methods for Addressing Anxiety

Anxiety is a common mental health concern affecting millions of people worldwide. While various approaches exist for managing anxiety, Solution-Focused Therapy (SFT) has emerged as an effective tool for helping individuals overcome anxiety and lead more fulfilling lives.

Solution-Focused Therapy is a goal-oriented, collaborative approach that identifies and builds upon an individual's strengths and resources to create positive change. Unlike traditional forms of therapy that often dwell on past problems, SFT focuses on the present and future, helping clients develop a clear vision of their desired outcomes and the steps needed to achieve them.

SFT is guided by the belief that individuals can solve problems and create meaningful change. By shifting the focus from the issue to the solution, SFT empowers clients to take an active role in their healing and growth.

When applied to managing anxiety, Solution-Focused Therapy offers an empowering alternative to traditional problem-focused approaches. By helping individuals identify their strengths, develop a clear vision of a preferred future, and take concrete steps toward achieving their goals, SFT provides a roadmap for overcoming anxiety and reclaiming a sense of control and well-being.

This chapter explores the key principles and techniques of Solution-Focused Therapy and how they can be applied to managing anxiety. Clear explanations, real-life examples, and step-by-step guidance are provided to help readers harness the power of SFT in their journey toward a more positive, anxiety-free future. The tools and strategies presented can help individuals tap into their resilience and resources to create lasting, meaningful change.

## Understanding Solution-Focused Therapy

Solution-Focused Therapy (SFT) is a relatively new approach to psychotherapy that has gained significant popularity since its inception in the 1980s. Developed by Steve de Shazer, Insoo Kim Berg, and their colleagues at the Brief Family Therapy Center in Milwaukee, Wisconsin, SFT emerged as a departure from traditional problem-focused therapies.

The history of Solution-Focused Therapy is rooted in a fundamental shift in perspective. Instead of focusing on the intricate details of the problems that brought clients to therapy, de Shazer, and his team began to explore what clients were already doing that was working. They discovered that by focusing on these exceptions to the problem and amplifying them, clients could make significant progress in a shorter amount of time.

Several key principles and assumptions guide the Solution-Focused Therapy approach. Central to SFT is the idea that focusing on solutions rather than problems is the most effective way to create positive change. By shifting the conversation away from what's wrong and toward what's desired, SFT helps clients tap into their strengths and resources to develop a more positive future.

Another core principle of Solution-Focused Therapy is the emphasis on strengths and resources. SFT operates on the belief that all individuals have the inherent capacity to solve their problems and possess unique strengths and resources to be leveraged to create change. By helping clients identify and build upon these strengths, SFT empowers them to become active agents in their growth and healing.

Clear, achievable goals are another hallmark of solution-focused therapy. In SFT, the therapist works collaboratively with the client to develop specific, measurable, and realistic goals that align with the client's values and desired outcomes. By breaking down larger goals into smaller, manageable steps, SFT helps clients build momentum and experience a sense of progress and accomplishment.

Exceptions play a key role in identifying solutions in Solution-Focused Therapy. Exceptions refer to times when the problem is absent or less severe, providing valuable insight into what works for the client. By exploring these exceptions and identifying the strategies and resources that contributed to them, SFT helps clients develop a roadmap for overcoming their challenges.

Finally, Solution-Focused Therapy emphasizes the importance of a collaborative therapist-client relationship. In SFT, the therapist is not seen as the expert with all the answers but rather as a facilitator who works alongside the client to explore possibilities and co-create solutions. This collaborative approach fosters a sense of empowerment and ownership in the therapeutic process.

By understanding the history, principles, and assumptions that underlie Solution-Focused Therapy, individuals seeking to manage their anxiety can begin to see the potential for change and growth in their own lives.

## The Solution-Focused Approach to Anxiety

The Solution-Focused approach to anxiety shifts the focus from the problem to desired outcomes and solutions, offering an empowering alternative to feeling stuck and helpless.

To apply Solution-Focused Therapy to anxiety, clients are encouraged to imagine a future where anxiety is no longer a problem instead of dwelling on anxiety symptoms or contributing factors. This shift in focus helps clients see possibilities for change and motivates them to take steps toward their desired outcomes.

Identifying exceptions, such as when anxiety is less severe or absent, is key in the solution-focused approach. Clients can uncover effective strategies and resources to manage anxiety by exploring these exceptions and what was different.

For example, a client with social anxiety may recall a recent event where they felt more at ease in conversation. Exploring the differences, such as being with a supportive friend or in a comfortable setting, can reveal strategies to reduce anxiety in social situations.

Another essential component is developing a clear vision of a preferred future where anxiety is no longer significant. Clients are encouraged to describe their lives in detail, serving as a powerful motivator and helping them stay focused on desired outcomes despite setbacks.

The Solution-Focused approach emphasizes setting realistic, achievable goals. While eliminating anxiety may be the ultimate goal, progress often happens in small steps. Setting specific, measurable goals aligned with desired outcomes allows clients to experience progress and build momentum.

A client struggling with panic attacks, for instance, may set a goal to practice a relaxation technique three times per week. While not eliminating panic attacks, it represents a concrete step toward managing anxiety and building control.

By shifting focus to desired outcomes, identifying exceptions, envisioning a preferred future, and setting realistic goals, the Solution-Focused approach empowers clients to engage in their healing and growth actively.

## Solution-Focused Techniques for Managing Anxiety

Solution-Focused Therapy offers powerful techniques to help individuals manage anxiety effectively by shifting focus from problems to solutions, strengths, and desired outcomes.

The Miracle Question is a well-known Solution-Focused technique that invites clients to imagine a future where their problem has been solved overnight. The therapist asks, "Suppose tonight, while you sleep, a miracle occurs. When you wake up tomorrow morning, what will be different?" This helps clients develop a clear vision of their preferred future and identify specific changes they want to see, serving as a powerful motivator.

When processing the client's response, the therapist helps identify specific behaviors, thoughts, and feelings in their preferred future. A client with anxiety might imagine waking up calm and confident, engaging in activities they currently avoid, or having more positive interactions with others.

Scaling Questions invite clients to assess their situation or progress on a 0-10 scale, with 0 representing the worst and 10 the best scenario. For example, "On a scale from 0-10, where 0 means anxiety completely controls your life and 10 means you manage anxiety effectively, where are you today?" This helps clients develop a nuanced understanding of their situation, identify areas for improvement, measure progress, and celebrate successes. Exploring what it would take to move up one point reveals specific strategies and resources for managing anxiety.

Exception Finding involves exploring times when the problem is absent or less severe to identify strategies and resources the client has successfully used to manage anxiety. A client with generalized anxiety might reflect on a recent day when they felt calmer than usual, exploring what was different, such as engaging in a relaxing hobby, spending time with a supportive friend, or practicing a relaxation technique. This helps develop a toolkit of effective strategies.

Goal Setting is a critical component of Solution-Focused Therapy for managing anxiety. Goals are developed collaboratively, designed to be SMART (Specific, Measurable, Achievable, Relevant, and Time-bound), and aligned with the client's desired outcomes. Breaking goals into manageable steps, such as attending one social event per week for a client with anxiety-related avoidance, makes them more achievable.

Celebrating progress and maintaining motivation are essential aspects of goal setting in Solution-Focused Therapy.

By using the Miracle Question, Scaling Questions, Exception Finding, and Goal Setting, Solution-Focused Therapy empowers individuals to manage anxiety and create positive change actively.

### Integrating Solution-Focused Therapy into Daily Life

Integrating Solution-Focused principles and practices into every day routines is crucial for individuals to continue building on the progress made in therapy and develop a resilient, proactive approach to managing anxiety.

Practicing solution-focused thinking will facilitate the integration of Solution-Focused Therapy into daily life. This involves consistently directing attention toward desired outcomes, strengths, and exceptions. When faced with anxiety-provoking situations, individuals can ask themselves, "What would I like to happen?" or "What strengths and resources can help me manage this challenge?" Repeatedly redirecting focus in this way develops a solution-oriented mindset over time.

Keeping a solutions journal is another powerful way to integrate Solution-Focused Therapy into daily life. Individuals can record successes, insights, and progress toward goals, explore exceptions to anxiety, and identify effective strategies and resources. Regular reflection on progress and celebrating successes maintain momentum and motivation.

Enlisting support from others is critical for integrating Solution-Focused Therapy into daily life. While SFT techniques empower individuals to take an active role in their growth and healing, sharing goals and progress with supportive friends, family, or peers provides encouragement, accountability, and fresh perspectives. Practicing Solution-Focused techniques in interactions, such as asking scaling questions or exploring exceptions, is also beneficial.

Maintaining progress and preventing relapse requires consistent effort and attention. Even after significant progress in managing anxiety, setbacks may occur. Continuing to practice Solution-Focused techniques and maintaining a solution-oriented mindset minimize the impact of setbacks and facilitate getting back on track.

Developing a personalized self-care plan incorporating Solution-Focused principles is a helpful strategy for maintaining progress. This plan may include regular check-ins to assess progress, identify areas for improvement, and engage in self-care activities that promote relaxation, resilience, and well-being. Prioritizing self-care and consistently working toward goals develops a stronger sense of control over anxiety and maintains progress over time.

Integrating Solution-Focused Therapy into daily life requires ongoing effort and commitment, but the benefits are substantial. Practicing solution-focused thinking, keeping a solutions journal, enlisting support from others, and maintaining progress through self-care and persistence allow individuals to build on skills and insights gained in therapy and develop a more empowered, proactive approach to managing anxiety.

## When to Seek Professional Help

While Solution-Focused Therapy techniques help manage anxiety, self-help strategies may not always be sufficient. There are times when seeking professional help is necessary.

Suppose anxiety significantly interferes with daily life and functioning, causing distress or making it difficult to fulfill responsibilities at work, school, or in relationships. In that case, it may be time to seek additional support.

The severity and duration of anxiety symptoms are also important considerations. If anxiety symptoms are severe, persistent, or worsening despite efforts to manage them, professional help may be necessary. If anxiety is accompanied by other concerning symptoms such as depression, substance abuse, or thoughts of self-harm, seeking professional help is critical.

When seeking professional help for anxiety, finding a qualified

Solution-Focused therapist is important. While many therapists may incorporate some Solution-Focused techniques, not all have specialized training in this approach. Individuals can ask for referrals from their primary care physician or search online directories such as the Psychology Today Therapy Directory or the Solution-Focused Brief Therapy Association website to find a qualified Solution-Focused therapist.

When interviewing potential therapists, individuals can ask about their training and experience with Solution-Focused Therapy and their approach to treating anxiety. Finding a therapist who is a good fit in terms of personality, communication style, and overall approach to treatment is also important.

Solution-Focused Therapy offers a powerful approach to managing anxiety. By shifting focus from problems to desired outcomes, strengths, and solutions, SFT helps individuals develop a more proactive mindset for managing anxiety.

This chapter explored the fundamental principles and techniques of Solution-Focused Therapy, including the Miracle Question, Scaling Questions, Exception Finding, and Goal Setting. It also discussed strategies for integrating these techniques into daily life, such as practicing solution-focused thinking, keeping a solutions journal, enlisting support from others, and maintaining progress through self-care and persistence.

Overcoming anxiety is a journey that requires ongoing effort and commitment. There may be setbacks and challenges, but by maintaining a solution-oriented mindset and seeking professional help, individuals can continue progressing and achieving their goals.

Readers are encouraged to approach managing anxiety with curiosity, compassion, and a commitment to finding what works for them. By embracing the principles and techniques of Solution-Focused Therapy and integrating them into daily life, individuals can develop a more empowered approach to managing anxiety and creating positive change.

# Week 8 Self-Help guide

## Solution –Focused Methods to Address Anxiety

Solution-focused therapy provides a practical approach to managing anxiety. This week-long self-help guide introduces key principles and techniques of solution-focused therapy, presenting strategies for shifting focus from anxiety-related problems to solutions. The guide explores goal setting, teaching how to identify and prioritize desired outcomes. It focuses on exceptions, examining times when anxiety is less severe and how to replicate those conditions. The guide introduces scaling questions, a tool for measuring progress and identifying small, achievable steps forward. It teaches the miracle question, a technique for envisioning a future without anxiety and working backward to identify necessary changes. The guide explores externalization, a method for separating oneself from anxiety and gaining a new perspective. It focuses on building resilience by identifying and leveraging personal strengths. The guide summarizes the key principles and techniques, providing a roadmap for ongoing progress. By incorporating these solution-focused strategies into daily life, individuals can develop a more empowered, proactive approach to managing anxiety.

# Week 8 Day 1

## Miracle Question Visualization

**Objective**: Harness the power of the Miracle Question, a Solution-Focused Therapy technique, to vividly imagine a desired future without anxiety and identify specific goals to work toward.

**Information**: The Miracle Question is a transformative tool that invites you to envision a future where your problems, such as anxiety, have miraculously vanished overnight. By engaging in this imaginative exercise, you can tap into your inner resources and wisdom to identify what a life free from anxiety would look and feel like for you.

This visualization technique helps you shift your focus from the current challenges of anxiety to a more positive, solution-oriented perspective. By exploring the details of your miracle day, you can gain clarity on the specific changes you desire in various aspects of your life, such as relationships, work, self-care, and personal growth.

The insights gained from the Miracle Question visualization can serve as a powerful guide for setting meaningful goals and identifying the small, manageable steps needed to move closer to your desired future. By regularly envisioning and connecting with this ideal scenario, you can cultivate hope, motivation, and a clear sense of direction in your journey toward managing anxiety.

**Instructions**:

1. Find a quiet, comfortable space where you can relax and focus

without distractions. You may choose to sit or lie down, which-ever allows you to feel most at ease.

2. Close your eyes and take a few deep, slow breaths to center your-self and let go of any tension or preoccupations. Allow yourself to fully arrive in the present moment.

3. Imagine that while you sleep tonight, a miracle occurs, and your anxiety completely disappears. When you wake up in the morn-ing, you discover that your life is free from anxiety's grip.

4. In your mind's eye, explore what this miracle day looks and feels like. Consider the following questions to guide your visu-alization:

    ◦ What is the first thing you notice that tells you the miracle has happened?
    ◦ How do you feel physically, emotionally, and mentally?
    ◦ What are you doing differently throughout your day?
    ◦ How are your interactions with others (family, friends, colleagues) different?
    ◦ What new activities or experiences do you engage in?
    ◦ How do you approach challenges or stressful situations?
    ◦ What positive changes do you notice in your self-talk and thoughts?

5. Allow yourself to fully immerse in the sensations, emotions, and details of this miracle day. Notice the small and significant changes that have taken place, and the sense of freedom and possibility that comes with a life unburdened by anxiety.

6. When you feel ready, gently open your eyes and return to the present moment. Take a few deep breaths to ground yourself.

7. In your journal or on a piece of paper, write about your miracle day experience in as much detail as possible. Capture the specific changes you noticed, the feelings you experienced, and the new possibilities that emerged.

**Reflection**: Take a moment to reflect on your Miracle Question visu-alization experience. Consider the following questions:

- How did it feel to imagine a life free from anxiety?
- What were the most significant or meaningful changes you noticed in your miracle day?
- What new insights or realizations did you gain about your desired future and the possibilities that exist for you?
- How can you use this experience as a source of inspiration and motivation in your journey toward managing anxiety?

**Integration**: Use your Miracle Question visualization as a powerful tool for setting specific, achievable goals in your anxiety management journey. Review the details of your miracle day and identify the key changes or experiences that resonated with you most.

Based on these insights, create a list of specific, measurable goals that align with your vision of a life free from anxiety. Break these goals down into small, manageable steps that you can start working on daily.

Regularly revisit your Miracle Question visualization and connect with the feelings of possibility and empowerment it evokes. Use this as a source of inspiration and guidance as you take consistent action toward your goals and desired future.

Remember, the Miracle Question is not about creating a perfect life overnight but rather about tapping into your inner wisdom and resources to identify what a more fulfilling, anxiety-free life could look like for you. By consistently working toward this vision, with self-compassion and patience, you can gradually transform your relationship with anxiety and create meaningful, lasting change.

# Week 8 Day 2

## Discovering Hidden Strengths and Resources through Exception Finding

**Objective**: Utilize the Solution-Focused Therapy technique of Exception Finding to identify times when anxiety is less severe or absent, and explore the unique factors contributing to these experiences, ultimately uncovering hidden strengths and resources.

**Information**: Exception Finding is a powerful tool that shifts the focus from the problem of anxiety to the times when it is less severe or absent. By exploring these exceptions in detail, you can gain valuable insights into the strategies, resources, and circumstances that contribute to better managing anxiety.

Exceptions are the moments, however brief or infrequent, when the problem is not as severe or is absent altogether. These instances hold the key to understanding what works for you in reducing anxiety and can serve as a foundation for building future success.

When engaging in Exception Finding, it's essential to approach the process with curiosity and openness. By asking yourself detailed questions about the exception, you can uncover the specific factors that made a difference, such as your thoughts, actions, environment, or support system.

As you identify these factors, you can begin to recognize the hidden strengths and resources that you already possess in managing anxiety.

These insights can be empowering, as they demonstrate your ability to influence your experience of anxiety positively.

By exploring exceptions, you can also challenge the belief that anxiety is constant and unmanageable. Recognizing that there are times when anxiety is less severe can instill hope and motivation, as it reveals the possibility of change and growth.

**Instructions:**

1. Reflect on a recent situation or moment when your anxiety was less severe or absent altogether. This could be a brief instance or a more extended period.
2. In your journal or on a piece of paper, write down a detailed description of this exception. Consider the following questions to guide your exploration:
    ○ What was different about this situation compared to times when anxiety is more severe?
    ○ What were you doing, thinking, or feeling during this time?
    ○ Who were you with, if anyone, and how did their presence impact your anxiety?
    ○ What was your environment like, and how did it contribute to your experience?
    ○ What specific actions, if any, did you take that helped manage your anxiety?
3. As you write, aim to capture as many details as possible about the exception. The more specific and comprehensive your description, the more insights you can gain.
4. Once you have thoroughly described the exception, review your notes and identify any specific strategies, resources, or strengths that contributed to the reduced anxiety. These could be internal factors, such as coping mechanisms or self-talk, or external factors, such as support from others or environmental modifications.

5. Make a list of these strategies, resources, and strengths, and consider how you can apply them to other situations where you typically experience anxiety.

**Reflection**: Take a moment to reflect on your Exception Finding experience. Consider the following questions:

- What new insights or realizations did you gain about your ability to manage anxiety?
- What specific strategies, resources, or strengths did you identify that contributed to the exception?
- How did it feel to recognize these hidden strengths and resources within yourself?
- What did you learn about the potential for change and growth in your relationship with anxiety?

**Integration**: Integrate the insights and strategies gained from Exception Finding into your daily life and anxiety management plan. Consider the following steps:

1. Review the list of strategies, resources, and strengths you identified during the exercise.
2. Choose one or two that resonate with you and feel most applicable to your current challenges with anxiety.
3. Brainstorm ways to incorporate these strategies or resources into your daily routines or anxiety-provoking situations. This could involve practicing a specific coping technique, seeking support from others, or modifying your environment.
4. Set small, achievable goals for implementing these strategies consistently. Start with manageable steps and gradually build upon your successes.
5. Regularly reflect on your progress and the impact of utilizing your identified strengths and resources. Celebrate your successes and use any setbacks as opportunities for learning and refinement.

Remember, Exception Finding is an ongoing process. As you continue to explore and learn from the times when anxiety is less severe, you can continually expand your repertoire of effective strategies and deepen your understanding of your own resilience and capacity for change.

By integrating Exception Finding into your anxiety management journey, you can cultivate a more empowered, solution-focused mindset that recognizes your inherent strengths and resources in the face of challenges. This shift in perspective can foster hope, motivation, and a greater sense of control over your experience with anxiety.

# Week 8 Day 3

## Measuring and Managing Anxiety with Scaling Questions

**Objective**: Utilize Scaling Questions, a Solution-Focused Therapy technique, to assess the severity of anxiety, identify specific strategies for improvement, and track progress over time.

**Information**: Scaling Questions are a powerful tool for gaining a more nuanced understanding of your anxiety and developing targeted strategies for managing it effectively. By rating your anxiety on a scale from 0 to 10, you can create a clear, measurable representation of your current experience.

The scale serves as a reference point, with 0 representing no anxiety at all and 10 representing the worst anxiety imaginable. By assigning a specific number to your anxiety level, you can begin to track changes and progress over time.

Scaling Questions go beyond merely measuring the severity of anxiety; they also encourage a solution-focused mindset. By imagining what it would take to move up one point on the scale, you can identify specific strategies, resources, or changes that could help alleviate your anxiety.

This process of envisioning improvement helps shift your focus from the problem to potential solutions. By breaking down the larger goal of managing anxiety into smaller, incremental steps, you can develop a more manageable and achievable plan for progress.

Scaling Questions also provide an opportunity for self-reflection and insight. As you consider your current rating and the factors influencing it, you may gain a deeper understanding of the specific triggers, thoughts, or situations contributing to your anxiety.

By regularly using Scaling Questions to assess your anxiety and track your progress, you can develop a more empowered, proactive approach to managing your mental health. This tool allows you to recognize patterns, celebrate successes, and adjust your strategies as needed.

**Instructions**:

1. Take a moment to reflect on your current experience of anxiety. Consider the thoughts, feelings, and physical sensations you are experiencing.
2. On a scale from 0 to 10, with 0 being no anxiety at all and 10 being the worst anxiety imaginable, rate your current level of anxiety.
3. In your journal or on a piece of paper, write down the number you have assigned to your current anxiety level.
4. Below your rating, write down any thoughts, feelings, or observations that come up for you as you consider your current anxiety level. This could include specific triggers, challenges, or factors contributing to your anxiety.
5. Now, imagine moving up one point on the scale. For example, if you rated your current anxiety as a 6, consider what it would take to reach a 7.
6. Write down what would be different at this higher rating. What specific changes, strategies, or resources would help you achieve this improvement? Consider factors such as coping techniques, support systems, lifestyle changes, or mindset shifts.
7. Break down these strategies or resources into specific, actionable steps. Identify what you can do in the short-term and long-term to work towards this one-point improvement.

**Reflection**: Take a moment to reflect on your experience with Scaling Questions. Consider the following questions:

- What insights did you gain about your current level of anxiety and the factors influencing it?
- What specific strategies or resources did you identify for moving up one point on the scale?
- How did it feel to envision improvement and break it down into manageable steps?
- What did you learn about your own capacity for change and growth in managing anxiety?

**Integration**: Integrate the strategies and resources you identified through Scaling Questions into your daily life and anxiety management plan. Consider the following steps:

1. Review the specific, actionable steps you identified for moving up one point on the anxiety scale.
2. Prioritize these steps based on their potential impact and feasibility. Choose one or two to focus on initially.
3. Develop a plan for implementing these strategies consistently. Set realistic goals and timelines for each step.
4. Regularly reassess your anxiety level using the scaling question. Notice any changes or improvements, and celebrate your progress.
5. As you make progress or encounter challenges, adjust your strategies and goals as needed. Use the scaling question as a tool for ongoing self-reflection and course correction.

Remember, Scaling Questions are a versatile and dynamic tool. As you become more comfortable with this technique, you can adapt it to various aspects of your anxiety management journey.

For example, you can use scaling questions to assess your confidence in managing anxiety, your motivation for change, or your satisfaction with your progress. By regularly incorporating this tool into your self-reflection practice, you can gain valuable insights and maintain a solution-focused, growth-oriented mindset.

Scaling Questions empower you to take an active role in understanding and managing your anxiety. By breaking down the complex experience of anxiety into a measurable scale, you can develop a more concrete, actionable plan for improvement. This process fosters a sense of control, self-efficacy, and hope in the face of challenges.

As you integrate Scaling Questions into your anxiety management toolbox, remember to approach the process with patience, self-compassion, and a willingness to learn and adapt. Celebrate your successes, no matter how small, and use setbacks as opportunities for growth and refinement. With consistent practice and a solution-focused mindset, you can harness the power of Scaling Questions to create meaningful, lasting change in your relationship with anxiety.

# Week 8 Day 4

## SMART Goals for Anxiety Management

**Objective**: Develop specific, achievable goals for managing anxiety and create a structured plan to reach them using the SMART goal framework.

**Information**: Goal setting is a crucial element of Solution-Focused Therapy, providing direction and purpose in the anxiety management journey. The SMART goal framework ensures that goals are Specific, Measurable, Achievable, Relevant, and Time-bound, making them more effective and manageable.

Specific goals clearly define the desired outcome, while measurable goals allow for tracking progress. Achievable goals are realistic and attainable, considering available resources and constraints. Relevant goals align with personal values and the overall aim of reducing anxiety. Time-bound goals have a clear timeline for completion, promoting accountability and motivation.

By breaking down larger goals into smaller, manageable steps, the process of working towards them becomes less overwhelming. This approach also allows for celebrating small successes along the way, maintaining momentum and building self-efficacy.

**Instructions**:

1. Identify a specific area of your anxiety management you'd like

to focus on, such as reducing avoidance behaviors or improving self-care.

2. Craft a SMART goal related to this area. Ensure your goal is:
   ○ Specific: Clearly define what you want to achieve.
   ○ Measurable: Identify how you will track your progress.
   ○ Achievable: Ensure the goal is realistic within your current resources and constraints.
   ○ Relevant: Confirm the goal aligns with your values and overall anxiety management objectives.
   ○ Time-bound: Set a specific timeline for achieving the goal.
3. Break your SMART goal down into smaller, manageable steps. Identify the specific actions you'll take to work towards your goal.
4. Create a timeline for achieving each of these smaller steps, setting specific target dates for completion.
5. Identify potential obstacles or challenges that may arise as you work towards your goal. Brainstorm strategies for overcoming these barriers.

**Reflection**: Reflect on your experience setting a SMART goal for managing anxiety. Consider how having a specific, achievable goal impacts your motivation and confidence. What challenges do you anticipate as you work towards this goal, and how will you address them?

**Integration**: Begin working on your SMART goal, focusing on one small step at a time. Regularly review your progress and celebrate your successes, no matter how small. If needed, adjust your plan based on your experiences, while maintaining a commitment to your overall goal.

# Week 8 Day 5

## Harnessing Personal Strengths and Resources

**Objective**: Identify and activate personal strengths and resources to build resilience and confidence in managing anxiety.

**Information**: Resource Activation, a key technique in Solution-Focused Therapy, involves recognizing and mobilizing existing strengths and resources to cope with challenges. By focusing on what's already working and available, individuals can build a more empowered and resilient approach to anxiety management.

Personal strengths and resources can take many forms, such as skills, knowledge, positive relationships, past successes, and character traits. These assets can provide a foundation for coping with anxiety and building confidence in one's ability to manage challenges.

Activating these strengths and resources involves consciously identifying them and finding ways to apply them in daily life and anxiety-provoking situations. By leveraging existing capacities, individuals can develop a stronger sense of self-efficacy and resilience.

**Instructions**:

1. Brainstorm a list of your personal strengths and resources. Consider skills, knowledge, positive relationships, past successes, and character traits that help you cope with challenges.
2. Choose one strength or resource from your list that you'd like to focus on activating today.

3. Identify specific ways you can apply this strength or resource in your daily life, particularly in situations that typically trigger anxiety.
4. Create a plan for actively using this strength or resource. Set intentions for when and how you'll apply it.
5. At the end of the day, reflect on your experiences activating this strength or resource. Note any positive impacts or insights gained.

**Reflection**: Consider what you learned about your personal strengths and resources through this exercise. How did it feel to consciously activate and apply them? How might continuing to harness these assets support your anxiety management?

**Integration**: Develop a habit of regularly identifying and activating your strengths and resources. Incorporate this practice into your daily routine, noting how it impacts your overall well-being and ability to cope with anxiety.

# Week 8 Day 6

## *Strengthening Coping Skills through Practice*

**Objective**: Identify and practice a specific coping skill to build mastery and confidence in managing anxiety.

**Information**: Coping skills are specific strategies or techniques used to manage anxiety symptoms and promote emotional regulation. Regular practice of these skills can enhance their effectiveness and build a stronger sense of self-efficacy in coping with anxiety.

Examples of coping skills include deep breathing exercises, progressive muscle relaxation, mindfulness meditation, grounding techniques, and cognitive reframing. The key is to find strategies that resonate personally and to practice them consistently, even in the absence of acute anxiety.

By setting aside dedicated time to practice coping skills, individuals can develop a stronger mastery of these tools. Regular practice also helps to make the application of these skills more automatic and accessible in moments of heightened anxiety.

**Instructions:**

1. Identify a specific coping skill you'd like to practice today. Consider strategies you've found helpful in the past or new techniques you'd like to explore.
2. Set aside 10-15 minutes in your day to practice this coping skill. Choose a time when you can focus without distractions.

3. Before beginning your practice, note your current emotional state and any anxiety symptoms.
4. Practice your chosen coping skill for the allotted time. Focus on fully engaging with the experience.
5. After your practice, note any changes in your emotional state, anxiety symptoms, or overall sense of well-being.

**Reflection**: Reflect on your experience practicing this coping skill. What felt effective or challenging about the process? What did you notice about your body's response? How might regular practice support your anxiety management?

**Integration**: Commit to practicing your chosen coping skill regularly, ideally daily. Experiment with applying the skill in various situations, both calm and anxious. Note any positive impacts on your overall anxiety levels and coping abilities.

# Week 8 Day 7

## Sustaining Progress and Navigating Setbacks

**Objective**: Develop a personalized plan for maintaining progress and coping with potential setbacks in anxiety management.

**Information**: Maintaining progress in anxiety management is an ongoing process that requires continued effort and strategies for coping with setbacks. By developing a personalized maintenance plan, individuals can proactively support their well-being and build resilience.

A maintenance plan may include regular self-care practices, ongoing use of effective coping skills, staying connected to supportive people, and monitoring signs of increased anxiety. It's also important to have a plan for responding to potential setbacks, which are a normal part of the growth process.

Preparing for setbacks involves identifying potential triggers, recognizing early warning signs, and having a repertoire of strategies to cope with heightened anxiety. This may include reaching out for support, adjusting self-care practices, or re-engaging with therapeutic tools.

By anticipating challenges and having a plan in place, individuals can feel more equipped to navigate difficulties and maintain their progress in anxiety management.

**Instructions**:

1. Reflect on the strategies, techniques, and insights that have been most helpful for you in managing anxiety over the past week.

2. Create a list of self-care practices and coping skills you'd like to continue using regularly to maintain your progress.
3. Identify potential triggers or high-stress situations that could increase your anxiety. Brainstorm specific strategies for coping with these scenarios.
4. Develop a plan for recognizing and responding to early warning signs of increased anxiety. What actions will you take to prioritize self-care and use your coping skills?
5. Identify your support system and consider how you can reach out for help when needed. Who can you turn to for emotional support or practical assistance?

**Reflection**: Reflect on your key takeaways and insights from the past week. What have you learned about yourself and your relationship with anxiety? How can you integrate these learnings into your ongoing anxiety management?

**Integration**: Implement your personalized maintenance plan, committing to regular self-care and use of coping skills. Regularly check in with yourself, noting your progress and any areas needing additional support. Remember to be compassionate with yourself during setbacks, recognizing them as opportunities for growth and recommitment to your well-being.

# Week 8 Tracking Progress

Week 8: Week 8 has emphasized solution-focused strategies. Reflect on your progress by identifying your position on the bridge and rating your anxiety level on the 0-10 scale. Recognize the practical steps you've taken toward resolving problems and creating meaningful change.

**Instructions**:

1. Take a moment to reflect on your progress and experiences.
2. Refer to the bridge illustration below.
3. Consider where you currently stand on your journey.
4. Place a mark on the bridge representing your current position.
5. Next, rate where your average anxiety level has been over this week.
6. Record your anxiety rating on the provided 0-10 scale, with 0 being no anxiety and 10 being the most intense anxiety you've experienced.
7. Reflect and journal.

**Reflection**: After marking your bridge position and anxiety rating, reflect on your progress. Examine skills learned, challenges faced, and changes in thoughts and behaviors. Journal your insights and observations. Identify successes, challenges, and areas requiring more attention. Determine if you need to slow down, revisit previous weeks or skills, or seek professional help to maintain progress. Assess your overall progress and consider if professional support is needed or how it's contributing to your journey.

| 0 | 1 | 2 | 3 | 4 | 5 | 6 | 7 | 8 | 9 | 10 |
|---|---|---|---|---|---|---|---|---|---|----|

No
Anxiety

Moderate
Anxiety

High
Anxiety

# 13

# *Emotional Intelligence*

Emotional Intelligence (EI) is the ability to recognize, understand, and manage one's own emotions, as well as the emotions of others. It plays a crucial role in overall mental health and well-being. Individuals with high EI are better equipped to navigate life's challenges, build strong relationships, and succeed in various aspects of their lives.

One area where EI is particularly relevant is in managing anxiety. Anxiety disorders are among the most common mental health issues, affecting millions of people worldwide. By developing and applying EI skills, individuals can gain a deeper understanding of their anxiety, learn effective coping strategies, and ultimately reduce the impact of anxiety on their daily lives.

This chapter will explore the concept of Emotional Intelligence in-depth, focusing on its four key domains and the specific skills associated with each. It will also examine the relationship between EI and anxiety, highlighting how EI can be a powerful tool in overcoming anxiety and promoting overall mental health. Through practical strategies and insights, readers will gain the knowledge and tools needed to enhance their own EI and take control of their emotional well-being.

## Understanding Emotional Intelligence

Emotional Intelligence consists of four key domains: self-awareness, self-management, social awareness, and relationship management. Each domain encompasses specific skills that contribute to overall EI.

Self-awareness involves recognizing and understanding one's emotions and the triggers and patterns associated with those emotions. This domain includes emotional self-awareness, accurate self-assessment, and self-confidence.

Self-management builds upon self-awareness and focuses on effectively regulating and controlling one's emotions. Essential skills in this domain include emotional self-control, adaptability, achievement orientation, and positive outlook.

Social awareness extends beyond the self and involves the ability to recognize and understand the emotions of others. This domain includes skills such as empathy, organizational awareness, and service orientation.

Relationship management combines the skills from the previous domains to build and maintain strong, positive relationships with others. This domain includes skills such as influence, conflict management, teamwork, and inspirational leadership.

Individuals with high Emotional Intelligence experience numerous benefits across various aspects of their lives. They tend to have better mental health and well-being, as they are more adept at managing stress and building resilience. They also enjoy more fulfilling interpersonal relationships, as they can communicate effectively, resolve conflicts, and build trust. Additionally, high EI is associated with increased success and performance in both personal and professional settings, as emotionally intelligent individuals can better navigate challenges, adapt to change, and inspire and motivate others.

## Emotional Intelligence and Anxiety

Emotional Intelligence plays a significant role in recognizing and understanding anxiety. Individuals with high EI are better equipped to identify the physical, emotional, and cognitive symptoms of anxiety, such as increased heart rate, feelings of worry or fear, and difficulty concentrating. They are also more attuned to the specific triggers and situations that contribute to their anxiety.

By developing EI skills, individuals can learn to manage and reduce their anxiety symptoms effectively. Self-awareness allows them to recognize the early signs of anxiety and take proactive steps to address it. Self-management skills, such as emotion regulation and stress-reduction techniques, help individuals control their anxiety and maintain a sense of calm and focus.

Social awareness skills, such as empathy and perspective-taking, can also be valuable in managing anxiety. By understanding the emotions and experiences of others, individuals can gain a more balanced perspective on their challenges and feel less alone in their struggles.

Relationship management skills, such as effective communication and conflict resolution, can help individuals build a strong support network and navigate difficult situations more easily. This sense of connection and support can be a powerful buffer against anxiety and promote overall mental health.

Conversely, low Emotional Intelligence can contribute to increased anxiety and poor mental health outcomes. Individuals with low EI may struggle to recognize and understand their emotions, leading to a sense of overwhelm and lack of control. They may also have difficulty regulating their emotions and may engage in unhealthy coping mechanisms, such as avoidance or substance abuse.

Low EI can also impact social relationships, leading to misunderstandings, conflicts, and a lack of support. This social isolation and lack of connection can further exacerbate anxiety and contribute to a negative cycle of emotional distress.

## Developing Self-Awareness

Developing self-awareness is a critical first step in enhancing Emotional Intelligence and managing anxiety. Self-awareness involves the ability to identify and label one's own emotions accurately. This skill allows individuals to recognize the specific emotions they are experiencing, such as fear, worry, or frustration, and to understand the intensity and duration of those emotions.

To develop self-awareness, individuals can practice mindfulness and self-reflection. Mindfulness involves paying attention to the present moment without judgment or distraction. By observing their thoughts, feelings, and physical sensations, individuals can better understand their emotional experiences.

Self-reflection involves considering one's thoughts, feelings, and behaviors and exploring the underlying patterns and triggers associated with those experiences. Journaling, meditation, and therapy can all be practical tools for promoting self-reflection and gaining insight into one's emotional life.

Recognizing emotional triggers and patterns is another route to self-awareness. Triggers are specific situations, people, or experiences that provoke strong emotional responses. By identifying these triggers, individuals can develop strategies for managing their emotional reactions and reducing their anxiety.

Seeking feedback from others can also be a valuable way to develop self-awareness. Asking trusted friends, family members, or colleagues for their observations and insights can provide a different perspective on one's emotional patterns and behaviors. This feedback can help individuals to identify blind spots or areas for growth and to develop a more accurate and comprehensive understanding of their emotional experiences.

## Enhancing Self-Management Skills

Self-management skills build upon self-awareness and enable individuals to regulate their emotions effectively, particularly in the face of stress and anxiety. Emotion regulation techniques, such as cognitive reappraisal, acceptance and commitment, and relaxation strategies, can help individuals manage their emotional responses and maintain a sense of calm and control.

Cognitive reappraisal involves reframing one's thoughts and perceptions about a situation to alter its emotional impact. By challenging negative or anxious thoughts and considering alternative perspectives, individuals can reduce the intensity of their emotional reactions and develop a more balanced outlook.

Acceptance and commitment techniques focus on accepting one's emotions without judgment or resistance while committing to actions that align with one's values and goals. This approach can help individuals to reduce the struggle against difficult emotions and to focus on constructive behaviors that promote well-being.

Relaxation and stress-reduction strategies, such as deep breathing, progressive muscle relaxation, and visualization, can help individuals calm their physiological responses to stress and anxiety. These techniques can be practiced regularly to build resilience and improve emotional regulation.

Impulse control and delay of gratification are also important self-management skills. Individuals can develop greater self-discipline and emotional stability by resisting immediate urges and temptations in favor of long-term goals and values.

Adaptability and flexibility are self-management skills that enable individuals to navigate change and uncertainty easily. By developing the ability to adjust one's thoughts, emotions, and behaviors in response to new situations and challenges, individuals can reduce anxiety and maintain a sense of control and resilience.

Cultivating optimism and positive self-talk can also be powerful tools for self-management. By focusing on the positive aspects of a situation and engaging in encouraging and supportive inner dialogue, individuals can boost their mood, reduce their anxiety, and develop a more resilient mindset.

Social awareness is an integral part of emotional intelligence, focusing on our ability to understand the social dynamics and emotional states of those around us. This awareness enhances our capacity to interact effectively and empathetically in various social contexts. Here, we delve into four crucial aspects of improving social awareness.

Empathy, the ability to comprehend and share the feelings of another, is at the core of social awareness. It involves more than just recognizing someone else's emotions; it requires immersing oneself in their emotional experience. Perspective-taking, a related skill, involves seeing situations from others' viewpoints. Enhancing these abilities can be achieved through active listening and engaging in dialogues that explore diverse personal experiences, thus fostering deeper interpersonal connections and understanding.

Nonverbal communication, including facial expressions, body language, and eye contact, plays a significant role in understanding others' thoughts and feelings. Improving our ability to interpret these cues requires mindful observation and practice. Activities such as watching films or plays with the sound off can sharpen our skills in reading these nonverbal signals, which are often more telling than words alone.

Social norms and expectations guide behavior in various groups and cultures, influencing interactions and social acceptance. Awareness of and sensitivity to these norms can prevent misunderstandings and foster smoother interactions. This understanding can be enhanced through cultural studies, travel, and social interactions that expose one to diverse social systems and values.

Appreciating diversity involves recognizing and valuing the differences that make each culture unique. This appreciation is crucial in a globalized world, leading to more inclusive and effective interactions. Educational programs, workshops, and direct engagement with diverse groups can deepen our understanding and appreciation of cultural differences, enriching our social interactions and expanding our worldviews.

Improving social awareness involves understanding the emotional and social dynamics that influence human interactions. By cultivating empathy, recognizing nonverbal cues, understanding social norms, and appreciating cultural diversity, we enhance our ability to navigate and thrive in our social environments.

***Strengthening Relationship Management Skills.*** Relationship management, a fundamental component of emotional intelligence, involves building and maintaining healthy, supportive relationships. This skill set is critical for achieving personal and professional success and fostering environments of cooperation and respect. The following sections outline essential techniques and strategies for enhancing relationship management capabilities.

*Effective Communication Techniques.* Effective communication is the backbone of solid relationships. It encompasses several vital techniques:

1. *Active Listening*: More than just hearing words, active listening involves fully concentrating on the speaker, understanding their message, providing feedback, and withholding judgment. This can be practiced by summarizing the speaker's words and asking clarifying questions to ensure complete comprehension.
2. *Assertiveness:* This involves expressing one's thoughts, feelings, and needs in a clear, direct, and respectful manner. It's about being honest and straightforward while still valuing the feelings and rights of others. Role-playing scenarios can help individuals practice assertiveness in a controlled, reflective manner.
3. *Conflict Resolution:* Effective conflict resolution requires identifying the root cause of a conflict, actively listening to different perspectives, and working collaboratively to find a mutually satisfying solution. Techniques such as mediation training and conflict resolution workshops can enhance these skills.

*Building and Maintaining Trust.* Trust is crucial for stable relationships and involves consistency, reliability, and integrity. It can be built and maintained by consistently being reliable in actions, transparent in motives, and sincere in communications. Regular team-building activities and open discussion forums can reinforce trust among group members.

*Leadership and Influence.* Good leaders inspire and motivate others while fostering an environment of accountability and empowerment. Leadership involves not just directing or managing but also inspiring trust and enthusiasm. Developing leadership skills can include mentorship programs, leadership workshops, and practical leadership roles in various settings.

***Teamwork and Collaboration.*** Successful teamwork involves working with others towards a common goal while respecting diverse viewpoints and sharing responsibilities. It requires clear communication, shared leadership, and cooperative problem-solving. Team-building exercises and collaborative projects are effective ways to enhance these skills.

In strengthening relationship management skills, focusing on open communication, trust-building, leadership development, and effective teamwork is vital. These components help individuals manage and deepen their relationships, leading to greater personal and professional success. These skills can be continuously improved through deliberate practice and engagement in various interactive settings, contributing significantly to one's emotional intelligence and overall life satisfaction.

## Strategies for Enhancing Emotional Intelligence

The development of emotional intelligence (EI) is an ongoing process that requires dedication and various approaches to ensure personal growth and effective interpersonal relationships. Here, we discuss several methods to enhance EI, focusing on experiential and reflective practices.

Engagement in structured EI training programs and workshops provides a foundational understanding and practical skills in emotional intelligence. These programs are designed to facilitate learning through interactive sessions that typically involve role-playing, simulations, and group discussions. These settings offer immediate feedback and insights from peers and instructors, crucial for improving emotional awareness and management skills.

One-on-one coaching or mentoring is a highly personalized approach that helps individuals identify their emotional intelligence strengths and weaknesses. A coach or mentor can guide individuals through personalized challenges and scenarios, offering tailored advice. This personalized attention helps deepen the understanding of emotional intelligence in various real-world contexts.

Experiential learning involves scenarios that mimic real-life interactions and challenges, encouraging participants to practice and refine their EI skills in a controlled environment. Role-playing exercises, in particular, allow individuals to experiment with different approaches to managing emotions, both their own and others, and to see the immediate consequences of these strategies. This method helps consolidate emotional intelligence skills by putting theory into practice.

Journaling is a reflective practice that helps individuals process their emotions and experiences through writing. This method facilitates a deeper exploration of one's emotional responses and the situations that trigger them. Reflective writing can also aid in tracking progress over time and identifying patterns in emotional reactions that may need further development or adjustment.

Broadening one's horizons by seeking diverse experiences and engaging with people from various backgrounds can significantly enhance one's emotional intelligence. Exposure to different cultures, environments, and social settings teaches adaptability and improves understanding and connecting with people with different perspectives and life experiences. This enriches one's social awareness and bolsters overall emotional intelligence by promoting empathy and diverse interpersonal interactions.

In cultivating emotional intelligence through these strategies, the aim is to integrate and apply EI skills in various settings, enhancing personal insight and social interaction capabilities. Each approach provides unique benefits and, when combined, can offer a comprehensive enhancement of one's emotional intelligence.

## Integrating Emotional Intelligence into Daily Life

To effectively integrate emotional intelligence (EI) into daily life, one must actively apply EI skills in both personal and professional spheres, strategically utilize them to address challenges, and commit to ongoing refinement and evaluation of their emotional competencies.

Applying EI enhances understanding and communication in personal relationships, fostering deeper connections through empathy and responsive interactions. Professionally, EI facilitates improved teamwork, efficient conflict resolution, and competent leadership, contributing to a productive workplace environment by understanding and managing emotional dynamics.

Navigating life's challenges and setbacks with EI involves self-awareness and self-regulation to maintain stability and perspective. Recognizing and managing one's emotional reactions to stress can lead to more effective problem-solving and decision-making, keeping one poised under pressure.

Continuous improvement of EI competencies is essential. Regular self-evaluation helps identify strengths and areas needing attention, guiding personal development. This process can be supported by peer feedback, utilizing self-help resources, and occasionally engaging in professional assessments to gain deeper insights.

Additionally, interacting with individuals who exhibit high emotional intelligence provides practical learning opportunities. Observing and engaging with such individuals helps understand effective emotional management and relationship-building practices. These interactions also offer emotional support, further aiding personal growth in EI.

By actively embedding EI into daily activities, individuals can significantly improve their quality of life and interpersonal relations, making emotional intelligence a fundamental part of their ongoing personal development and social interactions.

This discussion on emotional intelligence (EI) underscores its role in enhancing interpersonal interactions and personal growth. Emotional intelligence involves recognizing, understanding, managing, and utilizing emotions effectively, which benefits personal well-being and social relationships.

The development of EI is a continuous, lifelong endeavor enriched by learning and practice. The core competencies of EI, including self-awareness, self-regulation, social awareness, and relationship management, develop through persistent engagement with diverse challenges and experiences.

The strategies discussed for enhancing EI emphasize reflective practice, social engagement, and the pursuit of diverse experiences. Regularly applying these strategies can deepen understanding and improve the quality of both personal and professional interactions.

Further exploration of EI is encouraged, as the rewards extend into many aspects of life. Available resources such as books, workshops, and formal training programs provide structured support for those interested in developing their emotional intelligence. These resources are instrumental for ongoing learning and application of EI skills.

In conclusion, while our exploration here is complete, the journey of understanding and applying emotional intelligence is ongoing. Focusing on and investing in EI can lead to substantial benefits, including enhanced personal satisfaction and professional success.

# Week 9 Self-Help Guide

## *Enhancing Emotional Intelligence to Overcome Anxiety*

Welcome to Week Nine of your journey through understanding and managing anxiety with a focus on enhancing your emotional intelligence. This guide is designed to provide you with daily activities that build upon your ability to understand and regulate your emotions, an essential skill in mitigating feelings of anxiety. Each day's task will challenge you to engage deeply with your feelings and practice strategies to enhance your emotional agility.

At times, anxiety can be overwhelming, leading to acute bouts of panic or distress that may disrupt your daily functioning. In such instances, it is crucial to consider seeking help from a mental health professional. Accessing professional support can provide you with additional strategies and a therapeutic space to explore your anxiety more thoroughly.

By dedicating time each day to develop your emotional intelligence, you will equip yourself with valuable tools to not only confront anxiety but also to enhance your overall mental health. Let's embark on this week of self-discovery and growth together.

# Week 9 Day 1

## Naming Emotions

**Objective:** Enhance your ability to identify and name different emotions as they occur, which is the foundational skill in emotional intelligence necessary for managing anxiety effectively.

**Information:** Recognizing and accurately identifying your emotions is critical because it influences how you perceive the world and react to situations. Emotions color your thoughts and can significantly impact your decisions and interactions with others. By becoming more aware of your emotional states, you can start to understand the triggers behind your feelings, paving the way for better self-regulation and anxiety management.

**Instructions:**

1. **Preparation:** Carry a small notebook or use a digital note-taking app for this exercise.
2. **Monitoring:** Throughout the day, pause at set intervals (e.g., every hour) to reflect on your current emotional state. You can set a timer to remind yourself.
3. **Recording:** When you identify an emotion, record it in your notebook or app. Include:
4. The specific name of the emotion (e.g., joy, frustration, sadness).
   - The intensity of the emotion on a scale from 1 to 10.
   - The context or situation in which the emotion occurred.
   - Your physical responses (e.g., heart racing, stomach tightening).

- Any thoughts that were going through your mind at that moment?

5. **Trigger Identification:** Whenever possible, try to identify what triggered the emotion. Was it something someone said? A particular event? A memory?

6. **Pattern Recognition:** Look for patterns and triggers in various emotions. Are certain times of day more emotionally charged? Do specific environments or people trigger certain feelings?

**Reflection:** At the end of the day, review your entries. Reflect on the following questions:

- Were there any emotions that surprised you?
- What have you learned about how your feelings correlate with different times, situations, or people?
- How do the physical sensations you noted align with different emotional states?

**Integration:** Use the insights gained from today's exercise to begin predicting emotional responses and preparing for them. For instance, if you notice that meetings with a particular colleague often lead to frustration, plan a strategy to manage your emotional response before your next meeting. This might include techniques like deep breathing before the meeting or reframing your expectations.

# Week 9 Day 2

## *Analyzing Emotional Responses*

**Objective:** Develop a deeper understanding of the appropriateness of your emotional responses, focusing on whether these reactions are proportionate to the events that trigger them.

**Information:** Sometimes, our emotional responses can be disproportionate to the reality of the situation, influenced by past experiences, stress levels, or preconceived notions. By analyzing the appropriateness of your reactions, you can start to calibrate your responses to be more in line with the actual circumstances, which is a crucial step in managing anxiety and improving emotional intelligence.

**Instructions:**

1. **Preparation:** Continue using the notebook or digital app from Day 1 for consistency in recording your observations.
2. **Observation and Documentation:** Throughout the day, when you experience a notable emotion, document the following in detail:
    - The emotion felt and its intensity.
    - The triggering event or situation.
    - Your immediate thoughts during the emotional response.
    - The actions you took in response to the emotion.
3. **Evaluation of Proportionality:**
    - For each recorded emotion, assess whether the intensity of

your response felt appropriate to the trigger. Consider if someone else might have responded differently and why.

- ○ Reflect on what factors might have influenced your response—were you tired, hungry, already stressed, or perhaps influenced by past experiences?

4. **Alternative Responses:** For each disproportionate response identified, brainstorm alternative, more proportionate responses. Write down what a more balanced reaction could have looked like and what thoughts or actions might lead to that more balanced reaction in the future.

5. **Plan Implementation:** Select one typical disproportionate emotional response you identified and plan an intervention. For example, if you often react with anger to minor inconveniences, you might plan to take three deep breaths before responding to stressors or to remind yourself of the bigger picture to gain perspective.

**Reflection:** At the end of the day, review the emotions and situations you documented:

- Identify any common themes or triggers that often lead to disproportionate responses.
- Reflect on how these disproportionate responses affect your day-to-day life and relationships.
- Consider the alternative responses you brainstormed: how might implementing these influence your emotional well-being and interactions?

**Integration:** Commit to applying at least one of the alternative responses in an actual situation the next time a similar trigger occurs. Review this commitment in your journal the following morning to reinforce your intention. Continue to monitor this specific emotional response throughout the upcoming days, noting any progress or setbacks in adjusting your reaction.

# Week 9 Day 3

## The Role of Empathy

**Objective:** Enhance your ability to empathize with others, which can lead to better understanding and management of your own emotions, thereby reducing anxiety.

**Information:** Empathy is the ability to understand and share another person's feelings from their point of view. It is a crucial component of emotional intelligence that fosters stronger connections with others and can significantly influence your emotional reactions. Empathy can also serve as a tool for mitigating feelings of isolation or misunderstanding, which are common triggers for anxiety.

**Instructions:**

1. **Preparation:** As in previous weeks, use a dedicated notebook or digital app to record your experiences.
2. **Active Listening and Observation:**
    - Engage in at least one significant conversation each day where the goal is to understand the other person's perspective fully. Choose different people from various aspects of your life to broaden the scope of this exercise.
    - During these conversations, focus on listening rather than responding. Pay attention to verbal and non-verbal cues such as tone of voice, facial expressions, and body language.
3. **Documentation:**

- After each conversation, record what the other person said and how they felt.
- Note your interpretations of their emotional state and the thoughts or events they shared.
- Reflect on how this exercise made you feel and whether it changed your perspective or feelings toward the person or situation discussed.

4. **Empathy Expansion:**
   - Based on your notes, identify areas where you struggled to relate to or understand the other person's perspective.
   - Research or ask questions in follow-up conversations to gain a deeper understanding of these points.

5. **Reflection and Feedback:**
   - Review your interactions at the end of each day and reflect on what you learned about others and yourself through these exercises.
   - If possible, get feedback from the people you conversed with on how they felt about the interaction. Did they feel understood? What could you do better?

**Integration:** Try to apply the insights gained from these exercises to improve your interactions with others daily. Make a conscious effort to employ empathy in situations where you might typically become anxious or reactive, and observe how this affects both your feelings and the outcomes of the interactions.

# Week 9 Day 4

## Emotional Journaling

**Objective:** Develop a habit of emotional journaling to gain insights into your emotional patterns, which can help manage anxiety more effectively by identifying triggers and understanding emotional responses in depth.

**Information:** Journaling provides a reflective space where you can express feelings freely, explore your emotional responses, and discern patterns or triggers in a structured manner. This practice not only aids in emotional release but also fosters self-awareness, a key component in emotional intelligence and anxiety management.

**Instructions:**

1. **Preparation:** Use a designated journal or digital document reserved for this activity to maintain privacy and consistency.
2. **Daily Focus Emotion:**
    ◦ Select the most significant emotion you felt during the day—this could be due to its intensity, the situation's impact, or its novelty.
    ◦ Describe the emotion, including what you think triggered it, how you reacted, and other subsequent emotions.
3. **Contextual Analysis:**
    ◦ Detail the context in which this emotion arose. Include specific factors like time, location, people involved, and what happened immediately before the emotion surfaced.

- Analyze the appropriateness of your emotional response compared to the situation. Consider if external stresses or unrelated thoughts may have influenced your reaction.

4. **Physical Sensations and Actions:**
   - Note any physical sensations associated with the emotion (e.g., tension, nausea, warmth).
   - Record any actions you took in response to the emotion, whether they were constructive or something you might handle differently.

5. **Reflection and Patterns:**
   - Reflect on the emotion and your response to it. Was there something you could learn about yourself from this experience?
   - Look for patterns over the past entries. Do you need to address recurring emotions, triggers, or responses?

6. **Planning for Improvement:**
   - Based on your journal entries, identify one aspect of your emotional response that you wish to improve (e.g., reducing anger outbursts, not jumping to conclusions).
   - Outline a specific plan or strategy to work on this aspect. For instance, if reducing anger is the goal, you might decide to practice counting to ten before responding when you feel angry.

**Integration:** Apply the insights from your journal to better prepare for and respond to similar situations in the future. For example, if you notice that crowded places tend to increase your anxiety, you might plan to use calming techniques before entering such environments. Regularly revisit your journal entries weekly to assess progress and adjust your strategies as needed.

# Week 9 Day 5

## Exploring Emotional Influence

**Objective:** Investigate how emotions influence your decision-making processes, aiming to identify instances where emotions may lead to less optimal choices and learn methods to integrate more rational, balanced decision-making practices.

**Information:** Emotions can significantly impact decisions, sometimes leading to impulsive actions or choices that may not align with long-term goals or values. Understanding the interplay between emotions and decisions is crucial for managing anxiety and improving overall mental well-being. You can make more deliberate, thoughtful choices by becoming aware of these dynamics.

**Instructions:**

1. **Preparation:** Use a journal or digital app to document your decisions and their associated emotions.
2. **Daily Decision Tracking:**
   - Record at least three decisions you make each day, ranging from minor choices (like what to eat for lunch) to more significant decisions (such as handling a work assignment).
   - For each decision, note the following:
     - The decision made.
     - The emotion(s) felt before and after making the decision.
     - The rationale behind your choice, if any.

■ The outcome of the decision.

3. **Emotion-Decision Analysis:**
   - Review each recorded decision and assess how much your emotions influenced the choice.
   - Evaluate whether the decisions driven more strongly by emotions had different outcomes than those made with a more balanced or rational approach.

4. **Identifying Emotional Patterns:**
   - Look for patterns in how certain emotions influence specific types of decisions.
   - Identify whether negative or positive emotions are more likely to sway your decision-making in undesirable ways.

5. **Strategic Response Development:**
   - Based on your analysis, develop strategies for mitigating the undue influence of emotions on critical decisions.
   - These strategies might include taking a timeout to cool down, discussing the decision with a trusted friend for perspective, or writing down the pros and cons to visualize the rational side of the decision.

**Reflection:** At the end of the week, reflect on the following:

- How has your awareness of the emotional influences on your decisions changed?
- What impact have the newly implemented decision-making strategies had on your anxiety levels and overall decision satisfaction?
- What lessons were learned from this week that you can apply moving forward?

**Integration:** Commit to continuing the practice of monitoring your emotional influences on decision-making. Regular reflection can gradually help refine your ability to separate impulsive, emotional reactions from reasoned responses. Incorporate your new strategies into everyday decision-making processes, especially in situations that pro-voke anxiety or emotional responses.

# Week 9 Day 6

## *Managing Stress*

**Objective:** Enhance your ability to manage stress effectively, aiming to reduce its impact on your emotions and overall mental well-being, thereby mitigating anxiety.

**Information:** Effective stress management is essential for maintaining emotional balance and preventing anxiety from becoming overwhelming. Techniques that help manage stress can lead to improved emotional regulation, better focus, and increased resilience in facing daily challenges.

**Instructions:**

1. **Preparation:** Keep your journal or digital app handy to document your experiences and insights from the day's activities.
2. **Stress Reduction Technique Selection:**
   - Choose two to three stress reduction techniques to practice throughout the day. Options might include deep breathing exercises, progressive muscle relaxation, a short walk, or a few minutes of mindful meditation.
3. **Scheduled Practice:**
   - Set specific times to practice each selected technique. Ideally, incorporate these practices when you typically experience higher stress levels (e.g., before a meeting, after a commute, or when transitioning back home from work).
4. **Documentation:**

- Record each instance when you use a stress reduction technique. Note the following:
    - The time and context of the stressor.
    - The specific technique used.
    - Your emotional state before and after the method.
    - Any immediate outcomes noticeable in your stress levels and emotional responses.

5. **Effectiveness Assessment:**
    - Review your entries to assess the effectiveness of each technique. Consider questions like:
        - Which technique had the most noticeable impact on reducing stress?
        - Were there techniques that seemed less effective, and why might that be?
        - How did the stress reduction influence your emotional state and decision-making abilities?

6. **Plan for Regular Integration:**
    - Based on your assessments, decide which techniques you will integrate into your daily routine moving forward.
    - Schedule regular times or triggers (e.g., setting reminders or associating the practice with specific daily activities) to practice the most effective techniques.

**Reflection:** Reflect on how incorporating stress management techniques into your daily routine has affected your overall ability to handle anxiety and emotional ups and downs:

- Have you noticed any changes in your overall emotional stability?
- How have these practices affected your productivity and interpersonal relationships?
- Are there any adjustments you need to make to improve the effectiveness of your stress management?

**Integration:** Commit to maintaining the practice of these stress management techniques. Regular and consistent practice can significantly enhance their effectiveness in reducing stress and anxiety:

- Continuously evaluate the impact of these techniques on your emotional well-being and make adjustments as needed.
- Consider incorporating new techniques as you become more adept at recognizing your stress signals and needs.

# Week 9 Day 7

## *Positive Emotional Reinforcement*

**Objective:** Cultivate and reinforce positive emotional experiences to enhance mood, reduce anxiety, and improve overall mental well-being.

**Information:** Focusing on positive emotions such as joy, gratitude, and contentment can offset the intensity of negative emotions and provide a more balanced emotional landscape. This practice improves mood and contributes to resilience, helping you manage stress and anxiety more effectively.

**Instructions:**

1. **Preparation:** Use your dedicated journal or digital app to document your emotional experiences, focusing mainly on positive emotions for this day.
2. **Identification and Documentation:**
    - Throughout the day, actively look for moments that trigger positive emotions. These might include interactions with others, personal achievements, or simple pleasures like enjoying nature or a favorite activity.
    - Document each positive emotional experience, noting:
        - The specific emotion felt (e.g., happiness, pride, relief).
        - The context or situation that triggered the emotion.
        - Your physical and psychological responses.
3. **Enhancement Techniques:**
    - For each positive emotion identified, apply techniques

that enhance or prolong these feelings. Techniques might include sharing the experience with someone else, reflecting on the enjoyable situation, or even taking a moment to savor the emotion quietly.

4. **Reflection and Analysis:**
   - Review your documented positive emotions and the contexts in which they occurred.
   - Reflect on how these emotions impacted your overall mood and interactions with others.
   - Analyze the effectiveness of the enhancement techniques you employed. Determine which techniques were most effective in prolonging or intensifying the positive experiences.

5. **Plan for Future Application:**
   - Identify common themes or situations that frequently led to positive emotions. Make a plan to incorporate more of these situations into your routine intentionally.
   - Schedule regular activities known to evoke these positive emotions, whether daily, weekly, or monthly.

**Integration:** Commit to identifying and enhancing positive emotional experiences daily. Regular acknowledgment and reinforcement of positive emotions can shift your overall emotional perspective and reduce the frequency and intensity of negative responses. Utilize your insights to create environments and interactions that foster these positive experiences.

**Reflection:** Reflect on the overall impact of this focus on positive emotions:

- How has emphasizing positive emotions affected your anxiety levels and general disposition?
- What changes have you noticed in responding to stress or negative situations?

- Are there particular positive emotions or activities you want to focus on more intensively going forward?

# Week 9 Tracking Progress

As you complete this week's exercises on emotional intelligence, evaluate your progress. Mark your current position on the bridge and rate your anxiety level on the 0-10 scale. Acknowledge the growth in your understanding and management of emotions.

**Instructions**:

1. Take a moment to reflect on your progress and experiences.
2. Refer to the bridge illustration below.
3. Consider where you currently stand on your journey.
4. Place a mark on the bridge representing your current position.
5. Next, rate where your average anxiety level has been over this week.
6. Record your anxiety rating on the provided 0-10 scale, with 0 being no anxiety and 10 being the most intense anxiety you've experienced.
7. Reflect and journal.

**Reflection**: After marking your bridge position and anxiety rating, reflect on your progress. Examine skills learned, challenges faced, and changes in thoughts and behaviors. Journal your insights and observations. Identify successes, challenges, and areas requiring more attention. Determine if you need to slow down, revisit previous weeks or skills, or seek professional help to maintain progress. Assess your overall progress and consider if professional support is needed or how it's contributing to your journey.

| 0 | 1 | 2 | 3 | 4 | 5 | 6 | 7 | 8 | 9 | 10 |

No
Anxiety

Moderate
Anxiety

High
Anxiety

## 14

# *Progress Check*

Tracking progress enables you to evaluate your journey, recognize the non-linear nature of progress, and develop self-reflection and self-compassion. Assessing your experiences provides valuable insights into your growth and the steps to move forward.

Progress is rarely a straight line. Expect ups and downs, challenges and victories. Acknowledging this reality helps maintain a balanced perspective and prevents discouragement from temporary setbacks. Approach these moments as opportunities for learning and development.

Honest self-reflection is essential for tracking progress effectively. Examine your thoughts, feelings, and behaviors objectively. Celebrate your successes, regardless of their size. Recognize areas that still challenge you and address them with compassion and understanding. Self-compassion is vital for sustaining motivation and resilience when facing anxiety.

Approach this chapter with openness and self-kindness. Overcoming anxiety is a highly personal journey, and your progress will be unique. Trust the process and your ability to grow and heal. You will continue striving toward greater peace and freedom with patience, persistence, and self-love.

## Recap of the Previous Nine Weeks

Over the past nine weeks, you explored various strategies and approaches to manage anxiety. In week one, you learned about mindfulness, a powerful tool for staying present and aware of your thoughts and emotions. Week two focused on practical strategies for dealing with panic and acute anxiety, providing you with tools to navigate intense moments of distress.

Cognitive Behavioral Therapy (CBT) was introduced in week three, helping you understand the connection between thoughts, feelings, and behaviors. In week four, you examined defense mechanisms and how they can sometimes hinder growth and progress. Week five delved into cognitive distortions, teaching you to identify and challenge irrational thought patterns.

Acceptance and Commitment Therapy (ACT) was the focus of week six, encouraging you to embrace your experiences and take action aligned with your values. Week seven explored transpersonal and Buddhist psychology, offering a spiritual perspective on overcoming anxiety. Solution-Focused Therapy, introduced in week eight, emphasized your strengths and resources in creating positive change.

Finally, week nine centered on enhancing emotional intelligence, helping you develop greater self-awareness, and improving your relationships with others. Each approach provided unique insights and tools to support overcoming anxiety.

As you reflect on the past nine weeks, consider which strategies resonated with you most. Which concepts or techniques did you find particularly helpful? Keep these in mind as you build your personalized toolkit for managing anxiety.

## Assessing Your Progress

Now that you have reviewed the strategies and techniques from the previous nine weeks assess your progress. Reflect on your overall experience and consider the changes you have noticed in your thoughts, feelings, and anxiety-related behaviors. Identify areas of improvement, no matter how small. Acknowledge challenges or setbacks as opportunities for growth and learning.

Evaluate the effectiveness of each approach you explored. Reflect on the techniques that resonated with you and those that felt less helpful. Everyone's journey is unique, so trust your instincts and focus on the strategies that align with your values and goals.

To gain an objective view of your progress, chart your anxiety levels throughout the nine weeks. Use a scale from 0 to 10, with 0 representing no anxiety and 10 representing severe anxiety. Identify patterns or trends in your ratings, noting weeks or techniques that coincided with lower anxiety levels. Use this information to inform your ongoing anxiety management plan.

Progress will have ups and downs, and anxiety levels might remain steady or even increase at times. Be patient and trust that continued practice and self-reflection will develop greater resilience and coping skills.

Acknowledge your hard work and commitment to your well-being. Use this self-reflection to set new goals and refine your approach to overcoming anxiety.

## The Bridge: A Visual Representation of Your Journey

Earlier we introduced the concept of visualizing your journey to overcoming anxiety as crossing a bridge. This metaphor represents the path from your starting point to your desired destination—a life with reduced anxiety. As you reflect on your progress, imagine yourself standing on this bridge.

Reflect on the distance you have covered since beginning your journey. Consider the steps you have taken, the obstacles you have overcome, and the personal growth you have achieved. Recognize the courage to embark on this path and your dedication to your well-being.

Now, picture yourself at your current location on the bridge. Observe your surroundings and acknowledge the challenges that lie ahead.

Simultaneously, recognize how far you have come. Compare your current position to your starting point, and appreciate the distance you have traveled and the skills you have gained.

As you stand on the bridge and look back at your journey, allow yourself to feel a sense of accomplishment. You have taken significant steps towards a life of increased peace and resilience. You have demonstrated your commitment to well-being and willingness to confront your fears.

Looking ahead, remember that the journey continues. You will encounter more challenges and opportunities for growth. However, you now possess the tools and strategies to navigate the path ahead. Trust in your ability to take the following steps until you reach your destination.

Remember that your journey is unique, and your path may differ from others. Focus on your progress and trust the process. Each step brings you closer to a life of greater freedom and resilience.

## Redefining Goals and Expectations

As you continue to assess your progress, revisit your initial goals and expectations. When you began this journey, you likely had a vision of what overcoming anxiety would look like and may have set specific goals for yourself. These goals might have included reducing the frequency or intensity of anxiety symptoms or engaging in previously avoided activities.

With nine weeks of experience and self-reflection, you now have a more realistic understanding of progress. Some of your initial goals may have been too broad or not specific enough, while others may have been too ambitious, not accounting for the non-linear nature of progress.

Redefine your goals based on your progress and experiences. Set realistic, achievable targets for the future and break down larger goals into smaller, manageable steps. For example, instead of eliminating anxiety, focus on reducing its impact on your daily life. Break this down into smaller goals, such as practicing mindfulness for 10 minutes daily or challenging one negative thought pattern weekly.

Setting realistic goals is essential for maintaining motivation and avoiding frustration. Celebrate small victories and use them as stepping stones toward your larger objectives. Be patient with yourself and trust the process, recognizing that progress takes time.

Reassess your expectations and be honest about what you can achieve within a given timeframe. Remember that overcoming anxiety is a lifelong journey rather than a single destination. Accept the ups and downs as part of the process and focus on your commitment to moving forward.

You create a realistic and achievable roadmap for the future by redefining your goals and expectations. This approach allows you to focus on the journey rather than fixating solely on the end goal, promoting a more sustainable and fulfilling path to overcoming anxiety.

## Revisiting and Reinforcing Techniques

Throughout your journey, you have encountered various techniques and strategies that resonated with you. Others may have felt less impactful or required additional practice. As you move forward, identify areas where you need more support or guidance. Revisit concepts and techniques from previous weeks, considering how you can integrate them into your daily life.

For example, if mindfulness proved particularly helpful, commit to practicing it regularly. Set aside dedicated time each day for mindfulness exercises, such as deep breathing or body scans. If cognitive restructuring resonates with you, continue challenging negative thought patterns as they arise. Keep a thought journal to track your progress and identify recurring themes.

If specific techniques feel challenging or less intuitive, don't be discouraged. Learning new skills takes time and practice. Be patient with yourself and seek additional resources or support if needed. This may involve contacting a therapist, joining a support group, or exploring self-help books and online resources.

Remember, the techniques you have learned are not one-time solutions but rather lifelong tools for managing anxiety. The more you practice and integrate them into your daily routine, the more effective they will become. Approach this process with curiosity and self-compassion, knowing that setbacks and challenges are normal for growth.

As you revisit and reinforce these techniques, remember that what works for you may evolve. Be open to adapting your approach as needed, and trust your instincts. The goal is to develop a personalized strategies toolkit that supports your ongoing well-being and resilience.

## Celebrating Your Progress and Resilience

Take a moment to acknowledge your courage and effort in your journey. Overcoming anxiety is no small feat; every step forward is worth celebrating. Recognize the value of setbacks as opportunities for growth and the lessons they offer.

Cultivate self-compassion by treating yourself with kindness and understanding. Recognize that personal growth is a lifelong process, and be patient with yourself as you navigate the ups and downs. Celebrate your resilience in the face of challenges, and trust your ability to bounce back from difficult moments.

Remember that progress is not just about reaching a destination but also about the skills and insights you develop along the way. With each step, you are building a foundation of resilience and self-awareness that will serve you well beyond this journey.

## Looking Ahead: Maintaining and Building Upon Your Progress

As you move forward, focus on maintaining and expanding the progress you have made. Develop a personalized self-care plan that includes the strategies and techniques that have been most effective for you. This may involve setting aside time for regular mindfulness practice, scheduling enjoyable activities, or establishing a support system of trusted friends or professionals.

Continue to practice and refine the skills you have learned. Be mindful of the ongoing nature of personal growth, and approach new challenges as opportunities to deepen your understanding and resilience. Stay connected to supportive resources, such as therapy, support groups, or educational materials, to continue learning and growing.

Remember, overcoming anxiety is a journey of self-discovery and healing. Trust in the process, and have faith in your ability to navigate the path ahead. Each step brings you closer to a life of greater peace, purpose, and fulfillment.

Tracking your progress is essential in managing anxiety effectively. Reflect on your experiences regularly, refine your goals, and consistently apply the techniques you have learned. This process provides valuable insights into your development and outlines the necessary steps for continued progress.

Address challenges methodically, viewing them as opportunities to apply your skills. Acknowledge your efforts and progress as part of your journey toward better managing anxiety.

The techniques and strategies acquired are practical tools for lifelong anxiety management. Incorporate them into your daily routine, ensuring you have a supportive environment and access to resources that bolster your continued learning and growth.

Managing anxiety is an ongoing process that involves continuous self-discovery and adjustment. To maintain and build upon your progress, create a personalized self-care plan that includes practices and activities beneficial to you. Dedicate time for regular practice, pursue enjoyable activities, and sustain a supportive network.

Stay engaged with resources that facilitate ongoing development, such as therapy, support groups, or educational materials. Consistent application of the skills you have developed will enhance your resilience and improve your ability to lead a fulfilling life. Commit to your ongoing growth and well-being, trusting your capabilities to navigate life's challenges.

# Week 10 Self-Help Guide

## Week Ten Self-Help Guide

Welcome to Week 10 of our journey to manage and understand anxiety. This week's homework is designed to reinforce the skills you've developed, assess your progress, and ensure continued growth. Each assignment focuses on a different aspect of your journey, from visualizing your overall progress to establishing a routine for regular practice. These tasks will help you reflect on what strategies have been effective, identify areas for improvement, and solidify your commitment to managing anxiety as part of your daily life. Let's explore these exercises to strengthen your foundation and enhance your resilience against anxiety.

# Week 10 Day 1

**Tracking Progress on "The Bridge"**

**Objective:** Reflect on your journey thus far by visualizing your progress as crossing a metaphorical bridge from anxiety to a more managed state.

**Instructions:** Visualize your journey as a bridge that spans from the onset of your anxiety management efforts to your current state.

1. On the bridge below, chart the starting point, the end, and key milestones.
2. Reflect on the obstacles you've overcome and the progress you've made. Note any particular techniques or insights that significantly helped you move forward.
3. Assess your current position on the bridge and identify what remains to be addressed to continue your progress.
4. Set specific, realistic goals for the subsequent phases of your journey based on your current position.

**Reflection:** After visualizing your progress on the bridge, reflect on the key moments that stand out as turning points or milestones in your journey. Consider both successes and setbacks. What lessons can you draw from these experiences? How have they shaped your approach to managing anxiety? Acknowledge the courage to start this journey and the persistence to continue.

| 0 | 1 | 2 | 3 | 4 | 5 | 6 | 7 | 8 | 9 | 10 |

No
Anxiety

Moderate
Anxiety

High
Anxiety

# Week 10 Day 2

## Assessing Anxiety Levels

**Objective:** Evaluate changes in your anxiety levels from the beginning of the guide to the present, focusing on what methods have been effective.

**Information:** Regular assessment of your anxiety levels provides a quantifiable measure of change over time. This allows you to identify which strategies are most effective, recognize patterns in your emotional response, and adjust your approach accordingly. Reflecting on these changes helps to reinforce effective behaviors and modify or discard less helpful ones.

**Instructions:**

1. Review your notes or journal entries from the beginning of this guide to now.
2. On a scale from 0 (no anxiety) to 10 (severe anxiety), rate your weekly anxiety levels and document any fluctuations.
3. Reflect on what changes you notice and identify which techniques or strategies contributed to these changes.

   1. Consider any persistent challenges and plan how to address them moving forward.
   2. Summarize your findings and how they will influence your approach to managing anxiety.

**Reflection:** Reflect on the anxiety levels charted over the past weeks.

What trends do you notice? Are there certain weeks or activities that correspond to spikes or drops in anxiety levels? Evaluate how your perceptions of anxiety and your coping mechanisms have evolved. What strategies have you found most effective, and how can you further integrate these into your daily life?

| | | | | | | | | | |
|---|---|---|---|---|---|---|---|---|---|
| Week 1: 1 | 2 | 3 | 4 | 5 | 6 | 7 | 8 | 9 | 10 |
| Week 2: 1 | 2 | 3 | 4 | 5 | 6 | 7 | 8 | 9 | 10 |
| Week 3: 1 | 2 | 3 | 4 | 5 | 6 | 7 | 8 | 9 | 10 |
| Week 4: 1 | 2 | 3 | 4 | 5 | 6 | 7 | 8 | 9 | 10 |
| Week 5: 1 | 2 | 3 | 4 | 5 | 6 | 7 | 8 | 9 | 10 |
| Week 6: 1 | 2 | 3 | 4 | 5 | 6 | 7 | 8 | 9 | 10 |
| Week 7: 1 | 2 | 3 | 4 | 5 | 6 | 7 | 8 | 9 | 10 |
| Week 8: 1 | 2 | 3 | 4 | 5 | 6 | 7 | 8 | 9 | 10 |
| Week 9: 1 | 2 | 3 | 4 | 5 | 6 | 7 | 8 | 9 | 10 |
| Today:  1 | 2 | 3 | 4 | 5 | 6 | 7 | 8 | 9 | 10 |

**Integration**: Integrate the practice of regularly assessing your anxiety levels into your ongoing anxiety management plan. Set aside time each week to reflect on your anxiety levels and document any changes or patterns you notice. Use this information to continually refine your approach to managing anxiety.

Consider creating a visual representation of your anxiety levels over time like the one above, to help you identify trends and correlations between specific strategies and changes in your emotional state. Regularly review this data to reinforce the strategies that have been most effective for you and to identify areas where you may need to make adjustments or seek additional support.

When you notice a significant reduction in your anxiety levels, take time to celebrate your progress and acknowledge the hard work you've put into managing your anxiety. Use these successes as motivation to continue practicing the strategies that have been effective for you.

If you notice that your anxiety levels are consistently high or not improving despite your efforts, consider reaching out for additional support from a mental health professional. They can help you identify any underlying issues that may be contributing to your anxiety and provide personalized guidance on additional strategies to try.

Remember that managing anxiety is an ongoing process, and it's normal to experience ups and downs along the way. By regularly assessing your anxiety levels and using that information to inform your approach, you can develop a more effective and sustainable plan for managing your anxiety over time.

# Week 10 Day 3

## Role-Playing Challenging Scenarios

**Objective:** Develop practical responses to anxiety-inducing situations through role-playing.

**Information:** Role-playing is a practical approach to preparing for real-life situations that cause anxiety. Simulating these scenarios in a controlled environment allows you to experiment with different strategies and receive immediate feedback. This exercise helps build confidence and can make stressful situations more manageable.

**Instructions:**

1. Identify two to three scenarios that typically induce anxiety for you.
2. Outline how these situations usually unfold and how you have responded.
3. Role-play these scenarios with a friend or therapist, learning new techniques or responses from this guide.
4. Reflect on the role-play: What new strategies worked? What didn't? How did you feel during the role-play?
5. Adjust your strategy based on this practice and plan to implement these changes in real-life situations.

**Reflection:** After each role-playing session, reflect on the experience. How did you feel before, during, and after the scenario? Did the strategies you employed alter the outcome of the situation? What did you learn about your ability to handle stress in a simulated environment? Identify any emotions or reactions that surprised you and explore their origins and implications.

# Week 10 Day 4

## Creating an Anxiety Management Toolkit

**Objective:** Compile a personalized toolkit of strategies and techniques that have been most effective for you in managing anxiety.

**Information:** An anxiety management toolkit is a personalized collection of strategies and techniques that have proven effective in managing your specific symptoms of anxiety. A readily accessible toolkit allows for quick adaptation to various situations, ensuring you always have a strategy for managing stress and anxiety as they arise.

**Instructions:**

1. Review your notes to identify the strategies and techniques that have significantly helped reduce your anxiety.
2. Create a list of these methods and brief instructions on implementing each one.
3. Organize the tools into categories based on the situation they are most effective for, such as quick relief, long-term management, and crisis situations.
4. Keep this toolkit accessible in your journal or a digital format for easy reference.
5. Commit to regularly updating the toolkit as you discover what works for you.

**Reflection:** Once your toolkit is assembled, reflect on choosing these tools. Why did you select these specific strategies? How do they complement each other? Consider any gaps in your toolkit—areas of your anxiety that your current selections might not fully address. Think about how you can expand or modify your toolkit to suit your evolving needs better.

# Week 10 Day 5

## *Establishing a Routine for Regular Practice*

**Objective:** Develop a routine that incorporates regular practice of your anxiety management techniques to ensure ongoing progress.

**Information:** Consistency is key to managing anxiety effectively. Establishing a routine for regular practice of anxiety management techniques ensures that you maintain the skills you have learned and continue to build upon them. A structured routine also helps to normalize these practices, integrating them into your daily life as regular activities rather than reactions to crises. This ongoing practice promotes resilience and long-term improvement in managing anxiety.

**Instructions:**

1. Select techniques from your toolkit that require regular practice, such as mindfulness, deep breathing, or journaling.
2. Create a daily schedule that allocates specific times for these practices, ensuring they integrate smoothly into your daily routine.
3. Use reminders on your phone or calendar to help you stick to this schedule.
4. At the end of each week, reflect on your adherence to this routine and note any improvements in managing your anxiety.
5. Adjust the routine as necessary to accommodate changes in your lifestyle or insights from your ongoing practice.

These assignments are structured to provide a comprehensive approach to managing anxiety, encouraging continual reflection and adaptation of strategies to meet individual needs and circumstances.

**Reflection:** At the end of each week, reflect on your adherence to the established routine. How consistently did you practice the techniques? What barriers prevented you from following your routine, and how can these be overcome? Notice any changes in your anxiety levels or general well-being that correlate with your practice routine. Adjust the routine as necessary to enhance its effectiveness and sustainability.

# *Week 10 Tracking Progress*

**Instructions**:

1. Take a moment to reflect on your progress and experiences.
2. Refer to the bridge illustration below.
3. Consider where you currently stand on your journey.
4. Place a mark on the bridge representing your current position.
5. Next, rate where your average anxiety level has been over this week.
6. Record your anxiety rating on the provided 0-10 scale, with 0 being no anxiety and 10 being the most intense anxiety you've experienced.
7. Reflect and journal.

**Reflection**: After marking your bridge position and anxiety rating, reflect on your progress. Examine skills learned, challenges faced, and changes in thoughts and behaviors. Journal your insights and observations. Identify successes, challenges, and areas requiring more attention. Determine if you need to slow down, revisit previous weeks or skills, or seek professional help to maintain progress. Assess your overall progress and consider if professional support is needed or how it's contributing to your journey.

| 0 | 1 | 2 | 3 | 4 | 5 | 6 | 7 | 8 | 9 | 10 |
|---|---|---|---|---|---|---|---|---|---|----|

No
Anxiety

Moderate
Anxiety

High
Anxiety

# 15

# *Self-Care Social Connections*

Self-care and social support play critical roles in managing anxiety. Engaging in regular self-care practices and maintaining strong social connections can significantly reduce stress, improve emotional resilience, and enhance overall well-being. Conversely, neglecting self-care and lacking social support can exacerbate anxiety symptoms and hinder progress in managing the condition.

Self-care and social connections share a reciprocal relationship with anxiety. When individuals experience high levels of anxiety, they may find it challenging to prioritize self-care activities or engage in social interactions. However, by neglecting these essential aspects of well-being, anxiety can worsen over time. On the other hand, consistently practicing self-care and nurturing social relationships can help alleviate anxiety symptoms and foster a greater sense of emotional balance.

Integrating self-care and social support into a comprehensive anxiety management plan is crucial for long-term success. By developing a personalized self-care routine and actively cultivating supportive relationships, individuals can create a strong foundation for managing anxiety and improving their overall quality of life. Throughout this chapter, we will explore the importance of self-care and social connections, providing practical strategies for incorporating these practices into daily life and overcoming common barriers to prioritizing self-care and social engagement.

## Understanding Self-Care

Self-care encompasses the intentional actions and practices that promote physical, emotional, and mental well-being. It involves taking responsibility for one's health and happiness by prioritizing activities that nurture the body, mind, and spirit. Self-care is not selfish or indulgent. Self-care is a necessary component of a balanced and fulfilling life.

Engaging in regular self-care practices offers numerous benefits for individuals struggling with anxiety. First, self-care helps reduce stress and anxiety levels by providing opportunities for relaxation, reflection, and rejuvenation. When individuals take time to unwind and engage in activities they enjoy, they experience a greater sense of calm and emotional balance. Second, self-care enhances emotional resilience, enabling individuals to cope better with their challenges and stressors. By taking care of themselves during difficult times, individuals build the inner strength and resources needed to navigate anxiety-provoking situations. Finally, consistent self-care practices contribute to improved overall well-being and life satisfaction. When individuals prioritize their needs and engage in activities that bring them joy and fulfillment, they experience a greater sense of contentment and purpose.

Despite the clear benefits of self-care, many individuals struggle to prioritize it daily. Common barriers to self-care include time constraints, competing priorities, and feelings of guilt or selfishness. Some individuals may feel that taking time is a luxury they cannot afford. In contrast, others may struggle with the belief that self-care is selfish or indulgent. Overcoming these barriers requires a shift in mindset and a commitment to making self-care a non-negotiable part of one's daily routine. By recognizing the value of self-care and making it a priority, individuals can experience the transformative effects it has on their anxiety management and overall well-being.

## Developing a Personalized Self-Care Plan

Creating a personalized care plan will help to incorporate self-care into daily life. The first step in developing a self-care plan is to assess current self-care practices. This involves taking an honest look at how much time and energy is currently devoted to self-care activities and identifying areas where improvement is needed. Some individuals may find that they are neglecting certain aspects of self-care, such as physical exercise or time for relaxation. Others may discover that their self-care practices are inconsistent or sporadic.

Once current self-care practices have been assessed, the next step is to identify areas for improvement. This may involve setting specific goals related to self-care, such as committing to a daily meditation practice or scheduling regular social activities with friends and loved ones. When setting self-care goals, it is important to be realistic and start small, gradually building up to more challenging or time-intensive practices.

A well-rounded self-care plan should incorporate various strategies addressing different aspects of well-being. Physical self-care may include regular exercise, healthy eating habits, and adequate sleep. Emotional self-care may involve activities such as journaling, therapy, or creative pursuits. Spiritual self-care practices, such as meditation, prayer, or connecting with nature, can help individuals find purpose and meaning. Intellectual self-care may involve learning new skills or engaging in mentally stimulating hobbies.

By developing a personalized self-care plan that incorporates a range of strategies, individuals can create a comprehensive approach to anxiety management that addresses their unique needs and preferences. Regular review and adjustment of the self-care plan may be necessary as individuals' circumstances and priorities change. The key is to remain flexible and open to new strategies while consistently prioritizing self-care as an essential component of overall well-being.

## The Power of Social Connections

Social connections play a vital role in mental health and well-being. Humans are social beings, and their relationships with others provide a sense of belonging, support, and purpose. For individuals struggling with anxiety, social connections can be especially important in managing symptoms and building resilience.

The impact of social support on mental health is well-documented. Research has consistently shown that individuals with strong social networks and supportive relationships have better mental health outcomes than those who are socially isolated or lonely. Social support can take many forms, including emotional support, such as having someone to talk to about one's feelings and experiences; informational support, such as receiving advice or guidance from others; and tangible support, such as practical assistance with daily tasks or responsibilities.

The benefits of social support are numerous. Emotionally supportive relationships provide a sense of validation and acceptance, helping individuals feel understood and less alone in their struggles. Knowing that others care and are available to offer support can reduce anxiety and increase a sense of safety and security. Informational support can help individuals navigate challenges and make informed decisions, while tangible support can alleviate stress and lighten the burden of daily responsibilities.

Despite the clear benefits of social connections, many individuals with anxiety struggle to build and maintain supportive relationships. Social anxiety, fear of rejection, and difficulty opening up to others can all contribute to social isolation and loneliness. Individuals with anxiety must recognize the challenges they face in forming social connections and actively work to overcome these barriers. By prioritizing social interactions and taking steps to build and nurture supportive relationships, individuals can harness the power of social connections to enhance their mental health and well-being.

## Strategies for Strengthening Social Connections

Strengthening social connections begins with assessing your current social network. Take an inventory of the relationships in your life, considering the quality and depth of each connection. Identify areas where you may need to focus more attention, such as neglected friendships or family ties.

Next, identify specific areas for improvement. This may involve reaching out to friends you haven't spoken to in a while, making an effort to attend social gatherings, or opening up to others about your struggles with anxiety. Be honest about the steps you need to take to build stronger, more meaningful connections.

For many individuals with anxiety, the thought of building new social connections can be daunting. Social anxiety and fear of rejection are common barriers that prevent people from putting themselves out there. To overcome these challenges, start small and gradually push yourself out of your comfort zone. Attend a local meetup or join a club centered around one of your interests. Pursue activities that align with your values and passions, as this can help you connect with like-minded individuals.

Online platforms and social media can also be valuable tools for expanding your social circle. Engage in online communities related to your hobbies or join support groups for individuals with anxiety. However, be mindful of your time online and prioritize face-to-face interactions whenever possible.

As you work to build new connections, don't forget to nurture your existing relationships. Make an effort to regularly check in with friends and loved ones, even just a quick phone call or text message. Practice active listening and express genuine interest in their lives. Show your appreciation for their support and tell them how much you value their presence.

Remember, building and maintaining social connections is an ongoing process. It requires effort, vulnerability, and a willingness to step outside your comfort zone. By prioritizing social connections and consistently strengthening your relationships, you can cultivate a robust support system that will help you navigate the challenges of anxiety and enhance your overall well-being.

**Fostering Supportive Relationships**

Fostering supportive relationships is essential for building a robust social support system. Supportive relationships are characterized by trust, empathy, and mutual respect. In these relationships, individuals feel comfortable sharing their thoughts, feelings, and experiences without fear of judgment or rejection.

To cultivate supportive relationships, it is important to establish healthy boundaries. This involves communicating your needs and expectations clearly and respectfully. Let others know what you need from them regarding support, and be willing to listen to their needs as well. Remember that healthy relationships involve give and take, and it is important to be there for others just as you want them to be there for you.

When communicating with others, practice active listening and validate their experiences. Show genuine interest in their lives and offer support and encouragement when needed. Be honest and authentic in your interactions, and avoid gossiping or speaking negatively about others.

Being mindful of the time and energy you invest in your relationships is also important. Prioritize those most meaningful and supportive, and be willing to let go of draining or toxic relationships. Find yourself in a relationship that consistently leaves you feeling depleted or unsupported. It may be necessary to set boundaries or end the relationship altogether.

Seeking professional support can also be a valuable step in fostering supportive relationships. A therapist or counselor can guide you in building and maintaining healthy relationships and help you work through any challenges or barriers you may be facing.

Building supportive relationships requires vulnerability, effort, and a willingness to invest in the lives of others. By prioritizing your relationships and working to cultivate a strong support system, you can enhance your resilience in the face of anxiety and improve your overall well-being. Remember, the more you nurture your relationships, the more they will grow and flourish, providing you with a powerful source of strength and support in times of need.

## Integrating Self-Care and Social Connection into Your Daily Life

Integrating self-care and social connection into your daily life is crucial for managing anxiety and maintaining overall well-being. To make self-care a non-negotiable priority, schedule it into your daily routine. Treat self-care activities with the same importance as any other appointment or commitment. Block out time in your calendar for exercise, relaxation, hobbies, or other activities that nourish your mind, body, and spirit.

Similarly, make a conscious effort to schedule regular social activities and interactions. This may involve setting aside time each week for coffee with a friend, joining a weekly support group, or planning a monthly outing with family. By making social connection a regular part of your routine, you prioritize your relationships and ensure that you are consistently receiving the support and interaction you need.

Balancing solitude and social engagement is also important for maintaining well-being. While social connection is crucial, carving out time for solitude and self-reflection is equally important. Make sure to schedule quiet time for yourself each day, whether it's a few minutes of meditation in the morning or a relaxing bath in the evening. Use this time to tune into your own needs and recharge your batteries.

There may be times when you need extra support in managing your anxiety and integrating self-care and social connection into your life. Don't hesitate to seek professional help when needed. A therapist or counselor can provide valuable guidance and support in developing healthy self-care and social connection habits and navigating any challenges or setbacks you may encounter along the way.

Integrating self-care and social connection into your daily life is an ongoing process. It requires patience, persistence, and a willingness to prioritize your well-being. By making self-care and social connection a non-negotiable part of your routine, you create a strong foundation for managing anxiety and building a fulfilling, vibrant life.

## The Ripple Effect: How Self-Care and Social Connections Benefit Others

Prioritizing self-care and fostering social connections benefits individuals and positively impacts those around them. When you engage in healthy self-care practices, you model the importance of self-compassion and self-respect. This can inspire others to reflect on their self-care habits and make positive life changes.

By demonstrating the value of setting boundaries, engaging in hobbies, and taking time for relaxation, you send a powerful message to your loved ones. They may begin to recognize the significance of self-care in their own lives and feel encouraged to prioritize their well-being. This shift in perspective can lead to a domino effect, creating a supportive environment that promotes healthy habits and emotional resilience.

Furthermore, actively nurturing your social connections contributes to a more compassionate and empathetic community. You foster a sense of belonging and understanding by listening to others, offering support, and engaging in meaningful conversations. This can inspire others to extend the same kindness and support to those around them, creating a ripple effect of positive social interactions.

As you share your experiences and knowledge gained from your self-care and social connection practices, you have the opportunity to positively influence others who may be struggling with anxiety or other mental health challenges. By openly discussing your journey and providing practical advice, you can help reduce mental health stigma and encourage others to seek the support they need.

Prioritizing self-care and social connections contributes to a more caring and connected society. Your actions can inspire others, create positive change, and foster a sense of community that supports the well-being of all its members.

Self-care and social connections are essential components of an effective anxiety management plan. By prioritizing self-care practices and nurturing supportive relationships, individuals can reduce stress, improve emotional resilience, and enhance overall well-being. Developing a personalized self-care plan that incorporates a variety of strategies, such as physical exercise, healthy eating, and engaging in hobbies, can help individuals effectively manage anxiety symptoms and build a strong foundation for long-term well-being.

Social connections provide invaluable support, validation, and a sense of belonging, which are crucial for navigating the challenges of anxiety. Building and maintaining a broad social support system requires effort, vulnerability, and a willingness to invest in relationships. By actively cultivating supportive connections and setting healthy boundaries, individuals can harness the power of social support to enhance their mental health and overall quality of life.

Integrating self-care and social connection into daily life is an ongoing process that requires commitment and persistence. By making these practices a non-negotiable priority and consistently working to nurture both self-care and social relationships, individuals can create a strong foundation for managing anxiety and building a fulfilling life.

It is important to remember that everyone's journey of self-care and social connection is unique. What works for one person may not work for another, and it is essential to approach these practices with flexibility, patience, and self-compassion. By staying attuned to personal needs and preferences, individuals can develop a sustainable and practical approach to anxiety management that promotes long-term well-being and resilience.

Individuals improve their lives by prioritizing self-care and cultivating supportive relationships. This also contributes to a more compassionate and connected world. Through the ripple effect of positive self-care and social interaction, individuals have the power to inspire and support others in their journeys toward well-being and resilience.

# Week 11 Self-Help Guide

## Self-Care & Social Connections

Self-care and social connections play crucial roles in managing anxiety. This week-long self-help guide focuses on nurturing oneself and fostering supportive relationships. The guide explores the importance of self-care, teaching practical strategies for integrating self-care activities into daily life. It emphasizes the benefits of regular exercise, healthy eating, and sufficient sleep in reducing anxiety symptoms. The guide also highlights the value of social support, providing tips for building and maintaining meaningful connections with others. It teaches effective communication skills for expressing needs and boundaries assertively. The guide encourages readers to identify and engage in enjoyable social activities that promote a sense of belonging and reduce isolation. It also addresses the challenges of social anxiety, offering techniques for gradually exposing oneself to feared social situations. Throughout the week, the guide provides reflective exercises and practical tasks to help readers incorporate self-care and social connection strategies into their lives. By prioritizing self-care and cultivating supportive relationships, individuals can strengthen their resilience and better manage anxiety.

# Week 11 Day 1

## Assessing Your Current Self-Care Practices

**Objective:** Evaluate your current self-care habits to identify areas for improvement.

**Information:** Self-care is essential for managing anxiety and maintaining overall well-being. By assessing your current self-care practices, you can identify areas where you may need to focus more attention and make positive changes.

**Instructions:**

1. Set aside 20-30 minutes for this exercise.
2. Create a list of your self-care practices, including physical, emotional, spiritual, and intellectual activities.
3. Note how often you engage in each activity and how it makes you feel.
4. Identify areas where you lack self-care and brainstorm new activities to incorporate into your routine.

**Reflection:** In your journal, reflect on your current self-care practices. How do they contribute to your overall well-being? What areas do you feel you need to focus on more? What new activities would you like to try?

**Integration:** Commit to incorporate at least one new self-care activity into your daily routine this week. Set a reminder or schedule it in your calendar to ensure you follow through.

# Week 11 Day 2

*Building New Social Connections*

**Objective:** Identify opportunities to build new social connections and take steps to engage in them.

**Information:** Building new social connections can be challenging, especially for those struggling with anxiety. However, by stepping outside your comfort zone and engaging in activities that align with your interests and values, you can create opportunities to meet like-minded individuals and forge new relationships.

**Instructions:**

1. Brainstorm a list of activities, groups, or events that align with your interests and values.
2. Research online or ask friends and family for recommendations on local groups or organizations you can join.
3. Choose one activity or event to attend this week.
4. Prepare conversation starters or questions to help break the ice when meeting new people.
5. Attend the activity or event and focus on being present and engaged.

**Reflection:** After attending the activity or event, reflect on your experience in your journal. What did you enjoy about it? What did you find challenging? What did you learn about yourself?

**Integration:** Plan to attend at least one new social activity or event monthly. Continue to challenge yourself to step outside your comfort zone and engage with others.

# Week 11 Day 3

### Practicing Active Listening

**Objective:** Develop active listening skills to improve communication and strengthen social connections.

**Information:** Active listening will facilitate effective communication and building solid relationships. By fully concentrating on what others are saying, without interrupting or planning your response, you demonstrate respect and empathy, fostering deeper connections.

**Instructions:**

1. Choose a conversation partner, such as a friend, family member, or colleague.
2. During the conversation, focus on being fully present and engaged.
3. Pay attention to verbal and nonverbal cues, such as tone of voice and body language.
4. Avoid interrupting or planning your response while the other person is speaking.
5. Ask clarifying questions and summarize what you heard to ensure understanding.
6. Practice empathy by trying to understand the other person's perspective and feelings.

**Reflection:** After the conversation, reflect on your experience in your journal. How did it feel to practice active listening? What did you learn about the other person? What challenges did you face?

**Integration:** Make a conscious effort to practice active listening in all your conversations this week. Notice how it impacts your relationships and the quality of your interactions.

# Week 11 Day 4

*Cultivating Gratitude*

**Objective:** Develop a daily gratitude practice to increase positive emotions and enhance overall well-being.

**Information:** Cultivating gratitude has been shown to have numerous benefits for mental health, including increased positive emotions, improved relationships, and greater life satisfaction. By focusing on what you are thankful for, you shift your attention away from negative thoughts and experiences.

**Instructions:**

1. Set aside 5-10 minutes each day for this practice.
2. Find a quiet, comfortable space where you can reflect without distractions.
3. Think of three things you are grateful for today. These can be big or small, such as a supportive friend, a delicious meal, or a beautiful sunset.
4. Write these three things down in a gratitude journal or notebook.
5. For each item, take a moment to appreciate and savor the feeling of gratitude fully.

**Reflection:** At the end of the week, review your gratitude journal. What patterns or themes do you notice? How has focusing on gratitude impacted your overall mood and outlook?

**Integration:** Make gratitude a daily habit by writing down three things you are thankful for daily. Consider sharing your gratitude with others to spread positivity and strengthen your relationships.

# Week 11 day 5

## Setting Healthy Boundaries

**Objective:** Learn to set and communicate healthy boundaries to protect your time, energy, and well-being.

**Information:** Healthy boundaries are essential for maintaining positive relationships and preventing burnout. By clearly communicating your needs and limits, you ensure that your well-being remains a priority.

**Instructions:**

1. Reflect on areas where you feel your boundaries are being crossed or violated.
2. List your specific boundaries, such as saying no to unreasonable requests or protecting your time.
3. Identify the actions you need to take for each boundary to communicate and enforce it.
4. Practice communicating your boundaries assertively and respectfully with others.
5. Be prepared to follow through with consequences if your boundaries are not respected.

**Reflection:** In your journal, reflect on how setting and maintaining healthy boundaries makes you feel. What challenges do you face in communicating your boundaries? How can you continue to prioritize your well-being?

**Integration:** Commit to regularly reviewing and updating your boundaries as needed. Remember that setting boundaries is an ongoing process and requires consistent effort and communication.

# Week 11 Day 6

## Practicing Self-Compassion

**Objective:** Develop self-compassion to reduce self-criticism and increase emotional resilience.

**Information:** Self-compassion involves treating yourself with the same kindness, understanding, and support you would offer a good friend. By practicing self-compassion, you can reduce feelings of inadequacy and increase your ability to cope with challenges and setbacks.

**Instructions:**

1. Notice when you are engaging in self-criticism or negative self-talk.
2. When you catch yourself being self-critical, pause and acknowledge your pain or discomfort.
3. Remind yourself that everyone makes mistakes and experiences challenges.
4. Offer yourself words of kindness and understanding, such as "This is a difficult moment, but I am doing my best" or "I am worthy of compassion and understanding."
5. Place your hand on your heart or engage in another soothing gesture to offer yourself physical comfort.

**Reflection:** In your journal, reflect on your experience practicing self-compassion. What challenges did you face? How did offering yourself kindness and understanding impact your mood and outlook?

**Integration:** Make self-compassion a regular practice by incorporating it into your daily self-care routine. Consider using self-compassion affirmations or meditations to reinforce this habit.

# Week 11 Day 7

## Reflecting on Your Progress

**Objective:** Reflect on your progress and set intentions for continued growth and self-discovery.

**Information:** Reflecting on your progress and celebrating your accomplishments is an essential part of the self-care journey. Acknowledging how far you have come builds motivation and momentum to continue making positive changes.

**Instructions:**

1. Set aside 30 minutes for this reflection exercise.
2. Review your journal entries from the past week and reflect on the self-care and social connection activities you engaged in.
3. Celebrate your successes and acknowledge your progress, no matter how small.
4. Identify any challenges or obstacles you faced and brainstorm strategies for overcoming them in the future.
5. Set intentions for the coming week, focusing on the self-care and social connection practices you want to prioritize.

**Reflection:** Write about your overall experience with this week's self-care and social connection activities in your journal. What insights have you gained about yourself and your relationships? What areas do you want to continue focusing on?

**Integration:** Commit to prioritizing self-care and social connection in your daily life. Regularly check in with yourself and adjust your practices as needed to ensure they continue to support your well-being and growth.

# Week 11 Tracking Progress

With the conclusion of Week 11's focus on self-care and social connections, take a moment to reflect. Place a mark on the bridge representing your current position and rate your anxiety level on the 0-10 scale. Recognize the importance of nurturing yourself and your relationships.

**Instructions**:

1. Take a moment to reflect on your progress and experiences.
2. Refer to the bridge illustration below.
3. Consider where you currently stand on your journey.
4. Place a mark on the bridge representing your current position.
5. Next, rate where your average anxiety level has been over this week.
6. Record your anxiety rating on the provided 0-10 scale, with 0 being no anxiety and 10 being the most intense anxiety you've experienced.
7. Reflect and journal.

**Reflection**: After marking your bridge position and anxiety rating, reflect on your progress. Examine skills learned, challenges faced, and changes in thoughts and behaviors. Journal your insights and observations. Identify successes, challenges, and areas requiring more attention. Determine if you need to slow down, revisit previous weeks or skills, or seek professional help to maintain progress. Assess your overall progress and consider if professional support is needed or how it's contributing to your journey.

```
0    1    2    3    4    5    6    7    8    9    10
```

No                          Moderate                    High
Anxiety                     Anxiety                    Anxiety

## 16

# *Embracing an Anxiety-Free Life*

Completing the *ANXIETY FREE 12-Week Self-Help Guide to Overcome Anxiety* is a notable achievement that warrants acknowledgment. This guide has equipped you with various strategies and insights to manage anxiety effectively. However, the journey doesn't end here. Maintaining the progress you've made and continuing to apply the principles learned will be crucial as you move forward.

This chapter will serve as a bridge between the structured environment of the program and the ongoing practice that will integrate these techniques into your everyday life. It's important to continue practicing the skills that have been effective for you and to remain vigilant about your mental health.

We will discuss how to keep making progress in your anxiety management, how to identify and handle potential triggers, and how to adapt the skills learned to new challenges that may arise. This is an ongoing commitment to living a balanced and fulfilling life without the constraints of overwhelming anxiety.

In the past 12 weeks, you have learned various techniques to manage anxiety, such as mindfulness, cognitive behavioral therapy (CBT), acceptance and commitment therapy (ACT), and emotional intelligence.

Now is the time to assess how these strategies have impacted your daily life.

Begin by reviewing each method you have adopted. Reflect on how these practices have helped reduce your anxiety and consider which techniques were the most effective. It's helpful to note specific situations where you successfully applied these strategies and observed positive outcomes.

Assessment of your growth is not just about recognizing successes but also acknowledging the hurdles you've encountered. Identifying these challenges helps refine your approach to managing anxiety.

Celebrate the progress you've made. Acknowledging your efforts and outcomes reinforces your commitment to managing anxiety and promotes a positive mindset. This reflection will serve as a foundation for the ongoing adaptation and application of the anxiety management techniques you've learned.

Understanding the specific triggers that can escalate your anxiety is crucial for ongoing management. A trigger can be any event, situation, or emotional state that exacerbates feelings of anxiety. Common triggers include stressful life events, interpersonal conflicts, work pressures, health concerns, or environmental factors.

Begin by listing triggers that you've noticed during the program. Recognizing these allows you to anticipate and prepare for situations challenging your anxiety management skills.

It's equally important to identify early warning signs of anxiety. These can manifest physically, emotionally, cognitively, or behaviorally. For instance, you might experience tension, restlessness, irritability, mood swings, racing thoughts, or changes in sleep and appetite when anxiety begins to build.

By pinpointing these early signs, you can take proactive steps to apply the techniques you've learned before anxiety becomes overwhelming. This early intervention helps to maintain your progress and prevent setbacks.

Developing a proactive approach to managing anxiety involves maintaining a consistent routine that incorporates the strategies you have learned. Here are steps to manage triggers and respond to early warning signs effectively:

1. *Maintain Consistency in Self-care*: Consistency in your self-care routine is vital. Regular exercise, adequate sleep, healthy eating, and mindfulness practices are fundamental to sustaining mental health and reducing susceptibility to triggers.
2. *Utilize Learned Techniques*: Regularly practice mindfulness, relaxation techniques, and cognitive behavioral strategies. These tools can help you manage reactions to triggers and maintain emotional balance.
3. *Prepare for Known Triggers*: Plan ahead if certain situations trigger your anxiety. Develop coping strategies specific to these scenarios, such as deep breathing exercises or positive self-talk.
4. *Build a Support Network*: Stay connected with supportive friends, family, or a therapist who can provide encouragement and understanding. A strong support network is invaluable for resilience and recovery during challenging times.
5. *Create an Action Plan*: Develop a personalized plan that outlines specific steps to take when you detect early warning signs of anxiety. This plan might include activities that promote relaxation, reaching out to a friend, or adjusting your schedule to reduce stress.

By regularly employing these strategies, you can effectively manage your triggers and maintain the progress you've achieved in your anxiety management journey.

Remember that experiencing setbacks is a normal part of any long-term behavioral change, including anxiety management. How you handle these setbacks can significantly impact your overall resilience and ability to manage anxiety.

1. *Acknowledge Setbacks:* Recognize that setbacks are temporary and

an expected part of the process. Viewing them as opportunities for learning and growth can help reduce feelings of frustration or discouragement.

2. ***Utilize Learned Strategies***: When facing challenges, actively use the strategies you have found most effective. Whether it's mindfulness techniques, CBT methods, or relaxation practices, revisiting these tools can help you navigate challenging times.

3. ***Practice Self-Compassion***: Be kind to yourself during difficult moments. Self-compassion involves treating yourself with the same kindness and understanding you would offer a friend in a similar situation.

4. ***Seek Support***: Don't hesitate to contact your support network for help when needed. Sometimes, talking things through with someone can provide a new perspective and additional strategies to handle the situation.

5. ***Adjust Your Plan as Needed***: If a particular aspect of your action plan is not working, reassess and adjust it. Flexibility is key in dealing with anxiety effectively.

By approaching setbacks with a constructive attitude and using them as a learning experience, you can continue to progress toward managing anxiety effectively.

As you continue to apply the skills and techniques you've learned, envisioning your life without the constraints of overwhelming anxiety becomes more achievable. This section guides setting new goals and cultivating a positive outlook for sustained personal and professional growth.

1. ***Set New Goals***: Reflect on your aspirations beyond anxiety management. Setting new personal and professional goals can motivate you to apply your anxiety management skills in broader aspects of your life, fostering growth and development.

2. ***Cultivate Positivity and Gratitude***: Develop a mindset that

emphasizes gratitude and positivity. Focusing on positive aspects of your life and expressing gratitude can reinforce your mental resilience and reduce the impact of stress and anxiety.

3. *Prioritize Self-Care:* Continue to make self-care a priority. Engaging in activities that promote well-being, such as hobbies, exercise, and social interactions, supports mental health and prevents burnout.

4. *Inspire Others*: Share your journey and successes with others struggling with similar issues. Your experience can inspire and provide practical insights to those beginning their paths to an anxiety-free life.

5. *Stay Open to Learning:* Remain open to new methods and ongoing learning about anxiety management. The field is constantly advancing, and new techniques or insights can enhance your ability to manage stress and anxiety effectively.

By embracing these practices, you solidify your commitment to a lifestyle that supports lasting well-being and peace, empowering you to lead a fulfilling, anxiety-free life.

Committing to lifelong learning is essential for sustaining progress in managing anxiety and achieving personal growth. This commitment involves staying informed about new research, adapting to evolving methods and continually reassessing and adjusting your strategies.

1. *Stay Informed:* Keep up-to-date with the latest research and advancements in anxiety management. Attending workshops, reading relevant books, and subscribing to journals can provide you with new insights and techniques.

2. *Explore Additional Resources*: Consider exploring further therapeutic options like workshops or additional therapy sessions as needed. These can offer deeper insights and more specialized strategies tailored to your needs.

3. *Assess and Adjust Your Strategies*: Regular self-assessment is

crucial to understanding the effectiveness of your current anxiety management strategies. Be prepared to make adjustments based on what is most effective for you.

4. ***Engage in Community Learning***: Participate in community groups or online forums where experiences and strategies are shared. Learning from the experiences of others can provide support and introduce new coping mechanisms.

5. ***Reflect Regularly:*** Set aside time to reflect on your growth and the areas where you might still feel challenged. This reflection can guide your learning and help tailor your ongoing personal development plan.

By fostering an environment of continuous learning and adaptation, you ensure that your anxiety management skills remain effective and relevant, supporting a fulfilling and dynamic life.

As you approach the conclusion of this structured guide, conducting a final progress check and reflection can help solidify the gains you've made and prepare you for continued success on your terms.

1. ***Complete a Self-Assessment***: Evaluate your current anxiety level compared to the program's beginning. Assess areas of improvement and note any particularly effective techniques.

2. ***Compare Initial and Current States***: Reflect on your initial state of anxiety and compare it to where you stand now. This comparison can highlight both the progress made and the areas that may require ongoing attention.

3. ***Identify Key Lessons Learned***: Pinpoint the most valuable lessons and strategies that have significantly impacted your well-being. Recognizing these can reinforce their importance and encourage their use in the future.

4. ***Express Gratitude***: Acknowledge the support and resources that have aided you in this journey. Expressing gratitude can enhance your overall well-being and strengthen your social bonds.

5. ***Plan for Future Growth***: Outline steps for future growth and how to continue applying the skills learned to new challenges. Planning helps maintain the momentum of self-improvement and anxiety management.

This final reflection is a recap of your journey and a crucial step in transitioning from a structured program to self-guided growth. It's a time to celebrate your achievements and set the stage for your ongoing journey toward an anxiety-free life.

As we conclude this guide, it's important to recap the key points and strategies supporting your journey toward managing anxiety. This final chapter reinforces the lessons learned and encourages you to continue applying these strategies proactively.

1. ***Recap of Key Strategies:*** Reflect on the essential techniques—mindfulness, cognitive behavioral therapy, and emotional intelligence—that have been most effective in managing your anxiety. Reminding yourself of these strategies ensures they remain at the forefront of your daily routines.

2. ***Ongoing Application***: Encourage the continuous application of the learned strategies. Integrating these practices into different aspects of your life can help manage stress and anxiety in long-term scenarios.

3. ***Reminder of Your Strength and Resilience:*** Acknowledge the strength and resilience you demonstrated throughout this program. This acknowledgment is crucial as it empowers you to face future challenges confidently.

4. ***Celebration of Commitment:*** Celebrate your commitment to live an anxiety-free life. Recognizing this dedication is important for maintaining motivation and recognizing your capability to control your mental health.

By keeping these points in mind, you can continue to leverage your newfound skills and maintain the progress you've achieved. Let this guide be a foundation upon which you build a resilient, fulfilling life characterized by continued learning and self-discovery.

# 17

# *Week 12 Self-Help Guide*

## Week Twelve Self-Help Guide

This seven-day homework guide is designed to reinforce the techniques and strategies you've learned throughout *ANXIETY FREE*. Each assignment is crafted to help you solidify your understanding and practical application of these methods so that you may sustain an anxiety-free life. Congratulations on completing this journey. Remember that diligence and mindfulness are required to maintain peace of mind.

Keep this book handy and refer to it to reinforce your knowledge and skills, such as repetition, bills, endurance, and resilience, as with anything. The more you use these techniques, the more they become part of you. The more they become part of you, the more seamlessly they integrate into who you are. This is the point we strive for. When all the learning and all the effort becomes second nature, If you are committed and continue to work hard on implementing the knowledge and skills you have learned. *ANXIETY FREE:* you will one day look back and realize that you have lived anxiety-free, and you will continue to do so.

# Week 12 day 1

## Conducting a Self-Assessment

**Objective**: Evaluate your progress and identify areas for continued growth.

Information: Conducting a self-assessment is crucial for recognizing your achievements and identifying areas requiring ongoing attention. This exercise will help you solidify the gains you've made and prepare for continued success in managing anxiety.

**Instructions:**

1. Set aside 30 minutes for this self-assessment exercise.
2. Reflect on your anxiety levels at the beginning of the program and compare them to your current state. Note any significant improvements or changes.
3. List the techniques and strategies you found most effective in managing your anxiety throughout the program.
4. Identify any areas or situations where you still feel challenged or believe there is room for further growth.
5. Write down the most valuable lessons you've learned during this journey.

**Reflection:** In your journal, reflect on how far you've come in your journey towards managing anxiety. Celebrate your progress and acknowledge your hard work and dedication to this program.

**Integration:** Use the insights gained from this self-assessment to create a personalized plan for ongoing growth and anxiety management. Incorporate the most effective techniques into your daily routine and set realistic goals for addressing any areas that need further attention.

# Week 12 Day 2

*Developing a Maintenance Plan*

**Objective:** Create a personalized plan to maintain progress and apply anxiety management techniques.

**Information:** Developing a maintenance plan is essential for sustaining your progress and ensuring that you continue to apply the strategies learned throughout the program. This plan will be a roadmap for ongoing anxiety management and personal growth.

**Instructions:**

1. Review the techniques and strategies you've learned, such as mindfulness, CBT, ACT, and emotional intelligence.
2. Create a daily or weekly schedule that incorporates these practices into your routine. Be specific about the activities you will engage in and the time you will dedicate to each.
3. Identify potential challenges or obstacles that may arise and brainstorm solutions or coping mechanisms to address them.
4. Set realistic, achievable goals for maintaining progress and continuing personal growth. These goals should be specific, measurable, and time-bound.
5. Share your maintenance plan with a trusted friend, family member, or therapist for accountability and support.

**Reflection:** Reflect on how having a structured maintenance plan can support your ongoing journey towards an anxiety-free life. Consider how you can remain flexible and adapt your plan while remaining committed to your goals.

**Integration:** Begin implementing your maintenance plan, making adjustments as necessary. Regularly review your progress and celebrate your successes along the way.

# Week 12 Day 3

*Cultivating Resilience*

**Objective**: Develop strategies for building resilience and effectively navigating setbacks.

**Information:** Resilience is the ability to bounce back from adversity and adapt to challenges. Cultivating resilience is crucial for maintaining progress in anxiety management and fostering a positive outlook on personal growth.

**Instructions:**

1. Reflect on a recent setback or challenge in your anxiety management journey. Identify the thoughts, emotions, and behaviors that arose in response to this situation.
2. Reframe the setback as an opportunity for growth and learning. What insights can you gain from this experience?
3. Practice self-compassion by treating yourself with kindness and understanding. Write down three compassionate statements to support yourself during difficult times.
4. Identify three strategies you can use to build resilience: practicing mindfulness, seeking support from others, or engaging in activities that promote well-being.
5. Create a "resilience reminder" – a visual or written cue that prompts you to use these strategies when faced with challenges. Place this reminder in a prominent location.

**Reflection:** In your journal, reflect on how cultivating resilience can help you maintain progress and navigate the ups and downs of your anxiety management journey.

**Integration:** Incorporate resilience-building strategies into your daily life. When faced with setbacks, remember to practice self-compassion and reframe challenges as opportunities for growth.

# Week 12 Day 4

## Expanding Your Support Network

**Objective:** Identify and strengthen connections with individuals who can provide ongoing support and encouragement.

**Information:** A strong support network is essential for maintaining progress in anxiety management and fostering a sense of connection and belonging. Identifying and cultivating supportive relationships can provide a foundation of encouragement and understanding as you continue your journey.

**Instructions:**

1. Make a list of the people in your life who have been supportive and understanding throughout your anxiety management journey. Consider friends, family members, colleagues, or professionals.
2. Reach out to at least one person on your list and express gratitude for their support. Share an update on your progress and discuss how they can continue to support you moving forward.
3. Identify areas where you need additional support, such as a specific aspect of anxiety management or a particular life challenge.
4. Brainstorm ways to expand your support network, such as joining a support group, attending workshops or classes, or connecting with others with similar experiences.
5. Make a plan to regularly engage with your support network through in-person meetings, phone calls, or virtual check-ins.

**Reflection:** Reflect on the value of having a solid support network and how it can contribute to your overall well-being and progress in anxiety management.

**Integration:** Consistently nurture supportive relationships and remain open to expanding your network. Remember that seeking support is a sign of strength and self-awareness.

# Week 12 Day 5

## Embracing Lifelong Learning

**Objective:** Cultivate a mindset of curiosity and openness to ongoing learning and personal growth.

**Information:** Embracing lifelong learning is crucial for maintaining progress in anxiety management and fostering personal growth and development. By staying curious and open to new ideas and strategies, you can continue to expand your toolkit for effectively managing anxiety.

**Instructions:**

1. Identify a topic or skill related to anxiety management that you'd like to learn more about. This could be a specific therapy technique, a mindfulness practice, or a related area of personal growth.
2. Research resources for learning more about this topic, such as books, articles, podcasts, or online courses. Choose one resource to explore in-depth.
3. Set aside dedicated time for learning and engaging with your chosen resource. Take notes on insights and ideas that resonate with you.
4. Reflect on how you can apply what you've learned to your anxiety management practice. Identify one or two actionable steps you can take based on your learning.
5. Share your learning experience with a support network member

or in a journal entry. Discuss how embracing lifelong learning can support your ongoing growth and development.

**Reflection:** Reflect on the value of lifelong learning and how cultivating a curious and open mindset can enrich your anxiety management journey and overall personal growth.

**Integration:** Commit to engage in ongoing learning and personal growth. Set regular goals for exploring new topics and ideas related to anxiety management and self-discovery.

# Week 12 Day 6

## Practicing Gratitude

**Objective:** Develop a consistent gratitude practice to foster a positive outlook and enhance overall well-being.

**Information:** Practicing gratitude is a powerful way to shift your focus toward the positive aspects of life and cultivate a sense of appreciation and contentment. Incorporating gratitude into your daily routine can support your progress in anxiety management and contribute to overall well-being.

**Instructions:**

1. Set aside 10-15 minutes each day for a dedicated gratitude practice.
2. Begin by taking a few deep breaths and bringing your attention to the present moment.
3. Reflect on three things you are grateful for today. These can be simple, everyday experiences or more significant events or relationships.
4. For each item, take a moment to appreciate and savor the feeling of gratitude fully. Notice how it feels in your body and mind.
5. Write your gratitude reflections in a journal or share them with a loved one.
6. Throughout the day, look for opportunities to express gratitude towards others. This can be through a simple "thank you," a heartfelt compliment, or an act of kindness.

**Reflection:** In your journal, reflect on how practicing gratitude affects your overall outlook and well-being. Notice any shifts in your perspective or mood as you consistently engage in this practice.

**Integration:** Make gratitude a daily habit by incorporating it into your morning or evening routine. Consider keeping a gratitude journal or partnering with a friend or family member to share daily gratitude reflections.

# Week 12 Day 7

## Envisioning Your Future Self

**Objective:** Create a vivid, optimistic vision of your future self to inspire ongoing growth and progress.

**Information:** Envisioning your future self is a powerful exercise for clarifying your goals, values, and aspirations. By creating a detailed and positive vision of who you want to be, you can cultivate motivation and direction for your ongoing anxiety management journey.

**Instructions:**

1. Find a quiet, comfortable space where you can reflect without distractions.
2. Close your eyes and take a few deep breaths, allowing yourself to relax and focus.
3. Imagine yourself one year from now, having made significant progress in your anxiety management journey. What does this future version of yourself look like? How do they feel? What are they doing differently?
4. Visualize specific details of your future self's life, such as their daily routines, relationships, work or personal projects, and overall well-being.
5. Notice the qualities and strengths your future self embodies, such as resilience, self-compassion, and a growth mindset.
6. Open your eyes and write down a detailed description of your future self. Include specific goals, values, and qualities you want to cultivate.

**Reflection:** Reflect on how envisioning your future self can be a source of inspiration and motivation for your ongoing growth and progress. Consider how you can align your daily actions and choices with this vision.

**Integration:** Regularly revisit your future self-vision to stay connected to your goals and aspirations. Use this vision as a guide for setting intentions and making decisions that support your ongoing anxiety management journey.

Engaging in these daily exercises will reinforce the skills and mindset needed to maintain progress, build resilience, and embrace lifelong growth in your anxiety management journey. Remember to celebrate your successes, learn from challenges, and stay connected to your support network as you continue toward a more fulfilling, anxiety-free life.

# Week 12 Tracking Progress

As you complete the final week of the program, take a moment to reflect on your entire journey. Mark your current position on the bridge and rate your anxiety level on the 0-10 scale. Celebrate the progress you've made, the skills you've acquired, and the commitment you've shown to your well-being.

**Instructions**:

1. Take a moment to reflect on your progress and experiences.
2. Refer to the bridge illustration below.
3. Consider where you currently stand on your journey.
4. Place a mark on the bridge representing your current position.
5. Next, rate where your average anxiety level has been over this week.
6. Record your anxiety rating on the provided 0-10 scale, with 0 being no anxiety and 10 being the most intense anxiety you've experienced.
7. Reflect and journal.

**Reflection**: After marking your bridge position and anxiety rating, reflect on your progress. Examine skills learned, challenges faced, and changes in thoughts and behaviors. Journal your insights and observations. Identify successes, challenges, and areas requiring more attention. Determine if you need to slow down, revisit previous weeks or skills, or seek professional help to maintain progress. Assess your

overall progress and consider if professional support is needed or how it's contributing to your journey.

| 0 | 1 | 2 | 3 | 4 | 5 | 6 | 7 | 8 | 9 | 10 |
|---|---|---|---|---|---|---|---|---|---|----|

No
Anxiety

Moderate
Anxiety

High
Anxiety

# Final Words

# 18

# *Finding Meaning and Purpose*

In today's fast-paced, goal-driven society, people often chase external markers of success like wealth, status, and achievement. However, this pursuit frequently leaves individuals feeling anxious, unfulfilled, and disconnected from their true selves. To find lasting relief from anxiety and cultivate a deep sense of contentment, It's essential to turn inward and explore what truly matters: personal values, morals, and character.

Everyone yearns for a life of meaning and purpose. A profound sense of fulfillment and harmony emerges when actions and choices align with one's deepest values. This intrinsic motivation helps protect against anxiety, providing a stable foundation and clear direction.

However, it can be challenging to discover true values and purpose. Society, family, and media bombard individuals with messages about what they should want and who they should be. These external pressures can create cognitive distortions, leading to the adoption of inauthentic value systems. As a result, people may strive for goals that don't resonate with their true selves, leaving them anxious, empty, and lost.

To break free from this cycle of anxiety and disconnection,

embarking on an inner journey of self-discovery is crucial. This process involves examining beliefs, attitudes, and behaviors with honesty and curiosity to identify cognitive distortions that may hinder living a life of meaning and purpose.

One common distortion is the belief that a person's worth is contingent upon achievements or external validation. This belief can lead to pursuing goals that are not intrinsically meaningful, simply to gain approval or avoid rejection. As a result, individuals may feel constant pressure and anxiety, never feeling good enough or worthy of love and acceptance.

To counter this distortion, cultivating self-acceptance and self-compassion is essential. Learn to value yourself and others for who you are and who they are, not by social labels, careers, or income. Recognizing that inherent worth as a human being is not dependent on accomplishments, appearance, or social status is crucial. By treating oneself with kindness, understanding, and respect, individuals can develop a stable self-esteem that is not easily shaken by external circumstances.

Another cognitive distortion that can interfere with a sense of meaning and purpose is the belief that one must have a grand, world-changing mission to live a valuable life. This belief can create immense pressure and anxiety, leading to feelings of inadequacy or unfulfillment if a clear vision for making a significant impact on the world is lacking.

A life of meaning and purpose can take many forms and doesn't necessarily require grand gestures or global recognition. It can be as simple as cultivating loving relationships, engaging in fulfilling activities, and making a positive difference in the lives of those around you. Individuals can find a deep sense of purpose and satisfaction by shifting focus from grandiose expectations to small, everyday moments of connection and contribution.

Self-reflection and exploration are essential to discovering a unique path to meaning and purpose. This involves asking questions such as:

- What values are most important to me? What principles do I want to live by?

- What activities or experiences bring me joy, flow, and engagement?
- How do I want to contribute to the world and positively impact others?
- What legacy do I want to leave behind? How do I want to be remembered?

By contemplating these questions with openness and curiosity, individuals can gain clarity on what truly matters to them. They may discover that their deepest values include compassion, creativity, learning, or service to others. They may realize they feel most alive when engaging in art, nature, or meaningful conversation. Individuals can build a fulfilling and purposeful life by aligning choices and actions with these authentic values and passions.

Living a life of meaning and purpose requires courage, vulnerability, and a willingness to step outside one's comfort zone. It may involve taking risks, facing fears, and letting go of old patterns and beliefs that no longer serve them. However, the rewards of this inner work are immeasurable. When living in alignment with their deepest values and desires, individuals experience a sense of vitality, resilience, and inner peace that can weather any storm.

One of the most powerful benefits of living a life of meaning and purpose is its impact on mental health and well-being. When engaged in intrinsically meaningful activities, individuals experience a sense of flow and absorption that can be deeply satisfying and fulfilling. This sense of engagement and purpose is a natural antidote to anxiety, providing a sense of grounding and perspective.

In contrast, lacking a sense of meaning and purpose can make individuals more vulnerable to anxiety and other mental health challenges. Without a clear understanding of direction or intrinsic motivation, they may feel adrift and disconnected from themselves and others. They may be more susceptible to stress, worry, and rumination as they struggle to find a sense of control and coherence in their lives.

Cultivating meaning and purpose is an ongoing process of growth and self-discovery. As individuals move through different life stages, values and priorities may shift and evolve. What brought fulfillment in one's twenties may not be the same as what brings joy in one's forties or sixties. By staying open to new experiences and perspectives and continually reflecting on what matters most, individuals can maintain a sense of vitality and purpose throughout their lives.

In addition to reducing anxiety and promoting well-being, living a life of meaning and purpose can profoundly impact relationships and communities. When clear about values and passions, individuals are more likely to attract and connect with others who share their vision and priorities. They may build more profound, authentic relationships based on shared meaning and purpose rather than superficial interests or external markers of success.

Furthermore, when engaged in meaningful work or activities, individuals are more likely to impact the world around them positively. Whether through creative contributions, service to others, or commitment to personal growth and transformation, individuals can create ripples of positive change that extend far beyond themselves.

Finding meaning and purpose is not about achieving a specific goal or outcome but cultivating an authentic, fulfilling, and connected way of being in the world. It's about discovering what makes one come alive and pursuing it with passion and integrity. Committing to this inner work can help individuals reduce anxiety, enhance well-being, and contribute to a more compassionate, creative, and thriving world.

Finding meaning and purpose is deeply personal and transformative. It requires confronting fears, challenging assumptions, and letting go of beliefs and behaviors that no longer serve individuals. It invites exploring values, passions, and desires and aligning choices and actions with what truly matters. By doing so, individuals can cultivate intrinsic motivation, self-acceptance, and inner peace that act as buffers against anxiety and other mental health challenges.

This journey may involve setbacks, doubts, and challenges along the way. However, individuals can navigate these challenges with resilience and grace by staying committed to personal growth and self-discovery and surrounding themselves with supportive and inspiring others. They can learn to embrace life's uncertainty and complexity while staying anchored in their deepest values and purpose.

The rewards of living a life of meaning and purpose are immeasurable. Individuals experience greater joy, fulfillment, and well-being, and they also have the opportunity to impact the world around them in a positive way. By bringing unique gifts, passions, and perspectives to bear on the challenges and opportunities of our time, individuals can contribute to a more just, compassionate, and thriving world for all.

Embracing the journey of finding meaning and purpose with courage, curiosity, and an open heart is crucial. Being willing to ask deep questions, challenge assumptions, and take bold steps in the direction of one's dreams is essential. And remembering that no matter what challenges individuals face along the way, they can create a life of authenticity, connection, and purpose – one choice, one moment, one day at a time.

# 19

# *Final Chapter*

Congratulations on completing *ANXIETY FREE: A 12-Week Self-Help Guide to Overcome Anxiety*! Throughout these chapters, you have learned and practiced various evidence-based techniques, processes, and coping skills to manage and overcome anxiety. These strategies have provided a solid foundation for maintaining your progress and living an anxiety-free life.

As you embark on this new chapter, recognize that the journey to lasting change is not always linear. Setbacks are a normal part of the process. However, by remaining diligent, mindful, and committed to using your *ANXIETY FREE* strategies, you can continue to navigate life's challenges with greater ease and resilience. You should know that the information within *ANXIETY FREE* contains strategies and skills for life, not just to address anxiety.

During the program, you gained valuable insights into the nature of anxiety and its impact on your mind and body. You learned to identify and challenge negative thought patterns, practice mindfulness and relaxation techniques, and develop a more accepting and compassionate relationship with your thoughts and emotions. You also discovered the importance of self-care, building supportive social connections, and finding meaning and purpose in your life.

Moving forward, remember that most people live anxiety-free lives. Stress is a normal part of life, but you can manage it effectively with the right tools and mindset to prevent it from becoming chronic anxiety. The key is maintaining a proactive approach to your mental well-being and incorporating the strategies you have learned into your daily life.

One of the most powerful tools you have acquired is recognizing and reframing negative thoughts. When you find yourself slipping into anxious thought patterns, take a step back and challenge the accuracy and helpfulness of these thoughts. Practice replacing them with more balanced, realistic, and compassionate alternatives.

Continue to prioritize mindfulness and relaxation practices, such as deep breathing, progressive muscle relaxation, and meditation. These techniques reduce stress, promote emotional regulation, and enhance overall well-being. Make time for these practices daily, even just for a few minutes.

Regularly engage in activities promoting self-care and joy, such as exercise, hobbies, leisure time in nature, or connecting with loved ones. You build resilience and create a strong foundation for managing stress and anxiety by nurturing your physical, emotional, and social needs.

Remember, setbacks are opportunities for growth and learning. If you experience a surge of anxiety, approach it with curiosity and compassion. Reflect on what may have triggered the anxiety and how you can apply your learned skills to navigate the situation. Celebrate your successes, no matter how small, and use them as motivation to continue moving forward.

Finally, do not hesitate to seek support when needed. Whether it is reaching out to a trusted friend, family member, or mental health professional, having a supportive network can make all the difference in maintaining your progress and thriving in your anxiety-free life.

Your dedication and commitment to understanding and managing your anxiety have not only equipped you with valuable tools and strategies but have also revealed your innate strength and resilience. Your path to overcoming anxiety has been a catalyst for personal transformation. You have challenged limiting beliefs, developed new perspectives, and cultivated a more positive and empowering mindset. These profound changes extend far beyond the realm of anxiety management; they have the power to transform every aspect of your life.

As you step into this new chapter, recognize that your journey with anxiety has been a valuable teacher. It has taught you the importance of self-awareness, self-compassion, and adaptability. It has shown you that you can face challenges head-on and emerge stronger and wiser. Use these lessons to guide you through life's ups and downs.

Personal growth is an ongoing process, and your journey with anxiety has provided you with a solid foundation for continued self-discovery and development. Approach the opportunities that come your way, big and small, with the same courage, resilience, and self-compassion you have cultivated throughout this program.

Remember, you are the author of your own story. Your experience with anxiety is just one minor passage in your book of life. Embrace your unique journey and trust your ability to create a life that aligns with your values, passions, and dreams.

As you continue this lifelong journey of personal growth and well-being, trust in the knowledge and skills you have acquired. Welcome the challenges and opportunities that come your way, knowing you have the tools and resilience to handle them gracefully and confidently. As Booker T. Washington said, "Success is to be measured not so much by the position that one has reached in life as by the obstacles which he has overcome." This illustrates that overcoming challenges is a significant measure of success on your journey. Moreover, Michael Jordan's perspective, "Obstacles don't have to stop you. If you run into a wall, don't turn around and give up. Figure out how to climb it, go through it, or work around it," underscores the importance of facing challenges directly and finding ways to overcome them. By staying committed to your progress and practicing the strategies outlined in this book, you can maintain an anxiety-free life filled with joy, purpose, and endless possibilities.

# Appendix

About the Author
Defense Mechanisms
Cognitive Distortions
Anxiety FAQ
References

# *About The Author*

## About Dr. Dave

Dr. Dave Ferruolo combines a rich educational background with diverse clinical expertise to guide individuals to an Anxiety-Free life. With a BA in Psychology, a Masters in Clinical Social Work, and a Doctoral Degree, he is well-equipped as a Licensed Independent Clinical Social Worker (LICSW) and Master Licensed Alcohol and Drug Counselor (MLADC). His experience as a former Navy SEAL informs his dedicated approach to psychotherapy. Certified in various therapeutic modalities-including cognitive-behavioral therapy, mindfulness, trauma-focused therapies, and psychedelic-assisted therapies, Dr. Dave leverages his extensive knowledge to empower those struggling with Anxiety to lead a more balanced, calm life.

# Defense Mechanisms

**Avoidance:** Evading thoughts, emotions, or situations that are perceived as threatening or distressing. Example: Circumventing social events due to apprehension about rejection or humiliation.

**Behavioral Addictions:** Engaging in compulsive actions or habits (e.g., gambling, shopping, excessive exercise) as a means of managing stress, anxiety, or emotional distress.

**Catastrophizing:** Magnifying the potential adverse outcomes of a situation, resulting in heightened anxiety or distress. Example: Envisioning the direst possible consequence of a minor error or setback.

**Compartmentalization:** Isolating conflicting thoughts, emotions, or behaviors into distinct mental compartments to circumvent cognitive dissonance. Example: Justifying unethical conduct by separating it from one's moral principles.

**Compensation:** Accentuating strengths or accomplishments in one domain to counterbalance perceived deficiencies in another. Example: Excelling academically or athletically to offset feelings of social ineptitude.

**Conversion:** Transforming psychological distress or conflict into physical symptoms without a medical cause. Example: Developing blindness or paralysis as a consequence of unresolved trauma.

**Defensive Pessimism:** Embracing a negative outlook or anticipating the worst to shield oneself from disappointment or failure. Example:

Habitually expecting adverse outcomes to avoid being surprised by setbacks.

**Denial:** Disavowing or failing to acknowledge reality, particularly when it is unpleasant or upsetting. Example: Rejecting evidence of a substance abuse problem despite clear indications.

**Displacement:** Redirecting emotions or impulses from their original source to a less intimidating target. Example: Expressing anger towards a family member instead of the actual source of frustration, such as a boss.

**Dissociation:** Mentally disconnecting from reality or one's physical body to manage overwhelming emotions, trauma, or distressing experiences. Example: Experiencing a sense of detachment or observing oneself from an external perspective during a traumatic event.

**Distortion:** Construing reality in a manner that aligns with one's desires, beliefs, or expectations, often disregarding contradictory evidence. Example: Perceiving a romantic interest as perfect despite evidence of their flaws.

**Emotional Detachment:** Maintaining emotional distance or aloofness in relationships to avoid vulnerability, rejection, or intimacy. Example: Eschewing profound conversations or emotional expression to preserve control or autonomy.

**Emotional Eating:** Consuming food to alleviate or cope with challenging emotions, such as stress, sadness, or boredom. Example: Seeking comfort in ice cream or chocolate when feeling distressed or lonely.

**Emotional Inhibition:** Repressing or restraining the expression of emotions, especially negative or uncomfortable ones, to maintain composure or avoid vulnerability. Example: Withholding tears or anger during a confrontational conversation.

**Emotional Numbing:** Disengaging from or desensitizing oneself to emotional experiences to avoid pain or discomfort. Example: Emotionally shutting down after enduring repeated rejection or trauma.

**Emotional Overcontrol:** Exercising excessive restraint or control over one's emotions, often due to fear of losing control or appearing vulnerable. Example: Suppressing tears or anger even in situations where emotional expression would be appropriate or healthy.

**Emotional Suppression:** Repressing or concealing emotions, particularly negative or distressing ones, to project strength, composure, or control. Example: Pretending to be happy and content despite feeling sad or upset internally.

**Escapism:** Evading reality or unpleasant emotions by immersing oneself in distractions or fantasies. Example: Excessively watching television or playing video games to avoid confronting stress or anxiety.

**Exaggeration:** Overstating or embellishing one's accomplishments, abilities, or virtues to enhance self-esteem or gain approval from others. Example: Inflating one's contribution to a group project to appear more competent.

**Externalization:** Attributing one's own failures, mistakes, or shortcomings to external factors or circumstances, rather than accepting personal responsibility. Example: Blaming poor academic performance on a challenging teacher instead of acknowledging insufficient effort or preparation.

**Fantasy:** Constructing an imaginary world or scenarios to escape from reality. Example: Fantasizing about winning the lottery and never having to work again when dissatisfied with one's job.

**Humor:** Employing humor to navigate difficult or uncomfortable situations. Example: Cracking jokes about a stressful event to alleviate tension and improve the mood.

**Hypochondriasis:** Magnifying or fixating on minor physical symptoms to evade dealing with emotional distress. Example: Incessantly worrying about having a grave illness when experiencing anxiety.

**Idealization:** Perceiving someone or something as flawless, admirable, or perfect to avoid confronting reality. Example: Idolizing a celebrity without personally knowing them.

**Identification:** Imitating or aligning oneself with individuals or groups regarded as powerful or esteemed to boost self-esteem or mitigate anxiety. Example: Adopting the mannerisms and beliefs of an admired celebrity.

**Intellectualization:** Concentrating excessively on abstract or intellectual aspects of a situation while disregarding the emotional aspects. Example: Analyzing the technicalities of a breakup instead of acknowledging the emotional pain.

**Isolation:** Separating thoughts or emotions from their associated feelings, often through intellectualization or rationalization. Example: Recounting a traumatic event in a detached, factual manner without expressing emotional distress.

**Magical Thinking:** Subscribing to supernatural or irrational connections between thoughts, actions, or events to exert control or alleviate anxiety. Example: Trusting that wearing lucky socks will ensure success in a job interview.

**Minimization:** Understating the significance of one's thoughts, feelings, or actions. Example: Claiming to "only have a few drinks" each night despite engaging in heavy drinking.

**Obsessive-Compulsive Personality:** Adhering inflexibly to rules, routines, or rituals to exert control over one's environment or mitigate anxiety. Example: Meticulously organizing belongings or adhering to strict daily schedules to manage uncertainty or fear.

**Passive Acceptance:** Submitting to unfavorable circumstances without taking active steps to alter them. Example: Tolerating mistreatment in a relationship without establishing boundaries or seeking assistance.

**Passive-aggressiveness:** Expressing hostility or resentment indirectly through nonverbal behaviors, such as sarcasm, procrastination, or deliberate inefficiency. Example: Giving someone the silent treatment instead of directly addressing an issue.

**Perfectionism:** Establishing excessively high standards for oneself or others and becoming overly critical when those standards are not met. Example: Relentlessly pursuing flawlessness in academic, professional, or personal endeavors.

**Projection:** Assigning one's own unacceptable thoughts, feelings, or desires to others to avoid self-awareness or responsibility. Example: Accusing a partner of jealousy while denying one's own jealous feelings.

**Rationalization:** Devising logical explanations or justifications for behaviors or thoughts that are otherwise unacceptable. Example: Rationalizing excessive drinking by claiming to be merely "enjoying life."

**Reactive Formation:** Embracing beliefs or behaviors that are the opposite of one's true feelings or desires in response to anxiety or guilt. Example: Vociferously opposing LGBTQ rights due to internalized homophobia.

**Regression:** Reverting to an earlier developmental stage in the face of stress. Example: An adult sucking their thumb during periods of extreme anxiety.

**Repression:** Unconsciously suppressing disturbing or threatening thoughts, feelings, or memories from awareness. Example: Having no recollection of childhood trauma experienced.

**Rumination:** Persistently mulling over negative thoughts, feelings, or memories without finding resolution or relief, often leading to increased distress and anxiety. Example: Repeatedly replaying past mistakes or failures in one's mind.

**Scapegoating:** Holding others or external circumstances responsible for one's own mistakes or problems. Example: Blaming a coworker for a project's failure instead of acknowledging one's own role in the problem.

**Selective Attention:** Concentrating only on certain aspects of a situation while disregarding others, particularly those that elicit discomfort or conflict. Example: Ignoring evidence that contradicts one's political beliefs.

**Selective Memory:** Recalling only certain aspects of past events while conveniently forgetting or distorting others to protect oneself from painful or uncomfortable memories.

**Self-Handicapping:** Establishing obstacles or excuses to avoid exerting effort or taking responsibility for failure. Example: Procrastinating on studying for an exam and then attributing a low grade to insufficient preparation.

**Social Comparison:** Assessing one's own abilities, opinions, or accomplishments in relation to those of others to boost self-esteem or cope with feelings of inadequacy. Example: Feeling better about oneself by comparing oneself to others perceived as less successful or fortunate.

**Splitting:** Perceiving situations, people, or things as either entirely good or entirely bad, with no middle ground. Example: Viewing a friend as either perfect or completely flawed, depending on recent interactions.

**Sublimation:** Redirecting unacceptable impulses or emotions into socially acceptable activities. Example: An individual with aggressive tendencies becoming a successful athlete.

**Suppression:** Deliberately pushing unwanted thoughts, emotions, or memories out of awareness. Example: Consciously avoiding thinking about a traumatic event to prevent distress.

**Undoing:** Participating in actions or rituals to negate or counteract feelings of guilt or anxiety stemming from previous behaviors. Example: Engaging in charitable activities after behaving selfishly.

**Withdrawal:** Disengaging from social interactions or evading responsibilities to cope with stress or anxiety. Example: Isolating oneself from friends and family during periods of depression.

# Cognitive Distortions

**All-or-Nothing Thinking (Black and White Thinking):** Perceiving situations or people in absolute terms, without acknowledging the complexity or nuances of reality. Example: Believing that you're either a complete success or a total failure, with no middle ground.

**Always Being Right:** Insisting on being correct in every situation, even at the cost of damaging relationships or hindering personal growth. Example: Refusing to consider alternative viewpoints in a discussion.

**Assumed Constraints:** Limiting your potential based on perceived barriers that may not be accurate or insurmountable, such as age, gender, or past experiences. Example: Believing that you can't pursue a new hobby because you're "not talented enough."

**Attentional Bias:** Disproportionately focusing on negative or threatening information while disregarding positive or neutral stimuli. Example: Fixating on a single critical comment while overlooking numerous compliments.

**Attribution Errors:** Drawing inaccurate conclusions about the causes of events or behaviors, leading to misinterpretations and miscommunication. Example: Assuming someone's negative behavior is due to their personality rather than considering situational factors.

**Belief Perseverance:** Maintaining a belief despite contradictory evidence, often due to emotional attachment or cognitive dissonance. Example: Adhering to a political ideology despite facts that challenge its validity.

**Blaming:** Assigning responsibility for negative emotions or outcomes to others without acknowledging your own contributions. Example: Blaming a partner for your own unhappiness in a relationship.

**Catastrophizing:** Magnifying the negative aspects of a situation and anticipating the worst possible outcome. Example: Believing that a minor setback will lead to complete ruin.

**Cognitive Rigidity:** Struggling to modify your thoughts or beliefs in light of new information or changing circumstances. Example: Refusing to reconsider your stance on a controversial topic despite compelling evidence.

**Comparative Suffering:** Invalidating your own struggles or pain by comparing them to others who you believe have it worse. Example: Telling yourself that you have no right to feel anxious because others face more severe hardships.

**Comparison to Unattainable Standards:** Evaluating yourself or your life against unrealistic or perfectionistic benchmarks, leading to feelings of inadequacy or dissatisfaction. Example: Comparing your body to airbrushed images in media and feeling inferior as a result.

**Confirmation Bias:** Selectively seeking out information that supports your existing beliefs while disregarding evidence that contradicts them. Example: Only engaging with news sources that align with your political views and dismissing opposing perspectives.

**Control Fallacies:** Overestimating your control over external events or underestimating your control over your own actions and reactions. Example: Believing that you are solely responsible for someone else's happiness or that external factors entirely determine your success.

**Discounting the Positive:** Minimizing or dismissing positive experiences, qualities, or accomplishments. Example: Brushing off compliments by thinking they're insincere or undeserved.

**Emotional Reasoning:** Treating your emotions as evidence of truth, rather than objectively evaluating facts. Example: Concluding that a situation must be dangerous because it evokes anxiety, regardless of actual risk.

**Fallacy of Change:** Expecting others to change to meet your needs or believing that you can change others. Example: Assuming that if someone loves you, they should alter their behavior to suit your preferences.

**Fallacy of Fairness:** Insisting that life should be fair and finding any perceived injustice intolerable. Example: Feeling bitter because you believe you deserve better treatment than what you've experienced.

**False Consensus Effect:** Overestimating the extent to which others share your beliefs or opinions. Example: Assuming that everyone must agree with your perspective on a divisive issue because your immediate social circle does.

**Fatalistic Thinking:** Believing that outcomes are predetermined and efforts to change them are pointless. Example: Assuming that your actions won't make a difference because "it's just destiny."

**Forecasting Errors:** Drawing inaccurate conclusions about future events, often assuming the worst-case scenario without considering alternative possibilities. Example: Predicting that a presentation will be a disaster and ruminating about the potential consequences.

**Heaven's Reward Fallacy:** Believing that enduring suffering or making sacrifices will eventually lead to a reward. Example: Tolerating mistreatment in a relationship because you believe your patience will ultimately be recognized and appreciated.

**Hindsight Bias:** Perceiving past events as more predictable or inevitable than they were at the time, often after learning the outcome. Example: Believing that you knew a relationship would fail from the start, even though you were hopeful about it initially.

**Imposter Syndrome:** Doubting your accomplishments and fearing being exposed as a fraud, despite evidence of your competence. Example: Attributing your success to luck or external factors rather than recognizing your own skills and efforts.

**In-group Bias:** Favoring members of your own group over those outside of it, leading to prejudice or discrimination. Example: Giving preferential treatment to colleagues from your department while being dismissive of those from other departments.

**Jumping to Conclusions:** Drawing hasty conclusions without sufficient evidence, either by mind reading (assuming you know others' thoughts) or fortune telling (predicting negative outcomes). Example: Concluding that someone dislikes you based on a single interaction, without considering alternative explanations.

**Just World Fallacy:** Assuming that the world is inherently fair and people get what they deserve, leading to victim-blaming or overlooking systemic injustices. Example: Believing that someone who experiences misfortune must have done something to warrant it.

**Labeling:** Assigning global labels to yourself or others based on limited information or isolated events. Example: Calling yourself a "loser" because you faced a setback.

**Magnification and Minimization:** Exaggerating the significance of negative events while downplaying the importance of positive ones. Example: Ruminating on a single mistake while disregarding numerous successes.

**Memory Bias:** Recalling past events in a way that confirms your current beliefs or emotions, rather than accurately reflecting what happened. Example: Remembering a past failure as more catastrophic or defining than it actually was.

**Mind Reading:** Presuming to know what others are thinking or feeling, usually in a negative way, without any concrete evidence. Example: Assuming someone is annoyed with you without considering alternative explanations for their behavior.

**Need for Approval:** Seeking validation and approval from others to feel worthy or competent, and experiencing distress when it's not received. Example: Feeling devastated by criticism because it threatens your sense of self-worth.

**Overgeneralization:** Making sweeping conclusions based on limited evidence or isolated incidents. Example: Believing that you'll never succeed because you failed at one task.

**Perfectionism:** Holding yourself or others to unrealistically high standards and experiencing distress when those standards are not met. Example: Feeling like a failure because you made a minor error, despite overall strong performance.

**Personalization:** Assuming responsibility for events that are beyond your control or blaming yourself for external circumstances. Example: Believing that a friend's bad mood is a result of something you did wrong.

**Regret Avoidance:** Making decisions or engaging in behaviors to avoid potential regret, even if it means forgoing potential benefits or opportunities for growth. Example: Avoiding taking risks or trying new things out of fear of regretting the outcome.

**Selective Attention:** Focusing only on certain aspects of a situation while ignoring others. Example: Fixating on a single negative comment in a sea of positive feedback.

**Self-Blame:** Taking personal responsibility for negative outcomes or events, even when they are caused by factors beyond your control. Example: Blaming yourself for a company's financial troubles, despite external economic factors playing a significant role.

**Self-Serving Bias:** Interpreting information in a way that maintains or enhances your self-esteem, attributing positive outcomes to internal factors and negative outcomes to external factors. Example: Taking credit for a team's success while blaming failures on lack of resources or support.

**Should Statements:** Imposing unrealistic expectations on yourself or others with "should," "must," or "ought to" statements. Example: Thinking, "I should always put others' needs before my own," or "They ought to know what I want without me having to ask."

**Social Comparison:** Evaluating yourself in relation to others, often leading to feelings of inferiority or superiority. Example: Feeling inadequate because a coworker has a more impressive job title or feeling superior because you perceive yourself as more attractive than someone else.

**Tunnel Vision:** Narrowly focusing on a single aspect of a situation while neglecting the broader context or alternative perspectives. Example: Fixating on one potential obstacle to a goal and overlooking the resources and opportunities available to overcome it.

# Anxiety FAQ

**What is anxiety?**

Anxiety is a common mental health condition characterized by persistent and excessive worry, fear, and unease that can interfere with daily life.

**What are the different types of anxiety disorders?**

There are several types of anxiety disorders, including Generalized Anxiety Disorder (GAD), Panic Disorder, Social Anxiety Disorder, Specific Phobias, and Obsessive-Compulsive Disorder (OCD).

**What causes anxiety?**

Anxiety can result from a combination of genetic, biological, environmental, and psychological factors. Stressful life events, trauma, and certain medical conditions can also contribute to anxiety.

**What are the common symptoms of anxiety?**

Common symptoms include excessive worry, restlessness, irritability, difficulty concentrating, muscle tension, sleep disturbances, and physical symptoms like rapid heartbeat or sweating.

**How is anxiety diagnosed?**

Diagnosis typically involves a comprehensive evaluation by a mental health professional, including interviews and sometimes physical exams or questionnaires.

**Is anxiety treatable?**

Yes, anxiety is highly treatable with a combination of psychotherapy, medication, lifestyle changes, and other methods.

**What role does therapy play in treating anxiety?**

Therapy, such as cognitive-behavioral therapy (CBT) or exposure therapy, is crucial for addressing the underlying thoughts and behaviors contributing to anxiety.

**Are medications necessary for treating anxiety?**

While not everyone needs medication, anti-anxiety medications can be an effective part of treatment for some individuals, particularly those with severe or persistent symptoms.

**What are some common side effects of anti-anxiety medications?**

Side effects vary by medication but can include drowsiness, dizziness, nausea, weight gain, and sexual dysfunction.

**How important is social support in managing anxiety?**

Strong social support is vital, as it provides emotional comfort, reduces feelings of isolation, and can encourage treatment-seeking behavior.

**Can lifestyle changes affect anxiety?**

Yes, lifestyle changes such as regular exercise, a healthy diet, stress management techniques, and adequate sleep can positively impact anxiety symptoms.

**How can exercise help with anxiety?**

Regular physical activity has been shown to reduce anxiety symptoms by promoting relaxation, improving mood, and increasing self-efficacy.

**What are some strategies for coping with anxiety at work?**

Strategies include setting realistic goals, communicating with supervisors about accommodations, practicing relaxation techniques, and seeking support from colleagues or employee assistance programs.

**How can mindfulness and meditation help with anxiety?**

Mindfulness and meditation can reduce stress, promote relaxation, and help individuals develop a more accepting and non-judgmental relationship with their thoughts and feelings.

**What are some mindfulness exercises for anxiety?**

Mindfulness exercises include deep breathing, progressive muscle relaxation, body scans, and grounding techniques that focus on the present moment.

**Can nutrition impact anxiety?**

Yes, a balanced diet rich in whole foods, omega-3 fatty acids, and B vitamins can support mental health, while excessive caffeine and alcohol intake may worsen anxiety symptoms.

**Is there a connection between gut health and anxiety?**

Emerging research suggests a link between gut health and mood disorders, including anxiety, due to the gut-brain axis. Probiotics and a healthy diet may be beneficial for some individuals.

**How can journaling help with anxiety?**

Journaling offers a way to express thoughts and feelings, identify anxiety triggers, challenge negative thinking patterns, and track progress over time.

**What role does sleep play in managing anxiety?**

Quality sleep is essential for emotional regulation and coping with stress. Poor sleep can exacerbate anxiety symptoms, while good sleep hygiene can help reduce anxiety.

**How does anxiety impact daily life and relationships?**

Anxiety can affect one's ability to work, study, socialize, and enjoy life, often straining personal and professional relationships due to avoidance behaviors or excessive reassurance-seeking.

**Can major life events trigger anxiety?**

Yes, stressful life events such as job loss, relationship changes, or health issues can trigger or worsen anxiety symptoms in susceptible individuals.

**What is the impact of social media on anxiety?**

Excessive or negative social media use can increase feelings of inadequacy, FOMO (fear of missing out), and social comparison, potentially worsening anxiety symptoms.

**How can I support someone with anxiety?**

Offer empathy, listen without judgment, encourage them to seek professional help, and educate yourself about anxiety to better understand their experiences.

**What should I do if my anxiety feels overwhelming or unmanageable?**

Seek help from a mental health professional, reach out to supportive loved ones, and consider crisis resources like anxiety helplines or support groups.

**What is the difference between normal worry and an anxiety disorder?**

Normal worry is typically situational, short-lived, and does not significantly interfere with daily functioning, while anxiety disorders involve persistent, excessive, and often irrational worry that impacts quality of life.

## Can anxiety be prevented?

While not all cases can be prevented, managing stress, building resilience, and maintaining healthy lifestyle choices can reduce the risk of developing an anxiety disorder.

## What is the role of self-compassion in managing anxiety?

Practicing self-compassion can help reduce self-criticism, shame, and perfectionism that often fuel anxiety, promoting a more accepting and kind relationship with oneself.

## How can technology help in managing anxiety?

Mental health apps, online therapy platforms, and virtual support groups can provide accessible resources for coping with anxiety, tracking symptoms, and practicing relaxation techniques.

## What is exposure therapy, and how does it treat anxiety?

Exposure therapy involves gradually confronting feared situations, objects, or thoughts in a safe and controlled manner to reduce anxiety and build confidence over time.

## What is the difference between stress and anxiety?

Stress is typically a response to an external trigger or challenge, while anxiety is an internal emotional state characterized by persistent and often excessive worry or fear.

## Can caffeine worsen anxiety symptoms?

Yes, excessive caffeine intake can increase feelings of restlessness, nervousness, and racing thoughts, exacerbating anxiety symptoms for some individuals.

### How can I manage anxiety during public speaking or performances?

Strategies include practicing relaxation techniques like deep breathing, visualizing success, preparing thoroughly, and gradually exposing yourself to the feared situation to build confidence.

### What is the role of acceptance in coping with anxiety?

Accepting that some level of anxiety is a normal part of life and learning to tolerate uncomfortable feelings can help reduce the struggle and distress associated with anxiety.

### How can I handle anxiety in social situations?

Strategies include setting realistic expectations, practicing conversation skills, focusing on others rather than self-monitoring, and gradually exposing yourself to social situations.

### Can creative activities like art or music help with anxiety?

Yes, engaging in creative activities can provide a healthy outlet for self-expression, promote relaxation, and boost self-esteem, which can help manage anxiety symptoms.

### How can I manage anxiety related to health concerns?

Strategies include seeking accurate information from reliable sources, practicing relaxation techniques, challenging catastrophic thinking, and working with healthcare providers to address concerns.

### What is the link between anxiety and perfectionism?

Perfectionism can fuel anxiety by setting unrealistic standards, fear of failure, and self-criticism. Learning to embrace imperfection and practice self-compassion can help manage anxiety related to perfectionism.

**Can anxiety affect physical health?**

Yes, chronic anxiety can contribute to physical health problems like digestive issues, headaches, muscle tension, and weakened immune function.

**How can I manage anxiety while traveling?**

Strategies include planning ahead, practicing relaxation techniques, carrying calming items like music or essential oils, and challenging anxious thoughts about travel.

**What is the role of resilience in coping with anxiety?**

Building resilience through developing coping skills, maintaining a support network, and practicing self-care can help individuals better manage anxiety and bounce back from setbacks.

**Can pets help with anxiety?**

Yes, pets can provide companionship, emotional support, and a sense of routine that can be helpful for managing anxiety symptoms.

**How can I manage anxiety during significant life transitions?**

Strategies include seeking support from loved ones, maintaining self-care routines, setting realistic expectations, and focusing on the aspects of the transition that are within your control.

**What is the link between anxiety and procrastination?**

Anxiety can contribute to procrastination by fueling perfectionistic tendencies, fear of failure, or overwhelming feelings that lead to avoidance. Addressing underlying anxiety can help reduce procrastination.

**How can I manage anxiety in romantic relationships?**

Strategies include open communication with partners, setting healthy boundaries, practicing self-care, and seeking couples therapy if anxiety is significantly impacting the relationship.

**Can anxiety be genetic?**

Yes, research suggests that there may be a genetic component to anxiety disorders, though environmental and psychological factors also play a significant role.

**What is the role of assertiveness in managing anxiety?**

Developing assertiveness skills can help individuals set healthy boundaries, communicate needs, and reduce anxiety related to interpersonal conflicts or people-pleasing tendencies.

**How can I manage anxiety related to public transportation?**

Strategies include practicing relaxation techniques, carrying distracting items like books or music, gradually exposing yourself to public transportation, and challenging anxious thoughts about safety.

**Can anxiety be a side effect of certain medications?**

Yes, some medications like stimulants, steroids, or cold and flu remedies can have anxiety as a side effect. Always discuss any concerns with a healthcare provider.

**What is the role of self-care in managing anxiety?**

Engaging in regular self-care activities like exercise, hobbies, and stress management techniques can help reduce overall anxiety levels and improve coping skills.

**How can I manage anxiety related to job interviews or work presentations?**

Strategies include thorough preparation, practicing relaxation techniques, focusing on your strengths and qualifications, and reframing the situation as an opportunity rather than a threat.

# References

American Psychiatric Association. (2013). *Diagnostic and Statistical Manual of Mental Disorders (5th ed.)*. Washington, DC: American Psychiatric Publishing.

Anderson, F. G., Sweezy, M., & Schwartz, R. C. (2017). *Internal Family Systems Skills Training Manual: Trauma-Informed Treatment for Anxiety, Depression, PTSD & Substance Abuse*. PESI Publishing & Media.

Bandura, A. (1977). *Social learning theory*. Englewood Cliffs, N.J.: Prentice Hall.

Bannink, F. P. (2007). Solution-focused brief therapy. *Journal of contemporary psychotherapy, 37*(2), 87-94.

Bannink, F. P. (2015). *1001 solution-focused questions: Handbook for solution-focused interviewing*. New York, NY: Norton & Company.

Barlow, D., & Durand, V. (2009). Abnormal psychology; An integrative approach (5ed.). New York, NY: McGraw-Hill.

Beck, A. T., Rush, A. J., Shaw, B. F., & Emery, G. (1979). *Cognitive Therapy of Depression*. New York: Guilford Press.

Beck, J. S. (2011). *Cognitive behavior therapy: Basics and beyond* (2nd ed.). New York, NY: Guilford Press.

Beck, J. S., & Beck, A. T. (2011). *Cognitive behavior therapy: basics and beyond*. New York, NY: The Guilford Press.

Begley, S. (2007). *Train your mind, change your brain: How a new science reveals our extraordinary potential to transform ourselves*. New York: Ballantine Books.

Bell, A. C., & D'Zurilla, T. J. (2009). Problem-solving therapy for depression: a meta-analysis. *Clinical psychology review, 29*(4), 348-353..

Berger, K. S. (2010). *Invitation to the life span.* New York, N.Y.: Worth.

Blonna, R. (2017). *ACT on life not on anger: The new Acceptance and Commitment Therapy guide to problem anger.* New Harbinger Publications.

Brach, T. (2016). *Radical acceptance: Embracing your life with the heart of a Buddha.* New York, NY: Bantam Books.

Brackett, M. A. (2019). *Permission to feel: Unlocking the power of emotions to help our kids, ourselves, and our society thrive.* New York, NY: Celadon Books.

Brackett, M. A., Rivers, S. E., & Salovey, P. (2011). Emotional intelligence: Implications for personal, social, academic, and workplace success. *Social and Personality Psychology Compass, 5*(1), 88-103.

Burns, D. D. (1999). *The Feeling Good Handbook.* New York: Plume.

Butler, A. C., Chapman, J. E., Forman, F. M., & Beck, A. T. (2006). The empirical status of cognitive-behavioral therapy: A review of meta-analyses. Clinical Psychology Review, 26 (1), 17-31.

Capuzzi, D., & Stauffer, M. D. (Eds.). (2016). *Counseling and Psychotherapy: Theories and Interventions.* American Counseling Association.

Chödrön, P. (2016). *When things fall apart: Heart advice for difficult times.* Boston, MA: Shambhala Publications.

Clear, J. (2018). *Atomic habits: An easy & proven way to build good habits & break bad ones.* New York, NY: Avery.

Corcoran, J. (2006). *Cognitive-behavioral methods for social workers: A workbook.* Boston. Pearson/Allyn and Bacon.

Corcoran, J., & Pillai, V. (2018). *Social workers' desk reference* (3rd ed.). Oxford, UK: Oxford University Press.

Creswell, J. D. (2017). *Mindfulness interventions.* Annual Review of Psychology, 68, 491-516.

Cudzik, M., Soroka, E., & Olajossy, M. (2019). The impact of emotional intelligence level on the depression vulnerability. *Current Problems of Psychiatry, 20*(3), 179-186.

Cuijpers, P., Quero, S., Noma, H., Ciharova, M., Miguel, C., Karyotaki, E., ... &

Furukawa, T. A. (2021). Psychotherapies for depression: a network meta-analysis covering efficacy, acceptability and long-term outcomes of all main treatment types. *World Psychiatry, 20*(2), 283-293.

Dahl, J., Wilson, K. G., & Nilsson, A. (2015). Acceptance and Commitment Therapy and the treatment of persons at risk for long-term disability resulting from stress and pain symptoms: A preliminary randomized trial. *Behavior Therapy, 35*(4), 785-801.

Davidson, R. J., & Begley, S. (2012). *The emotional life of your brain: How its unique patterns affect the way you think, feel, and live--and how you can change them.* New York, NY: Hudson Street Press.

De Shazer, S. (1985). *Keys to solution in brief therapy.* New York, NY: Norton.

Dillon, C. (2003). *Learning from mistakes.* Belmont, CA: Brooks/Cole

Dindo, L., Van Liew, J. R., & Arch, J. J. (2017). Acceptance and Commitment Therapy: A transdiagnostic behavioral intervention for mental health and medical conditions. *Neurotherapeutics, 14*(3), 546-553.

Doran, J. M. (2015). *The Theory and Practice of Experiential Dynamic Psychotherapy.* Karnac Books.

Drisko, J. W., & Simmons, B. M. (2012). The evidence base for psychodynamic psychotherapy. *Smith College Studies in Social Work, 82*(4), 374-400.

Duckworth, A. (2016). *Grit: The power of passion and perseverance.* New York, NY: Scribner.

Ellis, A. (1962). *Reason and emotion in psychotherapy.* New York, NY: Lyle Stuart.

Elnitsky, C. A., Blevins, C. L., Fisher, M. P., & Magruder, K. (2017). Military service member and veteran reintegration: A critical review and adapted ecological model. *American Journal of Orthopsychiatry, 87*(2), 114–128. https://doi.org/10.1037/ort0000244

Espejo, E. P., Castriotta, N., Bessonov, D., Kawamura, M., Werdowatz, E. A., & Ayers, C. R. (2016). A pilot study of transdiagnostic group cognitive–behavioral therapy for anxiety in a veteran sample. *Psychological Services, 13*(2), 162–169. https://doi.org/10.1037/ser0000052

Feldman, C., & Kuyken, W. (2019). *Compassion in the landscape of suffering.* Contemporary Buddhism, 20(1), 143-155.

Ferruolo, D. (2015, April). *The Tao of equine facilitation.* PowerPoint presentation at the 12th Gathering on Equine Assisted Learning & Mental Health Practice, Prescott, AZ.

Ferruolo, D. (2016). Psychosocial Equine Program for Veterans. *Social Work, 61*(1), 53–60. https://doi.org/10.1093/sw/swv054

Flaxman, P. E., Blackledge, J. T., & Bond, F. W. (2016). *Acceptance and Commitment Therapy: Distinctive features.* Routledge.

Folke, F., Parling, T., & Melin, L. (2012). Acceptance and Commitment Therapy for Depression: A Preliminary Randomized Clinical Trial for Unemployed on Long-Term Sick Leave. *Cognitive and Behavioral Practice, 19*(4), 583-594.

Fonagy, P., & Allison, E. (2014). The role of mentalizing and epistemic trust in the therapeutic relationship. *Psychotherapy, 51*(3), 372-380.

Forsyth, J. P., & Eifert, G. H. (2016). *The Mindfulness and Acceptance Workbook for Anxiety: A Guide to Breaking Free from Anxiety, Phobias, and Worry Using Acceptance and Commitment Therapy,* Second Edition. New Harbinger Publications.

Franklin, C., Trepper, T. S., Gingerich, W. J., & McCollum, E. E. (Eds.). (2016). *Solution-focused brief therapy: A handbook of evidence-based practice.* Oxford, UK: Oxford University Press.

Fredrickson, B. L. (2013). *Love 2.0: Finding happiness and health in moments of connection.* New York, NY: Penguin Books.

Freud, A. (1936). *The Ego and the Mechanisms of Defense.* London: Hogarth Press and Institute of Psycho-Analysis.

Gabbard, G. O. (2017). *Gabbard's treatments of psychiatric disorders* (5th ed.). Arlington, VA: American Psychiatric Association Publishing.

Gallagher, M. W., Zvolensky, M. J., Long, L. J., Rogers, A. H., & Garey, L. (2019). *The impact of acceptance and commitment therapy on positive psychological outcomes: A systematic review and meta-analysis.* Journal of Contextual Behavioral Science, 14, 379-395.

Gerber, A. J., & Piers, C. (2019). *Neuropsychodynamic psychiatry.* New York, NY: Springer.

Germer, C. K. (2019). *The mindful path to self-compassion: Freeing yourself from destructive thoughts and emotions.* New York, NY: Guilford Press.

Germer, C. K., Siegel, R. D., & Fulton, P. R. (2013). *Mindfulness and psychotherapy.* New York, N.Y.: Guilford Press.

Gilbert, P. (2019). *Compassion: Concepts, research and applications.* London, UK: Routledge.

Gingerich, W. J., & Peterson, L. T. (2013). Effectiveness of solution-focused brief therapy: A systematic qualitative review of controlled outcome studies. *Research on Social Work Practice, 23*(3), 266-283.

Goleman, D. (1995). *Emotional intelligence.* New York, NY: Bantam Books.

Goleman, D., & Senge, P. (2014). *The triple focus: A new approach to education.* Florence, MA: More Than Sound.

Grant, A. (2016). *Originals: How non-conformists move the world.* New York, NY: Viking.

Grant, A. M., & Greene, J. (2018). *Solution-focused coaching: Managing people in a complex world.* New York, NY: Routledge.

Greenberg, L. S. (2015). *Emotion-focused therapy: Coaching clients to work through their feelings* (2nd ed.). Washington, DC: American Psychological Association.

Gross, J. J. (Ed.). (2007). *Handbook of Emotion Regulation.* New York: Guilford Press.

Haddock, S. A., Weiler, L. M., Trump, L. J., & Henry, K. L. (2017). The efficacy of internal family systems therapy in the treatment of depression among female college students: A pilot study. *Journal of marital and family therapy, 43*(1), 131-144.

Haidt, J. (2012). *The righteous mind: Why good people are divided by politics and religion.* New York, NY: Pantheon Books.

Hanson, R. (2015). *Hardwiring happiness: The new brain science of contentment, calm, and confidence.* New York, NY: Harmony.

Hanson, R. (2018). *Resilient: How to grow an unshakable core of calm, strength, and happiness.* New York, NY: Harmony Books.

Harris, R. (2019). *ACT Made Simple: An Easy-To-Read Primer on Acceptance and Commitment Therapy* (2nd ed.). New Harbinger Publications.

Hasler, G. (2010). Pathophysiology of depression: do we have any solid evidence of interest to clinicians? *World Psychiatry, 9*(3), 155-161.

Hayes, S. C., & Hofmann, S. G. (Eds.). (2018). *The third wave of cognitive behavioral therapy and the rise of process-based care.* Guilford Press.

Hayes, S. C., & Lillis, J. (2012). *Acceptance and Commitment Therapy.* Washington, DC: American Psychological Association.

Hayes, S. C., Levin, M. E., Plumb-Vilardaga, J., Villatte, J. L., & Pistorello, J. (2013). Acceptance and commitment therapy and contextual behavioral science: Examining the progress of a distinctive model of behavioral and cognitive therapy. *Behavior Therapy, 44*(2), 180-198.

Hayes, S. C., Strosahl, K. D., & Wilson, K. G. (1999). *Acceptance and Commitment Therapy: An Experiential Approach to Behavior Change.* New York, NY: Guilford Press.

Herbine-Blank, T., Kerpelman, D. C., & Sweezy, M. (2016). *Intimacy from the Inside Out: Courage and Compassion in Couple Therapy.* Routledge.

Hofmann, S. G., & Gómez, A. F. (2017). Mindfulness-based interventions for anxiety and depression. *Psychiatric Clinics of North America, 40*(4), 739-749.

Hofmann, S. G., Asmundson, G. J. G., & Beck, A. T. (2018). *The science of cognitive behavioral therapy.* San Diego, CA: Academic Press.

Hofmann, S. G., Asnaani, A., Vonk, I. J., Sawyer, A. T., & Fang, A. (2012). The efficacy of cognitive behavioral therapy: A review of meta-analyses. *Cognitive Therapy and Research, 36*(5), 427-440.

Hoge, C. W. (2010). *Once a warrior, always a warrior: navigating the transition from combat to home--including combat stress, PTSD, and mTBI.* Guilford, CT: Globe Pequot.

Holmes, J. (2002). All you need is cognitive behaviour therapy? *British Medical Journal, 324*(7332), 288–294.

Holmes, T. R. (2015). *Parts Work: An Illustrated Guide to Your Inner Life.* Winged Heart Press.

Honyashiki, M., Furukawa, T. A., Noma, H., Tanaka, S., Chen, P., Ichikawa, K., ... & Caldwell, D. M. (2014). Specificity of CBT for depression: a contribution from multiple treatments meta-analyses. *Cognitive therapy and research, 38,* 249-260.

Kabat-Zinn, J. (1990). *Full Catastrophe Living: Using the Wisdom of Your Body and Mind to Face Stress, Pain, and Illness.* New York: Delta.

Kabat-Zinn, J. (1994). *Wherever you go, there you are: Mindfulness meditation in everyday life.* New York, NY: Hyperion.

Kabat-Zinn, J. (2013). *Full catastrophe living: Using the wisdom of your body and mind to face stress, pain, and illness.* New York: Bantam

Kabat-Zinn, J. (2016). *Mindfulness for beginners: Reclaiming the present moment—and your life.* Boulder, CO: Sounds True.

Kabat-Zinn, J., & Davidson, R. J. (Eds.). (2019). *The Mind's Own Physician: A Scientific Dialogue with the Dalai Lama on the Healing Power of Meditation.* New Harbinger Publications.

Katz, M., Hilsenroth, M. J., Gold, J. R., Moore, M., Pitman, S. R., Levy, S. R., & Owen, J. (2019). Adherence, flexibility, and outcome in psychodynamic treatment of depression. *Journal of Counseling Psychology, 66*(1), 94.

Kelly, G.A. *The Psychology of Personal Constructs.* New York: Norton, 1955.

Keltner, D., Oatley, K., & Jenkins, J. M. (2019). *Understanding emotions* (4th ed.). Hoboken, NJ: Wiley.

Kim, J. S. (2008). Examining the effectiveness of solution-focused brief therapy: A meta-analysis. *Research on Social Work Practice, 18*(2), 107-116.

Kim, J. S. (2015). *Solution-focused brief therapy: A multicultural approach.* Thousand Oaks, CA: SAGE Publications.

Kirsch, I., Moore, T. J., Scoboria, A., & Nicholls, S. S. (2002). The emperor's new drugs: An analysis of antidepressant medication data submitted to the U.S. Food and Drug Administration. *Prevention & Treatment, 5*(1), 23.

Knox, J. (2015). *Self-Agency in Psychotherapy: Attachment, Autonomy, and Intimacy.* Norton & Company.

Kolassa, I., & Elbert, T. (2007). Structural and functional neuroplasticity in relation to traumatic stress. *Current    Directions In Psychological Science, 16*(6), 321-325. doi:10.1111/j.1467-8721.2007.00529.x

Koorankot, J., Moosa, A., Froerer, A., & Rajan, S. K. (2022). Solution focused vs problem focused questions on affect and processing speed among individuals with depression. *Journal of Contemporary Psychotherapy, 52*(4), 347-353.

Lebow, J., Chambers, A., Christensen, A., & Johnson, S. M. (Eds.). (2019). *Encyclopedia of couple and family therapy.* Switzerland: Springer International Publishing.

Leichsenring D Sc, F., Salzer, S., Jaeger, U., Kächele, H., Kreische, R., Leweke, F., ... & Leibing D Sc, E. (2009). Short-term psychodynamic psychotherapy and cognitive-behavioral therapy in generalized anxiety disorder: a randomized, controlled trial. *American Journal of Psychiatry, 166*(8), 875-881.

Lemma, A. (2016). *Introduction to the practice of psychoanalytic psychotherapy* (2nd ed.). Chichester, UK: Wiley Blackwell.

Linehan, M. M. (1993). *Cognitive-behavioral treatment of borderline personality disorder.* New York, NY: Guilford Press.

Lloyd, J., & Hertlein, K. M. (2015). *The complete systemic therapist: Integrating systemic approaches in psychotherapy.* Boston, MA: Cengage Learning.

Lopes, P. N., Salovey, P., & Straus, R. (2017). Emotional intelligence, personality, and the perceived quality of social relationships. *Personality and Individual Differences, 107*, 212-218.

López-López, J. A., Davies, S. R., Caldwell, D. M., Churchill, R., Peters, T. J., Tallon, D., ... & Welton, N. J. (2019). The process and delivery of CBT for depression in adults: a systematic review and network meta-analysis. *Psychological medicine, 49*(12), 1937-1947.

Luoma, J. B., Hayes, S. C., & Walser, R. D. (2017). *Learning ACT: An Acceptance and*

*Commitment Therapy skills-training manual for therapists* (2nd ed.). New Harbinger Publications.

Lutz, A. B. (2017). *Learning solution-focused therapy: An illustrated guide.* Washington, DC: American Psychiatric Association Publishing.

Lutz, W., Schiefele, A. K., Wucherpfennig, F., Rubel, J., & Stulz, N. (2016). Clinical effectiveness of cognitive behavioral therapy for depression in routine care: A propensity score based comparison between randomized controlled trials and clinical practice. *Journal of affective disorders, 189*, 150-158.

Luyten, P., Mayes, L. C., Fonagy, P., Target, M., & Blatt, S. J. (2015). Handbook of psychodynamic approaches to psychopathology. New York, NY: Guilford Press.

Lyubomirsky, S. (2013). *The myths of happiness: What should make you happy, but doesn't, what shouldn't make you happy, but does.* New York, NY: Penguin Press.

MacCann, C., & Roberts, R. D. (2008). New paradigms for assessing emotional intelligence: theory and data. *Emotion, 8*(4), 540.

MacLearn, C. (2008). Use of self in cognitive behavioral therapy. Clinical Social Work Journal , 36 (3), 245-253.

Maguire, L. (2002). Clinical social work: Beyond generalist practice with individuals, groups, and families. Pacific Grove, CA: Brooks/Cole.

Manber, R., Kraemer, H., Arnow, B., Trivedi, M., Rush, A., Thase, M., et al. (2008). Faster remission of chronic depression with combined psychotherapy and medication than with each therapy alone. Journal of Counseling and Clinical Psychology , 76 (3), 459-476.

Mansell, W., Harvey, A., Watkins, E., & Shafran, R. (2019). Conceptual foundations of the transdiagnostic approach to CBT. *Journal of Cognitive Psychotherapy, 33*(1), 14-33.

Manson, M. (2016). *The subtle art of not giving a f*ck: A counterintuitive approach to living a good life*. New York, NY: HarperOne.

McGinn, L. K. (2000). Cognitive behavioral therapy of depression: theory, treatment, and empirical status. *American journal of psychotherapy, 54*(2), 257-262.

McGonigal, K. (2015). *The upside of stress: Why stress is good for you, and how to get good at it.* New York, NY: Avery.

McKergow, M., & Korman, H. (2017). *In between: Neither inside nor outside the therapy room.* London, UK: Solutions Books.

McWilliams, N. (2016). *Psychoanalytic diagnosis: Understanding personality structure in the clinical process* (2nd ed.). New York, NY: The Guilford Press.

Michl, L. C., McLaughlin, K. A., Shepherd, K., & Nolen-Hoeksema, S. (2013). Rumination as a mechanism linking        stressful life events to symptoms of depression and anxiety: Longitudinal evidence in early adolescents and adults. *Journal Of Abnormal Psychology, 122*(2), 339-352. doi:10.1037/a0031994

Mikolajczak, M., Gross, J. J., & Roskam, I. (2019). Parental emotional regulation: The wider impact on family life. *Emotion Review, 11*(3), 230-243.

Miller, W. R., & Rollnick, S. (2002). Motivational interviewing: Preparing people for change (2nd ed.). New York: Guilford Press.

Neff, K. (2011). *Self-compassion: The proven power of being kind to yourself.* New York, NY: William Morrow.

Neff, K., & Germer, C. (2018). *The Mindful Self-Compassion Workbook: A Proven Way to Accept Yourself, Build Inner Strength, and Thrive.* The Guilford Press.

Nelis, D., Quoidbach, J., Mikolajczak, M., & Hansenne, M. (2011). Increasing emotional intelligence: (How) is it possible? *Personality and Individual Differences, 50*(1), 56-61.

Newport, C. (2016). *Deep work: Rules for focused success in a distracted world.* New York, NY: Grand Central Publishing.

Nezu, A. M., Nezu, C. M., & D'Zurilla, T. J. (2013). *Problem-solving therapy: A treatment manual.* New York, NY: Springer Publishing Company.

Otte, C. (2011). Cognitive behavioral therapy in anxiety disorders: current state of the evidence. *Dialogues in clinical neuroscience, 13*(4), 413-421.

Perry, B. D., & Pollard, R. (1998). Homeostasis, stress, trauma, and adaptation. A neurodevelopmental view of        childhood trauma. *Child And Adolescent Psychiatric Clinics Of North America, 7*(1), 33.

Perry, D., & Szalavitz, M. (2006). *The boy who was raised as a dog: and other stories from a child psychiatrist's notebook: What traumatized children can teach us about loss, love, and healing. New York Basic Books.*

Raes, F., & Williams, J. M. G. (2019). *The power of mindfulness: Mindfulness meditation training in sport (MMTS).* New York, NY: Springer.

Ratner, H., George, E., & Iveson, C. (2012). *Solution focused brief therapy: 100 key points and techniques.* New York, NY: Routledge.

Robichaud, M., Koerner, N., & Dugas, M. J. (2019). *Cognitive behavioral treatment for generalized anxiety disorder: From science to practice.* Routledge.

Ruiz, F. J. (2010). A review of Acceptance and Commitment Therapy (ACT) empirical evidence: Correlational, experimental psychopathology, component and outcome studies. *International Journal of Psychology and Psychological Therapy, 10*(1), 125-162.

Ryan, R. M., & Deci, E. L. (2017). *Self-determination theory: Basic psychological needs in motivation, development, and wellness.* New York, NY: Guilford Press.

Salzberg, S. (2017). *Real love: The art of mindful connection.* New York, NY: Flat-iron Books.

Schultz, D. P., & Schultz, S. E. (2009). *Theories of personality.* Belmont, CA: Wadsworth.

Schwartz, R. C. (1995). *Internal family systems therapy.* New York, NY: Guilford Press.

Schwartz, R. C., & Sweezy, M. (2019). *Internal Family Systems Therapy,* Second Edition. New York, NY: Guilford Press.

Segal, Z. V., Williams, J. M. G., & Teasdale, J. D. (2002). *Mindfulness-based cognitive therapy for depression: A new approach to preventing relapse.* New York, NY: Guilford Press.

Seligman, M. E. P. (2018). *The hope circuit: A psychologist's journey from helplessness to optimism.* New York, NY: Public Affairs.

Shedler, J. (2010). The efficacy of psychodynamic psychotherapy. *American Psychologist, 65*(2), 98-109.

Shulman, L. (2012). The skills of helping: Individuals, groups, and communities (7 ed.). Belmont, CA: Thomson Brooks/Cole.

Siegel, D. J. (2016). *Mind: A journey to the heart of being human.* New York, NY: W. W. Norton & Company.

Sinek, S. (2019). *The infinite game.* New York, NY: Portfolio/Penguin.

Slavin-Mulford, J., & Hilsenroth, M. J. (2012). Evidence-based psychodynamic treatments for anxiety disorders: A review. *Psychodynamic psychotherapy research: Evidence-based practice and practice-based evidence, 117-137.*

Smith, P. (2012). *The path of the centaur: Insights into facilitating partnership with horses to improve people's lives.*        Unpublished Dissertation, Prescott College.

Smock Jordan, S., Froerer, A. S., & Bavelas, J. B. (Eds.). (2019). *SFBT conversations: The art and practice of solution-focused brief therapy.* New York, NY: Routledge.

Stahl, J. V., Hill, C. E., Jacobs, T., Kleinman, S., Isenberg, D., & Stern, A. (2009). When the shoe is on the other foot: A qualitive study of intern-level treinees' preceived learning from clients. Psychotherapy: Theory, Research, Practice, Training , 46 (3), 376-38

Stevens, M., Lieschke, J., Cruwys, T., Cárdenas, D., Platow, M. J., & Reynolds, K. J. (2021). Better together: How group-based physical activity protects against depression. *Social science & medicine, 286,* 114337.

Stockton, D., Kellett, S., Berrios, R., Sirois, F., Wilkinson, N., & Miles, G. (2019). Identifying the underlying mechanisms of change during acceptance and commitment therapy (ACT): A systematic review of contemporary mediation studies. *Behavioural and cognitive psychotherapy, 47*(3), 332-362.

Stoddard, J. A., & Afari, N. (Eds.). (2014). *The big book of ACT metaphors: A practitioner's guide to experiential exercises and metaphors in acceptance and commitment therapy.* Oakland, CA: New Harbinger Publications.

Strosahl, K., Robinson, P. J., & Gustavsson, T. (2015). *Brief interventions for radical change: Principles and practice of focused acceptance and commitment therapy.* New Harbinger Publications.

Summers, F. (2016). *Transcending the legacies of childhood abuse: A psychodynamic view.* New York, NY: Guilford Press.

Sweezy, M., & Ziskind, E. L. (Eds.). (2016). *Innovations and Elaborations in Internal Family Systems Therapy*. Routledge.

Trivedi, M. H., Rush, A. J., Wisniewski, S. R., Nierenberg, A. A., Warden, D., Ritz, L., Norquist, G., Howland, R. H., Lebowitz, B., McGrath, P. J., Shores-Wilson, K., Biggs, M. M., Balasubramani, G. K., & Fava, M. (2006). Evaluation of outcomes with citalopram for depression using measurement-based care in STAR*D: implications for clinical practice. *American Journal of Psychiatry, 163*(1), 28-40.

Twohig, M. P., & Levin, M. E. (2017). Acceptance and Commitment Therapy as a treatment for anxiety and depression: A review. *Psychiatric Clinics of North America, 40*(4), 751-770.

Twomey, C., O'Reilly, G., & Byrne, M. (2015). Effectiveness of cognitive behavioural therapy for anxiety and depression in primary care: a meta-analysis. *Family practice, 32*(1), 3-15.

Vago, D. R., & Silbersweig, D. A. (2012). Self-awareness, self-regulation, and self-transcendence (S-ART): A framework for understanding the neurobiological mechanisms of mindfulness. *Frontiers in Human Neuroscience, 6,* 296.

Van Dam, N. T., van Vugt, M. K., Vago, D. R., Schmalzl, L., Saron, C. D., Olendzki, A., Meissner, T., Lazar, S. W., Kerr, C. E., Gorchov, J., Fox, K. C. R., Field, B. A., Britton, W. B., Brefczynski-Lewis, J. A., & Meyer, D. E. (2018). *Mind the hype: A critical evaluation and prescriptive agenda for research on mindfulness and meditation.* Perspectives on Psychological Science, 13(1), 36-61.

Van Dijk, S. (2018). *DBT made simple: A step-by-step guide to dialectical behavior therapy*. Oakland, CA: New Harbinger Publications.

Van Wormer, K. S. (2011). *Human behavior and the social environment, micro level: individuals and families*. New York, N.Y.: Oxford University Press.

Wallerstein, R. S. (2015). *Forty-two lives in treatment: A study of psychoanalysis and psychotherapy*. New York, NY: Routledge.

Walser, R. D., & Westrup, D. (2017). *Acceptance & Commitment Therapy for the treatment of post-traumatic stress disorder & trauma-related problems*. New Harbinger Publications.

Wenzel, A., Brown, G. K., & Karlin, B. E. (2011). *Cognitive behavioral therapy for depression in veterans and military servicemembers: Therapist manual.* Washington, DC: U.S. Department of Veterans Affairs.

Westen, D., Gabbard, G. O., & Blagov, P. (2015). *Psychodynamic diagnostic manual: PDM-2.* Silver Spring, MD: Alliance of Psychoanalytic Organizations.

Williams, M., & Penman, D. (2015). *Mindfulness: An eight-week plan for finding peace in a frantic world.* New York, NY: Rodale Books.

World Health Organization. (2017). *Depression and Other Common Mental Disorders: Global Health Estimates.* World Health Organization.

Wrzesniewski, A., Dutton, J. E., & Debebe, G. (Eds.). (2013). *Research in organizational behavior: Vol. 33. Purpose and meaning in the workplace.* Bingley

Xue, Y. (2023). Family System and Depression: Theoretical Perspectives and Intervention. *Journal of Education, Humanities and Social Sciences, 22,* 523-530.

Young, J. E., Klosko, J. S., & Weishaar, M. E. (2003). *Schema Therapy: A Practitioner's Guide.* New York: Guilford Press.

Zettle, R. D. (2015). Acceptance and commitment therapy for depression. *Current Opinion in Psychology, 2,* 65-69.

www.ingramcontent.com/pod-product-compliance
Lightning Source LLC
Chambersburg PA
CBHW070859120626
46546CB00001B/59